The Intext Series in PSYCHOLOGICAL ASSESSMENT

Series Editor: HAROLD J. VETTER
                  Loyola University of New Orleans

Individual Mental Testing

Part II Measurement

Individual Mental Testing

Part II   Measurement

ALLEN J. EDWARDS
University of Missouri at Columbia

INTEXT EDUCATIONAL PUBLISHERS
College Division of **Intext**
Scranton   San Francisco   Toronto   London

ISBN 0-7002-2399-1

Library of Congress Catalog Card Number: 77-166124

Copyright ©, 1972, International Textbook Company

Preface

This book is intended to describe the development and characteristics of the individual mental tests most commonly used in the training of psychometrists. As such, it is independent of the prior publication (Part I: History and Theories) and should be judged on its own merits. Relationships to historical and theoretical antecedents are marked, however, and so this volume assumes added meaning and utility when used in conjunction with Part I.

Because of limitations of space, scope, and purpose many excellent individual mental tests had to be excluded from the book. No apology is made for the decisions; at the same time, the psychometrist should realize that there are other available tests than the Stanford Revisions of the Binet-Simon Scales, the Wechsler Adult Intelligence Scale, the Wechsler Scale of Intelligence for Children, and the Wechsler Primary and Pre-school Scale. Under certain circumstances, some of these other tests may be more appropriate. The process of education and training should continue for the psychometrist.

Many persons have contributed to the completion of this book. Mrs. Mary Wiles has again assisted in obtaining permissions and clearances. My wife Jean, has remained a substantial contributor to whatever quality this book may have. My thanks are extended to those serving editorial functions: John Dugan, the late Roger Boulé, and Hal Vetter. Without the aid of such persons no book would be completed.

A. J. E.

Columbia, Missouri
February, 1972

Contents

Individual Mental Testing

Part II Measurement

1

Test Criteria

Tests—from the classroom variety administered by the teacher to determine academic gains to the most sophisticated of standardized forms—are used to obtain information that could not be gathered as easily or as precisely from another source. The test score is an indirect reflection, then, of a criterion behavior necessary to make decisions. When an appropriate test is selected, it will yield information that will predict with some degree of accuracy a relevant criterion. Yet a test measure is always indirect; the desired trait is inaccessible in most instances. For this reason certain other criteria are necessary in order to assure maximum accuracy and precision in prediction.

Test users, including clinicians and teachers, sometimes question the necessity and importance of explicit denotations of norming, score derivations, and statistical data such as reliability estimates and standard errors of measurement. However, these kinds of information are essential to achieving the goals desired by the test user, since they provide information about the limitations of the test. Although this may sound like a negative statement, in point of fact it is not. Where decisions must be made with less than perfect measurement, some degree of error influences the result. Control over the kind and degree of error which may be made by the test user is exercised by careful test building, norming, and determination of reliability and validity.

The well-trained psychometrist is not limited to proficiency at administering the tools of his trade. After all, care in following directions, scoring correctly, placing the examinee at ease so that he performs at his normal or best, and the like, are mechanical features. Accurate decisions must also be made in terms of the appropriate test to use for the referral problem, the limitations existing in the measures obtained with this particular examination, and the interpretation of the score for the best interest of the examinee. These latter matters are not merely mechanical procedures, and require that the psychometrist employ measurement and statistical tools as a means of providing for the best interest of the examinee.

The importance of the issues discussed here for test development and use are reflected in a publication by the American Psychological Association dealing with standards for tests used in both psychological and educational settings (French and Michael, 1966). This document should not only be familiar to every psychometrist but also be present for frequent reference in determining adequacy and suitability of tests, both new and old, for specific cases referred to him.

In developing the standards cited in most of the pamphlet, the committee members have made reference to a number of issues relevant to the purposes of testing. As a result, some discussion of these matters will be undertaken here. One of the first issues that must be faced is the fact that tests are administered as a means of decision making. The decision of a psychometrist and others who use the test results may have considerable influence on the present and future status of the individual tested. For this reason alone the committee members who wrote this pamphlet urge the necessity of applying the highest of standards when a test is selected, used, and interpreted.

Of course, the test constructor and publisher have responsibilities as well. Chief among these responsibilities is the provision of necessary information so that the psychometrist may determine the quality of the test for the purpose for which he needs it. Obviously, those tests which do not report necessary information about item selection, norming, reliability and validity, administration and scoring, and interpretation should at best be viewed with some suspicion and probably should not be used at all. Though such a statement might seem obvious, the fact is that a number of quite popular tests in recent years simply have not met adequate standards in terms of reporting to potential test users facts about the development and limitations of the test.

Admittedly, those who use test scores will not always be highly trained individuals. Though no apology is made in this volume for the position that the psychometrist should be skilled in all aspects of test administration, selection, and interpretation, results must be reported and interpreted to individuals not so well trained. Reporting highly technical information, for example, to a classroom teacher will contribute little to the problem directly involved or to the role of testing and decision making about students. But the alternatives, the suggestions, the implications which will be reported to the teacher in less complex terminology must be based upon the rigor of empirical evidence in the test itself.

In the most practical terms, the training needed by the psychometrist is reflected in the type of audience for which the APA standards are designed.

> These standards are intended to guide test development and reporting. A great amount of the information to be reported about tests is technical, and therefore the wording of the standards is of necessity technical. They should be meaningful to readers who have training approximately equivalent to a level between the master's degree and the doctorate in education or psychology at a superior institution of higher learning. It would be reasonable to expect that for most readers at least two and perhaps three courses in measurement have been taken along with at least two semesters of statistical methods. (French and Michael, 1966, p. 5)

Although other kinds of individuals may use this manual as well, the psychometrician is the essential individual for whom such a document is intended. In any practicum-type testing course, such as the one in Individual Mental Testing, such training and sophistication are necessary. The description of tests which follows will be concerned with the kinds of standards generally cited in this chapter and specifically described in the APA standards.

The committee members responsible for the standards have made the important point that even the best test may have quite negative results when used inappropriately. As they state, those who use tests bear the primary responsibility for any improvement that may occur in testing. For the psychometrist who is aware of necessary information about tests, who employs standards in test selection and use, the possibility of irresponsible decisions will be reduced. Test scores may be useful sources of information in making decisions about individuals. For the psychometrist employing appropriate standards in selection and use, this utility will be increased.

Reference

French, J. W., and W. B. Michael (co-chairmen). *Standards for Educational and Psychological Tests and Manuals.* Washington, D.C.: American Psychological Association, 1966.

2

The 1916 Stanford Revision of the Binet-Simon Scales

The Binet approach, as illustrated by test content, procedures, and scores, achieved full development in this country with the 1916 Revision of the Binet-Simon Scales done at Stanford by Lewis M. Terman. Initially popular for diagnosis and prediction in institutional settings, the test assumed increasing popularity in public school settings during the 1920's. Publication of the 1937 Revision signified the introduction of the most popular individual intelligence test ever devised. Probably never again will a single test be as widely used as the 1937 Revision of the Binet-Simon Scales.

The continuing popularity of the current 1960 Revision is to a large extent dependent upon the development and demonstrated utility of the prior scales. For that reason, in order to fully appreciate the strength and limitations of the 1960 Revision, it is necessary for the psychometrist to be familiar with both the preceding revisions. Assumptions, procedures, and even item content are strongly dependent upon the 1916 and 1937 Revisions.

The 1916 Revision

The test which was published as the 1916 revision of the Binet-Simon Intelligence Scale (Terman, 1916) had been preceded by considerable work by Terman and his colleagues and students (See Edwards, 1971, Chapter 4). These efforts bore fruition in the test published in 1916.

Purposes and Rationale

Translations of the Binet-Simon scales had received use in this country in at least restricted circumstances (Goddard, 1908; Terman and Childs, 1912). Despite apparent utility of the scales, limitations had been noted by users and it was obvious that in their present forms the scales could not be as efficient as desired. Terman reports that one of the major reasons for undertaking the revision was to correct imperfections that had been noted in the Binet-Simon scales as well as to provide a detailed guide for administration. As might be expected, the principal use for the translated scales had been in the diagnosis of retardation. Terman notes the increasing awareness of school personnel about educational retardation (Terman, 1916, pp. 3–5) and discusses proposed corrections which had been tried and found wanting. Failure rates had been noted from 30 to 50 percent in the elementary grades for children in public schools in the United States prior to 1915. Indeed, more than 5 percent of the children in schools in the United States were retarded educationally by at least three years, according to Terman. This represented not only a problem in terms of anxiety for pupils, parents and teachers but also a material loss, since over 10 percent of the budget in public school systems was devoted for reteaching material not learned originally by pupils. Concern over the problem had been reflected in a number of reforms attempted by school personnel; Terman specifically points to attempts at individualization of instruction, attempts at liberalizing promotion policies, and recognition of physical factors related to failure. Despite the fact that many of these approaches were progressive, they had not corrected the problem of educational retardation.

Terman states that the reason for failure of these procedures was a false assumption made by school personnel. They believed that if the right conditions were established all children were equally capable of satisfactory progress in the school. It is interesting to note the recurrence of this belief currently in school systems throughout our country. Terman rejected the assumption, basing his rejection upon the results of standardized tests of intelligence administered in school settings. According to him, there is not *one* level of child; all children are not able to learn at the same rate under appropriate circumstances. Nor are there even two well-defined groups, "normal" and "feeble-minded." Instead, Terman holds that there are many grades of intelligence, based upon test scores, ranging from such extreme retardation that custodial care is necessary to an opposite extreme which might be entitled genius. Even within subgroups, like the so-called "normal," there are vast differences among individuals found in mental ability. Terman believed these differences to be due to original endowment, but despite the lack of proof of this contention his position that such children within this subgroup would differ dramatically in their ability to achieve in school is a fact that can be illustrated. Again, in terms of current philosophies and attitudes, Terman's "proof" is almost completely rejected by those who believe that essentially all children are alike in learning ability. Perhaps this is a major reason why certain school systems, like New York City and Los Angeles, have abandoned the use of group intelligence tests at least at certain points, and have even questioned the use of individual tests.

Terman took the position that failure in school cannot be explained by lack of teaching competence or inadequate methodology. Certainly he would accept the premise that extremely competent teachers and the best in teaching methodologies would lead to better acquisition by all students. The point is that individual differences in acquisition would remain even under the most ideal educational procedures. He bases this position upon the belief that there are innate differences in ability from one child to another and that these differences are systematically related to academic achievement. All children who are failures or potential failures, he believes, should be administered a mental examination. The results may be used, in part, to make some decisions about the ability level of the child and to determine whether his failure is due to classroom procedures or his lack of ability to take advantage of classroom procedures. A large measure of the rationale for the development of the 1916 Revision, then, is to provide a systematic, accurate basis for making decisions about general mental level of the child.

To that date, intelligence tests had been used primarily for the purpose of identifying retardation and assigning a label descriptive of its degree. Indeed, almost without exception, these tests had been used in situations where extreme retardation had existed. Terman defends the use of tests in such settings on two bases: first, degree of retardation must be precisely determined before instruction suitable to the individual's level may be undertaken. Second, experience in such settings had indicated that degree of retardation extended close to normality and might be distinguished in subtle ways from normality by such tests. Particularly is this true for the child who, in the terminology of Terman's day, would be labeled high-grade moron and today would be considered borderline educable mentally handicapped. Such children represented an educational concern that had not been realized prior to the publication of the 1916 Revision.

In this regard, Terman reports that about 2 percent of children enrolled in school showed sufficient lack of mental development that school success is precluded for them beyond a certain level. Within this subgroup the child will rarely develop mentally beyond the level of the average child of eleven or twelve years, he thought. Most of these children will cease mental growth, Terman believed, between the mental level of the average seven-to-twelve-yeaɾ-old and most often between ages 9 and 12. Such retarded development had educational implications in the fact that most of these children rarely will be able to achieve beyond the sixth-grade level. The philosophy for the use of concrete materials in teaching such children is evident in Terman's statements that they will be unable to deal with abstract and difficult parts of most academic areas of study even by age 16 or so. Their learning, indeed, will represent a rote level so that they can learn to read to a minimal level and can deal with certain number combinations with facility. The generalizing ability necessary to think, to reason, or to make adequate judgments will not be possible, he believed, with such children. This assumption of inability to think, reason, and judge rings loudly of Binet's assumptions as well. It is worthy of note that the concrete philosophy of educational methods for mentally retarded children has been most popular, and remains so in most special classes, but has been questioned in recent years through experimentation using reinforcement procedures for conditioning purposes, even in institutional settings. Terman made assumptions about linear relationships between observed test score and learning proficiency that have remained popular, though questionable.

Intelligence and Delinquency

During the late nineteenth and early twentieth century a considerable amount of literature had been published on abnormal and aberrant behavior in relation to heredity (e. g., Goddard, 1914). Though weak in experimental methodology and lacking in convincing data, such publications had received a considerable amount of acceptance in this country. Terman equated the presence of delinquency in successive generations with a high degree of mental deficiency. Such a consistent relationship between delinquency and feeble-mindedness was found, he thought, because conscience and morality are dependent upon two conditions being present. The first of these was the ability to foresee and evaluate possible consequences of behavior. The second was some willingness and ability on the part of the individual to use self-control. Since the former may exist without the latter, many intelligent criminals may be found. However, the second of these, self-control, cannot exist in the absence of the first. For this reason, Terman believed, every severely retarded individual was at least a potential criminal. Indeed, the young child lacks moral responsibility. But for those children with sufficient intelligence, there develops an increasing ability and likelihood of relating present desires and actions to future consequences and generalizing from the particular to the general. Since delinquency in all its forms leads to considerable loss in human effort and money, diagnostic and ameliorative procedures are necessary. To Terman, one part of the procedure should be the administration of an intelligence test, such as the Stanford Revision, as a part of the psychological diagnosis of the criminal.

Superior Intelligence

Terman believed that there are as many children of superior ability in this country as there are retarded children. The importance of such a group of individuals is reflected in the leadership and direction which each can offer to the country's future. Progress of civilization depends upon creative thinking in the fields of the sciences, politics, the arts, and so on. As he states it, those individuals of average ability can follow but there must be superior individuals in mental ability to lead the way. To Terman, much of the superior mental ability in this country is unfortunately being wasted through poor environmental conditions or inadequate provisions educationally. For example, he speaks of the handicapping influences of poverty, social neglect, physical defects, and educational maladjustment as leading to a lack of development of leadership in the various fields despite the potential ability of many individuals.

His concern about the waste of human potential is reflected in the fact that he points out a flaw in the old saying "genius will out." To Terman this statement represented a dangerous half-truth. Educationally most children of superior intelligence are actually placed below the grade level at which they might accomplish if their abilities were sufficiently challenged. Under such circumstances Terman believed boredom and withdrawal might result. In these instances the potential represented by intellectual superiority would be partially wasted. He even advocated the use of grade skipping and special classes for mentally superior children so that they might move at a rate commensurate with their abilities. As he points out, probably the special class is the better procedure because rapid but continuous progress may be maintained. It should be noted here that although Terman in a number of places makes the point that an intelligence test is only one criterion which should be used in making decisions, he leaves the impression that an intelligence test alone can be most usable for most decisions to be made. It is rather easy to see why many school personnel, in reading Terman's work and that of others, drew the conclusion that the intelligence test may well be the answer to all problems. That it was not the intention of such writers to leave this impression seems clear in some respects, not so clear in others.

Other Uses of Intelligence Tests

Terman also advocated the utility of intelligence tests for decisions about grade placement in cases of children who transfer among school systems, making decisions about vocational fitness, the study of factors which influence mental development, questions of hereditary influences, social class factors, and so on. Thus intelligence tests should be applied to ever-increasing numbers of problems in our society with consequent gains in knowledge and decisions. Since he felt that the mental test did not operate as a threat to the child—indeed, the tasks were found to be very interesting and pleasant—such information would be superior to that obtained from other sources which represented more of a threat to the child.

To many persons of Terman's day, intelligence tests were superfluous; indeed, any reasonably intelligent person, according to these critics, should be able to make judgments about intellectual level of children by observation. Terman felt this position had some basis in fact since facility may be gained in coarse differentiation of individuals for degrees of intelligence. But such decisions are to a large degree subjective, with the result that they must contain a considerable amount of error. Tests of the type of the Stanford Revision will help to specify, control, and eliminate such error in judging individual differences.

One source of such error lies in the fact that the individual left to his own devices may assume a standard of what is average or normal intelligence that differs systematically from others making the same judgment about the same individual. It is necessary, then, to have some widely accepted standard as to what constitutes normal ability. A carefully normed test will provide just such a basis for comparison. Though not perfect, it will be much more precise than the estimates made by parents and teachers about the capabilities of children. Even with a trained and experienced teacher, judgments of intellectual ability are apt to be subject to grave error. According to Terman, this kind of error is most frequently demonstrated by the fact that teachers tend to overestimate the intelligence of the child who is overage for his grade. The teacher frequently estimates the intelligence of a child on the basis of his performance in the school grade in which he is placed. If he is a year or two older than other children in the classroom, it might be easy to conclude that he is of average ability when in point of fact he will not be.

Terman holds that the quality of the work done by the child academically cannot be estimated accurately unless his age is taken into account. The question for Terman is not whether the child works well in school but in what grade a child of his age should be able to do satisfactory work.

This position reflects the belief in the level idea of the mental-age concept.

Just as children of below average intelligence may be overestimated, so may children of above average intelligence be underestimated. Again, the issue is not one of the quality of the work which the child currently does but one of comparison of the quality of his work to his age mates and to older individuals. The young child who can accomplish at the level of an older child but is not allowed to do so may be educationally retarded in the school setting.

There are external conditions which also influence decisions by the individual, particularly the teacher, about intellectual competence of another person. Terman says that one of these is the inability of most of us to distinguish what is actual mental dullness from a condition resulting from unfavorable social environment or lack of educational opportunity. Although he does not pursue this issue further, it seems apparent that Terman felt that some estimation of the effects of environment should be taken into account in determining educational decisions. However, he does not discuss the effects of environmental lack on actual test performance. The question remains an important one even today: to what degree does environmental lack seriously depress the obtained score on an intelligence test?

According to Terman, adults pass judgment too frequently upon children's intellectual abilities in terms of superficial characteristics; for example, if the child is talkative and appears very alert, his intelligence may be overestimated. The child who is somewhat more withdrawn, who reacts slowly, who rarely expresses his thoughts or feelings may be underestimated in terms of intellectual ability. Terman reviewed the Binet study of teacher judgments of intelligence (see Edwards, 1971, Chapter 3), pointing to the error and lack of consistency between teachers in judging intellectual competence. Terman accepted Binet's conclusions and generalized them to the American society in which he lives.

Since error so frequently dominates subjective judgment, it is necessary for a more precise judgment of intellectual competence to be available to those who must make decisions about individuals. From this standpoint, Terman advocates the use of the Binet method which he characterizes as being nothing more than common sense but with a good portion of system and scientific exactness applied to this common sense. Science, as Terman maintains, does things better because it is more accurate. The Binet method and the test developed from this method will have considerable strength because it is not only common sense, it is also systematic and scientific. It seems clear that what Terman had in mind was really not a determination of "intelligence" but an objective measure of behaviors that could be related to specific goals, outcomes, and social situations. It is unfortunate that this matter was not more explicitly stated and that it did not have more direct influence on writings which followed, both for Terman and for other individuals in the field. Many of the problems which are currently being encountered in the administration and interpretation of intelligence tests today might have been avoided had this more specific and objective position become dominant.

Building a Test

Terman describes the antecedent of the 1916 Revision, the Binet-Simon scales, as an extended series of problems which must be solved by the child. To successfully solve these problems, which he also calls "stunts," requires the presence and use of intelligence. To avoid problems of formal school training or home exposure, Terman says that the problems used in the test are intended to test "native intelligence." But he goes on to point out that essentially the problems are designed to answer a question: How intelligent is the child? Essentially, then, the Binet-Simon scales give an indication of the child's ability to learn more of the same kinds of things reflected in test content. This latter goal did not require the inclusion of a reference to "native intelligence." Indeed, the ability to deal with specific kinds of problems as a predictor of similar behavior in the future is defensible in its own right. It is within this context that such tasks frequently predict academic achievement, since the kinds of items found in the test, though not directly attributable to formal learning, do apparently reflect skills necessary for accomplishment in the school setting.

Terman refers to Binet's position that intelligence may have many aspects and expressions. As a result, no one particular kind of item or test will reflect adequately the construct desired. To reflect some general picture of such abilities, Binet used items of different types. He thus included items intended to reflect memory, reasoning ability, comparisons, comprehension, number facility, general knowledge and the like. Just which items reflect which of these qualities Binet did not make clear, primarily because he was more interested in the general combination than any specific aspects.

The Binet scales could be used to judge the ability of a child by comparing his performance with average performance on the scale by normal children of different ages. This kind of examination represents an age scale, reflected in the 1911 Binet-Simon scale from age 3 through what was called adult. Each age level had a specific number of items so selected and tested as to reflect performance for the average child of that age. Since rarely did a given child ever perform successfully on all items at one age level and fail all items at the next age level, it was necessary to establish the highest age level at which all items are passed (the basal age) and the lowest age level at which all items are failed (the ceiling age). The summation of credits between these extremes would then yield the actual obtained mental age for the child. This obtained MA could be compared to performances for normal children of the same age in order to determine whether or not the child tested is accelerated or retarded or at the norm for his age group. The procedure is maintained in the 1916 Stanford Revision and all revisions following.

The Success of the Approach

The assumptions and procedures of the Binet-Simon method, according to Terman, are successful in a way that no prior testing procedures had been. At least three reasons account for this superiority of the Binet methodology. First, as Terman says, Binet was the first to use the idea of age standards in measuring ability. It is not possible in a limited number of items to design specific age-level tests in such a way that the average ten-year-old will pass items at that year level and at no others. Some approximation of the correct mental-age level for the child is obtained by his summation of successes over several year levels, beginning with items very easy for him so that he passes them all and continuing until items are too difficult and he fails them all. This procedure is practical, as Terman points out, because the percentage passing concept is employed (see Table 2-1).For, say, three items which we wish to use in

TABLE 2-1
HYPOTHETICAL ILLUSTRATION OF THE PERCENTAGE-PASSING CONCEPT

Age Group	A (Percent Correct)	Items B (Percent Correct)	C (Percent Correct)
6	0	0	62
7	4	2	80
8	13	6	98
9	28	9	98
10	44	12	98
11	62	90	71
12	81	95	50

an age scale, it is necessary to determine the age at which the items are successully passed by an age group. If we have representative samples of children from ages 6 through 12, we administer the item to each child in each age group and compute the number who can effectively pass the item. For item A it will be noted that there is a rather steady increment in percentage passing through age 12. Though not perfect, the increments are of sufficient quantity that this item probably is a good item to use in an age scale. The problem now is: at which age level should the item be placed? Theoretically, each item placed at a given age level should be passed by exactly 50 percent of that age group. In practical terms, however, this is not an adequate criterion to use since a 50 percent level is too difficult for total test placement. Experience has shown that items need to be passed by approximately 60 percent of an age group for the item to work effectively at that age level. Item A, then, might well be placed at the eleven-year group.

By the standards cited for item selection and placement, neither item B nor item C would be usable in an age scale. The psychometrist can realize that, even with limited number of items at each age level, a large pool of items must be assembled in building the test. Though some procedures can be used to permit utilization of some marginal items, such as varying scoring standards, the test constructor will begin with many more items than he finds usable in his test.

Such an empirical approach also has significance in another direction. It is possible for us to derive a large number of items which on a logical basis we believe should be suitable for testing youngsters of any given age. However, the percentage-passing concept for selection and inclusion of items frequently discloses the limitations of our logic. Binet in his experience and Terman in his both report that many items which they considered excellent ones turned out to be poor, while those which on a logical basis might seem poor worked well in discriminating youngsters of given ages. Since the Binet-Simon scales and their revisions had as a purpose the comparison of a child's performance with his age peers, the procedure followed here is both justifiable and necessary.

There is a further strength in this use of age standards as cited by Terman. Mental age is a concept which is readily understood by laymen as well as professionals. If the mental-age concept is valid (and this is a matter which still is not completely resolved), the denotation of a mental age should describe expectations for any given child. Thus, to say that a child has a mental age of eight should signify to us that he can "do" those things which the average child of eight years of age can do.

To make this expectation functional requires two additional conditions. First, the test content must truthfully reflect intellectual behavior of children of different ages such that the average is accurate. Second, we must be able to describe what it is that an average eight-year-old child can "do." If these conditions are met, then the mental-age concept is highly useful and meaningful. The value of the mental-age concept has frequently been questioned, however, most often on logical rather than empirical grounds. Systematic study has been very limited. In any event, Terman describes the derivation of the mental-age concept by Binet as perhaps the most important discovery in the history of psychology.

A second reason cited by Terman for the success of the Binet-Simon method involves the kinds of mental abilities used in testing with the scales. Principally this strength involves what Binet calls more complex mental processes rather than the simpler sensorimotor ones. Binet felt that considerably more information about intellectual competency could be gathered by rather inaccurate measurement of reasoning ability, ingenuity, judgment, and the like than with precise measurement of reaction time, sensory discrimination, and so on (see Edwards, 1971, Chapter 2). Binet maintains (and Terman agrees with him) that even severely retarded children do not differ very markedly from average children of the same age in many of the sensorimotor task performances utilized by Galton and others. Differences in use of the so-called complex mental processes, however, are very readily discovered and quantified.

A final reason given by Terman for the success of the Binet-Simon procedure was the fact that Binet attempted measurement of level of intelligence in a general form. Subtests, each of which was designed to measure a different faculty, were not used by Binet. His reason for this is the belief that, though faculties may exist, they are not independent of one another. There may be a faculty of reasoning and a separate power of judgment but the two are constantly interacting, since judgment cannot exist without reasoning and vice versa. Thus every function must include to some degree every other function of an intellectual nature. In the Binet approach, measurement will be both more meaningful and accurate if some general expression of the action of all faculties is obtained. One must include a variety of types of items in the test, sampling as many different traits as possible without attempting distinct measurement. The total score obtained, in this case the mental age, will represent the best estimate of the general intellectual functioning of the individual. Again, though this position is widely debated and in some quarters rejected, Terman accepted it and employed it in all the subsequent revisions of the scale.

Limitations of the Binet Approach

Terman points out that a number of criticisms had been offered of the Binet-Simon scales which were unfair simply because they reflected use of the scales for purposes not intended by the test. There were certain limitations built in by the procedures followed which would be as applicable to the Stanford revisions as they would for the original scales. Terman did not believe these to be totally limiting factors, however, only restrictive in the situations in which they might be used. For example, the Binet scales were intended to measure general intelligence. Thus the personality, the emotional instability, the physical limitations of the individual cannot be inferred directly from the score on the Stanford-Binet. Insofar as these factors influence test score they will of course be operative. But to criticize the scale for not giving accurate information on such factors is unjust. Indeed, in standardization Binet had made it clear that certain cases of emotional instability and of physical deformity were purposely excluded from the norms group so as not to influence the test scores. The score of the Binet scales, and of the Stanford revisions, is intended to reflect some general intellectual level of the person without implying diagnostic significance for inadequate performance. If, say, from some performance by the child the psychometrist suspects that there may be some emotional instability, then separate measurement should be undertaken. Such statements may also be made about presumed organicity or other conditions which might explain a kind of mental function or performance not acceptable to the psychometrist.

A second limitation in the scale which led to misunderstanding applies to the identification of special abilities and talents. Specific kinds of performance such as high ability in painting, music, mathematics, or whatever else are not easily identifiable from the Binet scale or the Stanford revisions. The reason for this, again, is because no effort was made to include kinds of items for that specific type of diagnosis. As Terman points out, the performance on the Binet scale can never be used as a means of determining the vocational inclinations of children and therefore cannot be used for any kind of vocational selection and guidance. Terman makes this point by stating that the Binet scales are not a "new kind of phrenology" (Terman, 1916, p. 49). However, Terman did believe that the score would give some indication of the degree of abstraction with which the individual might be successful. The later investigations entitled "The Genetic Studies of Genius" (see Edwards, 1971, Chapter 4) not only seem to be an outgrowth of this position but a support of it.

A third limitation follows somewhat along the same lines. Terman makes the point that the Binet scales cannot be used as a kind of predictor for educational methods desirable for any given child. Though the general level of ability reflected in the mental age will be useful to the teacher in deciding at what point he may begin to deal with a given child, the specific methods and content to be used with the child are not reflected from the score.

A final limitation cited by Terman is the need for many other kinds of information in decision making. The Binet method is not all-sufficient, as he points out, but does yield useful information when combined with other forms of information.

Norming the Test

The Binet scales, designed to identify retarded children for educational purposes (see Edwards, 1971, Chapter 3), had contained limitations which restricted their usefulness for other than its most direct purpose. There was very little "top" to the test and research had indicated misplacement of a number of items within the scale. Additionally, interpretation of results appeared to be easier and more valid than in point of fact was true. According to Terman, these limitations represented a central purpose for the Stanford Revision.

The Sample

Initial work in the translation and adaptation of the Binet-Simon scales had been begun by Terman as early as 1910. From that time until the appearance of the 1916 Revision, about 2,300 subjects were examined by various psychometrists using highly specific administration procedures. Of the total sample, Terman reports 1,700 of them as being normal children with about 200 members of the sample being designated defective or superior and over 400 being adult.

Apparently beginning about 1912 (Terman, 1916, p. 52), a systematic and detailed procedure began to develop the data necessary to an acceptable revision. Five major steps were followed to insure that the results would be a scale which would include appropriate items, yielding accurate scores, and consistent with the purposes of the Binet method. There was first a search of all sources where results for the items of the Binet-Simon scales had been tabulated and recorded. As a result of this phase of the investigation, each item was reported in terms of percentage passing by various ages with further information about administrative conditions and methods of procedure. On the basis of this information, including a considerable amount from other countries than the United States, items were provisionally arranged by age levels in order to do the first tryout.

A second step, and preceding the actual tryout, was to devise forty additional items. These added items would allow substitutions where certain items were not satisfactory and provided as well a minimum of six items for each year level. Terman does not report the source of the forty additional items.

The third step then involved the selection of a sample which Terman desired to be as representative as possible. To attain this criterion Terman reports the following procedure:

> . . . The method was to select a school in a community of average social status, a school attended by all or practically all the children in the

district where it was located. In order to get clear pictures of age differences the tests were confined to children who were within two months of a birthday. To avoid accidental selection, *all* the children within two months of a birthday were tested, in whatever grade enrolled. Tests of foreign-born children, however, were eliminated in the treatment of results. There remained tests of approximately one thousand children, of which nine hundred and five were between five and fourteen years of age. (Terman, 1916, pp. 52–53).

It is clear that the procedure followed to obtain a "representative sample" left out a number of sources of variation in test scores and thereby represented something less than true representation for score purposes. Using only schools in those communities of so-called average social status and where a single school represented all of the children of the district allows results and norms which restrict their applicability and predictive validity. Further, to exclude all children of foreign birth delimits the situations in which the scores may be used. However, these statements are intended not so much as an indictment of Terman as a denotation that limitations were built in, specified explicitly, and available to test users. Misapplication of the measure and misinterpretation are not Terman's responsibility.

The fourth step constituted recording as completely as possible every response by every child. Having complete information on what each child said allowed means of scoring items under various criteria. Though an item might not fit very well at an age level given one set of scoring criteria, under a slightly different one it might fit quite well. As an example, a given item might have five subparts. The item might be too easy for one age level because most of the children got all subparts right. At an age level one or two years younger, perhaps, only 60 percent of the children answered as many as three of the subparts. This item would be more appropriate for the lower age level. Not only could such quantitative matters be considered, but qualitative differences in the responses might also lead to placement at one age level to make it more appropriate than it would have been at some other age level.

Finally, considerable emphasis was placed on standardization of administration. The examiners were trained for six months and supervised for another six months. To make certain of as much final uniformity as possible, Terman himself scored every test record of every child.

Item Placement

For the placement of the items below the level of fourteen years, data from the one thousand children cited above were used. The procedure followed is actually a definition of what constitutes mental age. The items were so arranged with an appropriate scoring standard that the median mental age of unselected children of a given age group would correspond with the median chronological age. Though several age levels would be encompassed in the administration, the average child of chronological age eight, say, should obtain a mental age of eight if the scale is appropriate. The score that is obtained with the Stanford Revision of 1916, as well as those following, is a mental age. From this an intelligence quotient may be obtained and in both the 1916 and 1937 Revisions ratio IQ's were possible. Since the ratio IQ depends upon both mental age and chronological age, the median intelligence quotient should be one hundred for unselected children of each age. The formula for computing a ratio IQ is

$$\frac{MA}{CA} \times 100 = IQ$$

The ratio IQ is dependent upon accurate measurement of mental age and correct placement of items within the scale.

Even with the care taken, some problems of correct item placement remained. As Terman reports, where the median mental age from provisional arrangement of items appeared to be too high or too low, certain items could be changed to a different mental age level, or standards of scoring might be qualified somewhat until the correct placement was found which would yield a median mental age appropriate for the chronological age. Even with these procedures, however, three successive revisions were necessary, including independent scoring of data, before an accurate enough scale was obtained to meet Terman's specification.

Placement of items above age 14 and their norms constituted a different type of problem. School children over age 14 used in the original sample were students who had failed at least one grade. Since there would be some bias in the sample, either intellectual or academic or both, Terman determined to use adults available to him for purposes of item placement in the adult scale. About 30 business men and 150 so-called migrating unemployed men comprised one part of this sample, another part consisted of 150 adolescent delinquents, while the final subsample was of some 50 high school students, apparently without major problems. The sample for determining adult norms for the 1916 Revision consisted of 380 individuals, reflecting bias in the sample and consequent error in the norms. The mental-age concept is inappropriate above age 14 and has no true expression for the adult.

Effects of the Revision on Mental Ages

One of the problems with the Binet-Simon scales was that the tests tended to overestimate mental ability of young children and underestimate mental abilities of older children. The 1916 Revision, according to Terman, overcame this major defect. Not only would there no longer be an appearance of decline of mental age with increasing chronological age, but a very serious matter of misinterpretation would also be corrected. In the scales where overestimation of mental ability occurs at younger age levels, it would be possible to assume that a given youngster is of near average mentality at the time he becomes of school age. This would lead to expectations of performance which might not be congruent were the scale more precisely normed. Terman makes the point that an error of ten months in the mental age of a five-year-old child is as serious as an error of twenty months in the age of a ten-year-old child. Just as one would not wish to underestimate seriously the competence of a child, neither would one wish to seriously overestimate it. Though in recent years there has been an increasing belief in the power of expectations on performance, and even some limited support, major discrepancies between expectations and reasonable performance can lead to greater problems than solutions.

Terman reviews the consequences of the original Binet-Simon scale with inaccurate measurement at both the younger and older age levels. For young children, higher levels of retardation tended to be overlooked, since these children obtained test scores closer to normal than they should. With older children, however, and with adults, the proportion of retardation was overestimated. As a result of these deficiences, mental growth of children was difficult to trace with any degree of accuracy. As Terman states, ". . . By other versions of the Binet Scale an average five-year-old will show an intelligence quotient probably not far from 110 or 115; at nine, an intelligence quotient of about 100; and at fourteen, an intelligence quotient of about 85 or 90" (Terman, 1916, p. 63).

In the same way the child of borderline ability would present a picture somewhat as follows. At age 5 the IQ obtained by him would be approximately 90, by age 9 it would have dropped to 75, and at age 14 the obtained IQ would be about 65. As Terman says, such flaws in the test can lead to some very serious consequences. The 1916 Stanford Revision, then, corrects for such faults. Data available to Terman indicated that intelligence quotients obtained by children were consistent over periods up to four years. The matter of stability in the IQ has remained a problem of more than theoretical concern and is still the source of some debate. Certainly in the absence of stability, much prediction about future intellectual behavior of children from their test scores is loaded with error.

Distribution of Intelligence

The obtained intelligence quotients on the 1916 Revision for the 1,000 children used in the sample were plotted in frequency distributions for each age separately. Each distribution obtained was fairly symmetrical between ages 5 and 14. As might be expected, the combined distribution for all ages is very symmetrical and meets criteria for the normal curve. This finding led Terman to three conclusions.

First, the distribution indicated the gradual increase in grades of intelligence. As a result, only arbitrary points can be designated as division points between any particular grades. This matter assumes considerable importance for defining the difference between the normal child and the retarded child, or the normal child and the accelerated one. As Terman observes, a mentally defective child does not belong to a distinct psychological type. Neither does the exceptionally gifted child. As a result, the number of children who will be called mentally defective or mentally accelerated will depend upon some arbitrary standard designated by those who must make decisions about the individual. Some external behavioral criteria then must be designated as to what constitutes defective behavior. Performance of such individuals on a test like the 1916 Revision will indicate what cutoff point might be used, assuming that their performance is consistent. In the same way, mental superiority may be defined and compared to test measures.

A rather common opinion at the time held that there were more extreme deviations in ability below the median than above. The second conclusion drawn by Terman relates to this matter. In point of fact, he reports, the data do not support any such contention. At least with the kind of sample he used there will be a child equally high above the median as there is one below the median.

Finally, Terman rejects the idea that variability in mental traits becomes more evident during adolescence. At least for intelligence, the distribution of IQ is practically the same for all ages up through age 14. From this fact he infers that no increasing intellectual variability should be found above this point for the next few years.

Validity

Terman used the term *validity* not only as a reflection of statistical procedures but as a reflection of predictability in performance as well. For example, one means of determining the validity of the 1916 Revision was to divide the subjects at each level into three groups according to intelligence quotient. One group was composed of youngsters with IQ's below 90, another between 90 and 109, and the third those with IQ's above 110. A check was then made to determine the percentage of passes on each item for the given age level or those year levels immediately adjacent. For purposes of this kind of validity, it was necessary that performance by the high-IQ group be decidedly superior on each item to the performance of the low-IQ group. Where this finding held, the item was considered adequate in terms of its validity. Terman states that unless this kind of validity is found and accepted, the entire scale must be rejected.

In much the same way, Terman took the position that stability of the IQ over time for a given child was a reflection of validity of the intelligence quotient. One necessary procedure to indicate the validity of his scale, then, was to indicate that retests of children of different ability levels were consistent. Such measures were taken at intervals from two to five years and Terman reports that consistency of the IQ indicated that the inference made by him was acceptable. Since mental age according to Terman has little meaning unless considered a part of the chronological age, the ratio IQ is a significant feature of the test. The method of utilizing mental age with chronological age to achieve a ratio IQ transforms the test to a point-scale method if one wishes to use it in that fashion. Terman declares that such a procedure makes it superior to any other point scale available at least to 1916. His primary reasoning for this is that a larger number of tasks will be utilized with each child and the point (that is, IQ) determined for each child has more explicit meaning.

Sex Differences

One issue of the day, and one still not fully settled, is whether or not differences exist between the sexes in general intellectual ability. Terman makes the point that consistently throughout man's development the assumption has been made that men are superior in intelligence. The development of tests had indicated, however, that on the average women achieve about as well intellectually as do men. Explanations for disparities in achievement in eminence had emphasized first that women were not allowed opportunities to achieve despite their abilities, and second that more extreme variations are found in males than in females. Thus, just as there are more eminent men than women, there are also more males in institutions for the mentally defective.

Such arguments Terman described as interesting but in total less valuable than one could desire. The data available for the performance of 1,000 children on the 1916 Stanford Revision give him an opportunity to look at the issue of sex differences and whether or not they are found. His analysis indicated several factors of some interest and importance. First, comparisons of intelligence quotients between boys and girls to age 13 showed a small but fairly consistent superiority of girls. Beginning with age 14, however, the boys achieved superiority over the girls. With further analysis Terman concluded that girls probably are superior in ability to boys up to and including age 14. The change at fourteen is due not to actual superiority of males but to the fact that girls tend to be promoted promptly to high school.

Despite this finding of consistent differences to age 14, Terman dismisses the importance of such a finding by the fact that the differences are really very slight. At most ages only two or three points in IQ account for the differences between the sexes. As he is aware, such a difference is negligible. As a third point, and supporting the preceding one, the distributions of intelligence for boys and girls were found to be very similar. This finding offers little support to the contention that there is greater variability in the intelligence of males than females. Finally, individual items did not show large differences in terms of percentage of boys and girls passing. In a few instances, the difference was marked; e.g., the boys were better in arithmetical reasoning, giving differences between a president and a king, solving the formboard, making change, reversing hands of the clock, finding similarities, and solving the induction test. The girls, by contrast, achieved better than the boys on such tasks as drawing designs from memory, esthetic comparison, comparing objects from memory, answering the comprehension questions, repeating digits and sentences, tying a bowknot, and finding lines. The differences which occurred are not explicitly stated in this source. However, in the 1937 Revision the issue is faced more squarely and specific items favoring boys and girls are cited by McNemar (1942).

From the fact that so few items disclose sex differences, Terman concludes that intellectual differences between males and females, at least to age 14, are insignificant at best. Differences between the sexes in obtaining eminence, then, must be due to certain kinds of discrimination in business or choice by women for home life and family.

Social Class Differences

As a means of determing the validity of the intelligence quotient, comparisons between social classes within the sample were also made. Approximately half of the sample (the total was 492) were classified by teachers in terms of a social-class scale. This scale, crude and subjective in its application, consisted of five social levels: very inferior, inferior, average, superior, and very superior. The findings, despite the limitations in procedure, were accepted by Terman as indicating superiority of children from superior social class. The findings indicated that children from better homes were about seven IQ points above the median while those from inferior homes were about seven IQ points below the median on the average. By age 14, then, children from an inferior social class will be approximately one year below the median mental age for the total group. Those children who come from superior homes will average about one year above the median age. Terman offers as an explanation of this difference superiority in original endowment for the children from the upper social class.

Supporting evidence referred to by him includes teacher rankings of children according to intelligence, age-grade progress, quality of school work, and comparison of older and younger children and bright and dull children in the same family. Much of this support would seem tenuous since social factors may be as responsible as intellectual ones. Terman takes the position that, for comparative purposes, the intelligence of children of all social classes should be considered in terms of the same objective scale. This scale should be based on the median for all the social classes combined. Such a position seems defensible where all classes are appropriately represented. Unfortunately, most tests, even to the current date, have simply not been representative of all kinds of social conditions and therefore have not yielded median scores which would be most usable for comparative and predictive purposes.

Terman does make one point of some significance where he had found consistency. He reports that children of a given social class who obtain a given intelligence quotient were not distinguishable in their responses to individual items from children of the same intelligence in some other social class. This finding allows performance comparisons which are not possible otherwise. The importance of determining empirically differences and similarities in performance cannot be overstressed. Simply dismissing the issue as social bias will correct no problems.

Quality of School Work

Among the supportive evidence reported by Terman was the use of the quality of a child's school work as a means of determining adequacy of measurement with the scale. A sample of some 504 school children from the norms group was used for this purpose. Teachers scaled their work from very superior through very inferior. Terman then compared this judgment by teachers with the obtained IQ of the child, and reports fairly close agreement. About 10 percent of the time, however, rather serious disagreement was found. Thus a child might be reported as doing average work when his test score indicated that he was inferior in ability. Such differences, Terman explained, were due to the fact that teachers graded work without taking into account the age of the child. Thus a child over age in grade might be doing average work for that grade. The teacher would not consider the fact that he might be one or two years older than other children who are also doing average work for their age level. When correction for this discrepancy was made, Terman reported no serious disagreements remain.

Grade Progress

The entire sample of 1,000 children was used for the analysis of the relationship between intelligence quotient and grade progress. Again, Terman reports a fairly high correlation but some large discrepancies as well. For example, he reports that an intelligence level of nine years was found all the way from grade 1 to grade 7. A mental age of 12 was found all the way from grade 3 through 8. The procedures of the schools in assigning children to grade yield highly heterogenous groups in terms of mental ability. This is merely another way of saying that chronological age has been used as the basis for grade placement.

Discrepancies between mental age and grade placement were inevitably due to exceptional brightness or exceptional dullness, Terman reports. Seldom was any child with an IQ between 95 and 105 seriously misplaced. Those children who were intellectually dull, however, tended to be one to three grades in placement above their mental-age level. The greater the departure from average ability the greater the degree of misplacement. At the same time, very bright children tended to be located from one to three grades below their mental-age level. Again, the brighter the child the more serious the misplacement by the school. Terman makes the point that this condition exists because schools tend to promote children by age rather than ability. To a degree, bright children are "held back" while dull children are "socially promoted." Educationally, then, according to Terman, the retardation problem is the opposite of what was generally believed: bright children are the ones who are retarded, dull children are the ones who are accelerated. The solution to this dilemma, Terman states, is to be found in differentiated courses or special classes for both kinds of children; it is as important to have special classes for intellectually very bright children as it is to have special classes for intellectually dull ones.

Terman makes some observations about specific levels of intelligence as well. He refers to a special study of children who obtained IQ's between 70 and 79, regardless of chronological age, and reports that such a child never does satisfactory work in the grade where his chronological age would place him. After four or five years of school attendance, a child of this intellectual level tends to do very inferior work even if he has been retained a year or two. At best he does only average work for grades two to four years below his chronological age. By constrast, according to Terman, a child with an IQ of 120 or above is very rarely found below the grade for his chronological age in terms of achievement. Sometimes, by placement, he will be one or two grades above his chronological age. Wherever his grade placement, such a child displays work which is judged by teachers to be superior and Terman concludes that this work would remain superior even if he were grade skipped.

Teacher Estimates of Ability

Terman had teachers rank the children in their classes and compared these rankings with the actual obtained IQ. In this instance he reports the Pearson correlation coefficient as being .48. Although this value is of moderate magnitude, as he points out, either the teacher or the test must have made a number of mistakes for so little of the variance to be accounted for by this coefficient. He concludes that the problem is with the teacher rankings, not the test. He assumes that the disagreements found favor the validity of the test method rather than to cast doubt on its adequacies.

Classifying Intelligence Quotients

Though descriptive labels are considered prejudicial by many persons, they may act as an effective shorthand if the label signifies a performance and behavioral level demonstrably independent of the score and label itself. Terman points out that boundary lines determined either on IQ or labels, or both, are completely arbitrary. Indeed, the evidence is overwhelming that the individuals falling into one of the groups cited will not be homogeneous. Since labels of one kind or another are convenient and are frequently used, they should be given as much definitiveness as possible. This means describing behaviors applicable to the use of the label so that an independent determination of the adequacy of the label may be made. The terminology used by Terman in 1916 has changed somewhat. The essential cutoff points, though arbitrary, have remained fairly consistent however.

The classification scheme advocated by Terman in 1916 is as follows:

IQ	Classification
Above 140	"Near" genius or genius
120–140	Very superior intelligence
110–120	Superior intelligence
90–110	Normal, or average intelligence
80–90	Dullness, rarely classifiable as feeble-minded
70–80	Borderline deficiency, sometimes classifiable as dullness, often as feeble-mindedness
Below 70	Definite feeble-mindedness (Terman, 1916, p. 79)

Terman further subdivides the degrees of feeble-mindedness. Children who obtain IQ's between 50 and 70 and for whom the IQ's are consistent and meaningful, he calls *morons* (or, in today's terminology, "educable mentally handicapped"). Children who obtain IQ's between 25 and 50 will usually be classified as *imbeciles*, according to Terman (or today, "trainable"). Children obtaining IQ's below 25 he calls *idiots* (in comparable terms today, "custodial"). In agreement with Binet, the mature individual for whom the label "idiot" is appropriate will have a maximum intelligence at the three-year level, an adult "imbecile" will have a mental level somewhere between three and seven years, and an adult "moron" would achieve intellectual development between seven and eleven years. Regardless of the terminology used, and regardless of the emotional attitudes toward such terms, the general descriptions may be checked and verified. If they are adequate, the fault is not in the designation of a label.

As Terman points out, exact grading of these degrees of feeble-mindedness are of no great importance to the schools. The only categories of essential importance in the school setting are those of the so-called moron and borderline children. Such individuals a classroom teacher should at least tentatively identify so that proper referral may be made for intellectual evaluation and decisions about an appropriate educational program. For this reason, Terman describes behaviors appropriate to the various levels from feeble-minded through near genius. Case studies are also given by him for each of the labels within the scheme.

Feeble-mindedness

Terman begins his discussion of feeble-mindedness by quoting the most commonly used definition of this intellectual level. This definition, originating with the Royal College of Physicians and Surgeons of London, had emphasized lack of competition on equal terms with normal individuals by the feeble-minded person and of an inability to manage himself or his affairs with ordinary prudence. Terman criticized this definition as leading to many cases of unidentified "feeble-mindedness." Particularly does he quarrel with the matter of management of self and affairs with ordinary prudence. Terman states that the popular standard of ordinary prudence is so low that perhaps hundreds of thousands of high-grade mental defectives are not identified. Particularly would this be true in terms of social and industrial competition. He makes the point that many individuals seemingly are normal when considered in the crude environment in which they are raised. However, when they must compete with more normal individuals either in a school or occupational setting, deficiency on their part becomes much more evident. Some psychological criterion must be established which will be consistent. For this purpose he advocates, as might be expected, the use of the intelligence quotient as derived from the 1916 Stanford Revision.

Terman gives brief case studies of a dozen children identified by the

1916 Revision as obtaining IQ's of 75 or below and determined behaviorally as feeble-minded. As an example of one of these case studies (Terman, 1916, pp. 85–86):

> H. S.; boy, age 11; mental age 8–3; I.Q. approximately 75. At eight years tested at 6. Parents highly educated, father a scholar. Brother and sister of very superior intelligence. Started to school at seven, but was withdrawn because of lack of progress. Started again at eight and is now doing poor work in the second grade. Weakly and nervous. Painfully aware of his inability to learn. During the test keeps saying, "I tried anyway," "Its all I can do if I try my best, ain't it," et cetera. Regarded defective by other children. Will probably never be able to do the work beyond the fourth or fifth grade and is not likely to develop above the eleven-year level, if as high.

Such cases, Terman believes, would not lead to disagreement among any set of competent judges in terms of their classification. Individuals of this intellectual level Terman believed to be better suited for institutional care than for some kind of provisions in the school. Certainly, according to him, they must not be allowed to participate in regular classes, for their own good as well as for the good of the more competent students. Even in a special class progress will be slow. By adolescence, Terman states such children should be under custodial care.

Borderline

These cases, though difficult to identify, are those about which the school must be most concerned and for whom special education programs would be most usable. The IQ limit stated by Terman (between 70 and 80) is tenuous. As will be noted in the preceding case of "feeble-mindedness," for example, the given IQ was 75. Yet Terman considered this child, because of behaviors, to be better suited for institutional care than a special class of borderline children. In some instances, according to Terman, children with IQ's as low as 70 will be better suited for the borderline definition than the feeble-minded one. The matter of social interaction in competition becomes a significant one in making this decision. In this matter intelligence is not sufficient. Terman cites such things as moral traits, industry, the environment within which the individual must function, personal appearance, and so on as being significant along with intelligence. It is because of deficiencies in these areas that a child like H. S. cited above, must be considered feeble-minded. The borderline cases, however, may possess a high enough level of these other factors to allow the individual to function in society at large.

As with the category of feeble-mindedness, a case study will be cited here to illustrate the difference between borderline and the lower category (Terman, 1916, p. 90).

C. P.; boy, age 10–2; mental age 7–11; IQ 78. Portuguese boy, son of a skilled laborer. One of eleven children, most of whom have above this same grade of intelligence. Has attended school regularly for four years. Is in the third grade, but cannot do the work. Except for extreme stubbornness his social development is fairly normal. Capable in plays and games, but is regarded as impossible in his school work. Like his brother, M. P., the next case to be described, he will doubtless become a fairly reliable laborer at unskilled work and will not be regarded, in his rather simple environment, as a defective. From the psychological point of view, however, his deficiency is real. He will probably never develop beyond the eleven or twelve year level or be able to do satisfactory school work beyond the fifth or sixth grade.

Although one might argue that in this latter case environment may be a much more significant issue than the intellectual one, functionally the findings would probably be about the same. Whether or not—regardless of source—changes may be brought about of a significant nature in a child already age ten is debatable at best. Obviously, if environments can be restructured from much earlier in life so as to produce significant change, then this step should be taken.

In any event, Terman maintains that in cases like that of C. P., functioning in a normal, rather uncomplicated social environment is highly probable. In this regard, then, such a child may not be considered a defective. He points to the fact that in the laboring force there are probably thousands upon thousands of individuals of the same intellectual level and performance as C. P. Unfortunately, Terman takes a position that such differences are very commonly found on a "racial" basis. He predicts that investigations of "racial" differences and mental traits will yield large and significant differences in general ability. This regrettable position by him has at least one saving grace: that he advocates some kind of experimentation on the issue. Because there are problems of determining what a race is, such investigations have been slow in coming and inconclusive in results. There seems to be no valid reason for accepting differences even where some definitive position about what constitutes a race is undertaken. To call a child of Portuguese extraction of a given "race" is an unfortunate step indeed.

Whatever the cause of the functioning, and whatever the relations with given subgroups, Terman advocates the use of the special class as the best means of instruction for such children. He further states that the curriculum should concentrate on the concrete and practical, since such children will not be able to manage abstractions. This position has been widely accepted in special educational though, fortunately, some slow change in attitude is beginning. It seems reasonable that under appropriate circumstances children who are borderline in ability can "abstract." Indeed any generalizing procedure on their part must represent abstraction. Some current research in training programs in institutions has indicated that even severely retarded children may be able to perform at an intellectual level frequently not believed, much less tried, before. Under conditions of appropriate conditioning, some more realistic limits for retarded children may be discovered and implemented.

Dull Normal

This group will have difficulty in academic performance in school but probably should remain in regular classrooms. Terman reports that the majority of the group will be successful through at least the eighth grade though the degree of success may reflect some retardation along the way. He does advocate that even within the regular classroom they have somewhat differentiated courses of study. Failure and nonpromotion should be avoided if at all possible.

Average Intelligence

Since about 60 percent of all school children will test between 90 and 110 IQ, this represents the largest group in the schools. According to Terman, such children seldom are school problems so far as ability and even achievement are concerned. Rarely do they represent discipline problems in the school, and it would appear that school programs are largely designed for their ability level. Some degree of selectivity begins in the high school, and even a child of normal intelligence will have difficulties if he attempts the college program, according to Terman, since a high degree of selectivity enters in at this educational level.

Superior Intelligence

These children are highly successful in school; indeed, they often become the best scholars. Rarely are they allowed to proceed at a rate in school which is consistent with their mental ability.

Very Superior

This rare group should achieve at the highest level in the schools, though Terman says they do not do so simply because they are not given sufficient opportunities. The competencies of children of very high ability might be illustrated by the following case study (Terman, 1916, p. 100):

E. M; boy, age 6–11; mental age 10; IQ 145. Learned to read at age of five without instruction and shortly afterward had learned from geography maps the capitols of all the states of the union. Started to school at seven and one-half. Entered the first grade at 9:00 a.m. and had been promoted to the fourth grade by 3:00 p.m. of the same day! Has now attended school a half year and is in the fifth grade, age seven years, eight months. Father is on the faculty of a university.

E. M. is as superior in personal and moral traits as in intelligence. Responsible, sturdy, playful, full of humor, loving, obedient. Health is excellent. Has had no home instruction in school work. His progress has been perfectly natural.

Terman makes the point that children of very high ability frequently are like the child described in the case study of E. M. Such children are superior not only intellectually, according to him, but also in all kinds of moral and social traits.

Genius and Near Genius

Terman states that a case of this nature will rarely occur more than once in each ten thousand children. Indeed so rare are such cases that intelligence tests do not define very well what behaviors may be expected from the score. At certain age levels it is possible that the Stanford Revisions will yield a ratio IQ as high as 200. Such cases are, of course, extremely rare and Terman reports the highest IQ obtained in his study of a thousand children was an IQ of 160.

Terman summarizes this section dealing with classification by pointing out that children with IQ's below 80 within the sample were unable to do satisfactory school work in a grade equivalent to the chronological age. By age 12 most children of this degree of retardation will be educationally retarded by from two to three grades. By contrast, a child with an IQ of 120 or above is almost never found below the grade level for his chronological age and occasionally he will be somewhat above this. Wherever located, this child will do superior school work. Terman strongly advocates use of grade skipping as a means of allowing such children to express their competence. That large group which tests between 90 and 110, and especially between 96 and 105, are probably very aptly placed by age level in grade and may be expected to do normal work at this level.

It must be noted that though Terman makes frequent reference to social factors, vocational factors, and the like, nearly all of his discussion and "proof" is dependent upon school behavior.

Reliability

Previously, reference has been made to the determination of reliability of IQ's by a test-retest method covering up to four years. But Terman also considers reliability from the standpoint of examiner stability. He specifically mentions that an examiner who can apply items correctly and who has been trained in psychological interpretation of responses can achieve a fairly accurate judgment of an individual's intelligence in a span less than an hour. In fact, this estimate would be better than one dependent upon observation even over a period of several months (Terman, 1916, p. 106). This introduces the matter of psychometric training in the use of an instrument like the Stanford Revision.

Two extremes found in the matter of test administration and interpretation are cited by Terman. There was a group of psychologists at the time who believed that only the most thoroughly trained psychometrists should have access to tests, since interpretations by any other individual would be worthless. By contrast, there was a group who felt that any competent teacher or physician could interpret estimates of a child's intelligence after only a minimum amount of training.

As Terman notes, these issues are matters of opinion and at the time few investigations had been undertaken to indicate the need for extensive training or what would constitute minimum training. He does cite cases of training programs with teachers which indicated that competent administration and interpretation could occur in a training program of about six weeks.

Terman agrees with Binet and others that an individual with intelligence enough to be a teacher, and one who is willing to study the techniques leading to correct administration, scoring and interpretation, should be able to use the scale with sufficient accuracy to determine the mental ability of a child. In such cases, however, individuals must recognize the lack of experience they possess and not make important decisions on invalid results. Certainly the inexperienced, untrained individual should not be allowed to make decisions of a major nature about an individual. This position assumes further importance from the standpoint that the procedure is not merely a mechanical one, as important as mechanical procedures may be. Terman takes the position that a classroom teacher would be a better person to use the test and make a decision about children than would a physician, since the teacher at least has some personal acquaintance with the children whom he will be testing. Regardless of training, Terman insists upon the necessity of the examiner being able to communicate with the child who is to be tested, to establish adequate rapport so that the child is at ease and performs at a realistic level.

Examinee Attitudes

One possible source of unreliability in the obtained test score is the attitude of the child at the time of testing. Issues related to whether or not the child performed at his best possible level, whether or not the child was anxious over the test setting, or whether or not illness may have

influenced his performance and the like must be given some consideration. Terman maintains that these kinds of questions will be adequately
handled by the experienced and competent examiner. Such an individual
will recognize some rather obvious symptoms of these conditions, and if
he cannot correct them he will not attempt a test.

Coaching

The matter of practice effect from one testing to another has remained an issue even today. There was a belief among some individuals
at the time of publication of the 1916 Revision that after the test was used
with a few students in a school the word would rapidly spread about the
content of the items. Terman relates that experience had demonstrated
that this is the case only rarely and then it is restricted to but a few specific
items. He points out that experimentation in the area of the psychology
of testimony indicates the qualitative matters influencing retention of
specific experiences. Since any child will receive a fairly sizable number
of items (perhaps as many as 30 or 36 if he covers five or six age levels)
it would be the rare individual indeed who could recall any sizable number of the items and report them to other children.

Terman relates that a number of children were interviewed by him
an hour or so after they had taken an examination. He would ask them
how many of the tests they could actually recall. With the young preschool-age child, the retention was quite poor and very general. For the
primary-grade child, a few items were remembered with some degree of
specificity but not reported very accurately. With the child in the upper
elementary grades, somewhat more accurate reporting was done but still
quite limited. For example, Terman says:

> A boy of twelve years said: "He told me to say all the words I could
> think of. He said some foolish things and asked what was foolish (he
> could not repeat a single absurdity). I had to put some blocks together.
> I had to do some problems in arithmetic (he could not repeat a single
> problem). He read some fables to me (asked about the fables, he was
> able to recall only part of one, that of the fox and the crow). He showed
> me the picture of a field and wanted to know how to find a ball. (Terman,
> 1916, p. 112)

If these are typical comments, as Terman reports, then practice effects
must be very small.

There is the added matter that direct feedback is not given to a child
in terms of his performance. There is no way that the child will discriminate whether his answer is correct or incorrect, except as he is unable to
answer questions. If the child assumes, since the examiner is very accepting, that the answers he gives are all correct ones, the chances are excel-

lent that on a retesting he will tend to give the same responses. This will maintain high reliability of the test, so long as some change in the child's knowledge does not actually occur.

Terman does state that there is a possibility that certain items when used repeatedly with the same child may yield practice effects. By and large he believes that consistency will occur, but the age and intelligence of the child plus the time interval between administrations will have some influence on how much consistency is found. Again he resorts to material reported by others to illustrate good-to-excellent consistency, particularly with low-ability children. Even over a period of a few days, Terman reports only small increments at best. He suggests the possibility of an alternate form to overcome any possibility of practice effects, and such an alternate form was provided with the 1937 Revision. It is interesting to note that in the 1960 Revision we again use only one form.

Social Advantages

Terman agrees that children who come from economically more favorable homes and with higher educational backgrounds will consistently perform better than children from less favorable conditions. He does not accept the argument, however, that this difference is due to some intrinsic bias in the test favoring such children. Instead, he makes the claim that hereditary factors are important not only in the test score but in the social status of the individual as well. Though extreme differences may lead to depression of a child's ability function, he maintains that the ordinary differences fround in social environment, as demonstrated in children from different backgrounds attending the same school, would have little or no effect on the validity of the scale. He specifically describes the kind of study which was later conducted by individuals such as Skeels and Skodak (Skeels, 1938; Skodak, 1939) as necessary to demonstrate the influence of different environmental conditions. This issue continues to be a major one in determing whether or not test scores are valid, and even whether or not tests should be used in the schools for educational decisions.

References

Edwards, A. J. *Individual Mental Testing. Part I: History and Theories.* Scranton, Pa.: Intext Educational Publishers, 1971.

Goddard, H. H. "The Binet and Simon Tests of Intellectual Capacity," *The Training School,* Vol. 5 (1908), 3–9.

Goddard, H. H. *Feeble-mindedness.* New York: Macmillan, 1914.

McNemar, Q. *The Revision of the Stanford-Binet Scale.* Boston: Houghton, 1942.

Skeels, H. J. "Mental Development of Children in Foster Homes," *Journal of Consulting Psychology,* Vol. 2 (1938) pp. 33–43.

Skodak, Marie, "Children in Foster Homes: A Study of Mental Development," University of Iowa *Studies in Child Welfare,* (1939). Vol. 16, No. 1.

Terman, L. M. *The Measurement of Intelligence.* Boston: Houghton, 1916.

Terman, L. M., and H. G. Childs. "Tentative Revision and Extension of the Binet-Simon Measuring Scale of Intelligence," *Journal of Educational Psychology,* 3 (1912), pp. 61–74, 133–143, 198–208, 277–289.

3

The 1937 Stanford Revision of the Binet-Simon Scales

The second revision of the Binet-Simon scales, appearing in 1937, was the most widely used individual intelligence scale until the publication of the 1960 Revision. Available in alternate forms, the test offered a measure of intellectual level in children employing and refining the methods of Binet. The 1937 Stanford Revision appeared at a time when it was apparently ideally suited to both educational and psychological needs. Its importance is not limited only to its wide popularity but its influence upon the development of other scales as well.

Features of the New Revision

Almost as soon as the 1916 Revision of the Binet-Simon scales appeared, criticisms were reported. As limitations were found in actual testing situations and verified through repetition, the need for a new revision became apparent. Terman and Merrill (1937) report that the 1916 Revision had proven to be reasonably valid and certainly reliable in the intermediate years from six through twelve. At preschool ages and above age 12 or so, however, the 1916 Revision had proven to be defective in many respects. This crudeness of measurement at both extremes was a major reason for undertaking a new revision. Specifically, problems had been found with mental levels under four and at average adult and above. Between mental levels of five and ten years, the procedures followed had yielded a test which gave quite usable scores. With increases above age 10, however, scores tended to be progressively too low. This matter of underestimating the mental abilities of children at ages 12 and above, particularly, had been a flaw cited in the Binet scales since the first one of 1905. Though the 1916 Revision was considerably better than the earlier scales, the same problem still existed.

In addition to this general matter of poor measurement at extremes, there was also the matter of some specific flaws. For one thing, a number of items in the scale had proven unsatisfactory because of insufficient validity, problems in scoring, and practice effects. Additionally, for certain items the instructions provided were too general to lead to complete objectivity on the part of examiners and comparability of results from one examiner to another. A major lack in the 1916 Revision, according to Terman and Merrill, was the absence of an alternate form which could be used for retesting of given children immediately following an original testing.

Characteristics of the Test

One of the strengths of the 1937 Revision was the availability of two forms, differing almost completely in content and yet prepared in such a way that mutually equivalent scores would be obtained. The forms were prepared in such a manner that item difficulty (percentage passing by age), range (from year II to Superior Adult III), and reliability and validity were equivalent. It is more than an interesting historical footnote that users of the 1937 Revision tended to rely almost exclusively on one form (Form L) rather than the other (Form M). The lack of a need for an equivalent form, in point of fact, led to the combination in most recent form of the Binet scales, the 1960 Revision.

In any event, Terman and Merrill point out that the two forms are essentially equal and either may be used. Of greater importance is the fact that they believed they had corrected many of the faults found in the 1916 Revision. A wider range of abilities in ages is covered in the 1937 Revision, with more accurate standardization. The procedures of administration and scoring are defined much more specifically than in the prior revision. There was an attempt to reduce the verbal nature of the scale, particularly in the preschool years.

One matter which remains unchanged, however, is the use of the procedures and principals proposed by Binet for an age scale. As with prior such scales, the essential procedure is that of a standardized interview, placing the child in a situation where he must deal with aspects of prior experiences in an intelligent fashion.

Extensions from the 1916 Scale

The 1937 Revision contains 129 items, some 39 items more than appeared in the 1916 Revision. Though all items are not administered to every child, there is now provided the possibility of a wider range of performances than had been true before. Below mental level V, items were provided at half-year intervals, beginning at year II and continuing through year IV-6. Items are also provided for years XI and XIII, levels which had not been included in the 1916 Revision. To provide further top, Superior Adults II and III are also included.

Essentially, the test remained highly verbal in its content. Though there was a serious effort to reduce the verbal nature of items at ages below five, the inclusion of verbal behavior is an increasing function as one proceeds from year VI up the remainder of the mental-age scale. Terman and Merrill make the point that in the upper age levels among children and as one enters maturity, intellectual differences among individuals become reflected increasingly in the ability to deal with verbal symbols and concepts. ". . . Language, essentially, is the shorthand of the higher thought processes, and the level at which this shorthand functions is one of the most important determinates of the level of the processes themselves" (Terman and Merrill, 1937, p. 5).

Scoring

One of the criticisms leveled against the 1916 Revision, with considerable validity, was the problem of objectivity in scoring. Terman and Merrill made a major effort to correct this flaw with the 1937 Revision. The problem of objectivity in scoring can never be avoided in this kind of test, since there will always be a certain amount of subjectivity and individual judgment in decisions about the adequacy of responses. The matter of subjectivity in scoring is a greater problem in an individual test than it is in a group test, since the individual test will allow for a greater variety of correctness in responses. Terman and Merrill attempted to reduce the amount of subjectivity as much as possible in the 1937 Revision by providing a number of examples for each item, illustrating acceptable and unacceptable responses, as well as stating the general principles which the examiner should follow in scoring. Indeed, many items which might have been very workable in the scale were excluded simply because it would be too difficult to achieve objectivity in scoring.

Sampling Procedures

To achieve norms which are usable in educational settings throughout the entire country requires a representative sampling of children to establish the norms. The 1937 Revision represented a considerable improvement over the 1916 Revision in this regard, though it is true that there were still some very limiting aspects to sampling procedures. Terman and Merrill attempted to acquire a representative sampling of the white child population of the United States between the ages of two and eighteen. Control variables used in the selection of the sample included age, grade location, nationality, and geographical distribution. Using these controls, 100 children were used at each half-year level below age 6, 200 children were used at each year level between 6 and 14, and there were 100 individuals at each level from age 15 to 18. Though there is currently much quarrel with the use of only white children in such norming, and the nature of control variables selected, the procedures followed by Terman and Merrill in the 1937 Revision represent such an improvement over any prior attempts that they are a landmark in the field of testing.

Development of the 1937 Revision

The same procedures followed with the initial steps of the 1916 Revision were also followed here. Specifically, the literature dealing with the use of the 1916 Stanford-Binet Revision was surveyed extensively. All kinds of test and item content were also considered if proposed as a measure of ability. As a result of this search, literally thousands of test items were acquired, a number of which were untried. The decision as to which items to consider for inclusion in this scale was based upon an essential principle: items to be considered in the tryout must reflect the kinds of experiences systematically related to widely accepted criteria of intellectual abilities. Such items, particularly of a nonverbal nature, reflected as wide a variety as could be obtained. Where problems with the item were evident in scoring, interest to the subject, time limitations, and administrative convenience, the items were excluded.

Once a large pool of seemingly usable items was available, an experimental trial was begun. The major purpose in this tryout was to determine those items which might initally be excluded so as to reduce the pool to a more usable number. For the purpose, approximately 1,000 children who had been tested with the 1916 Revision were used. This procedure allowed some preliminary determination of mental-age level for an item based upon performance of children whose mental ages had already been determined. Since all such items could not be administered to all children, each item was administered to at least twenty children of each mental-age range where it might be usable. Performances on these items were plotted in terms of percentage passing at tested mental ages. The slope of the resulting curves gave Terman and Merrill an indication of the probable validity of the item. The items included for further tryouts were placed at a level where approximately fifty percent of the children passed the item.

This procedure allowed tentative placement of items in a provisional scale. Terman and Merrill used three criteria for determining whether or not an item would be retained. The first of these was validity in terms of percent passing, the second dealt with ease and objectivity of scoring, and the third reflected more mundane but necessary matters such as economy in time of administration, interest to the child, and the like.

Terman and Merrill discuss their definition of validity in greater detail. As mentioned, the primary determination of the "validity of an item" was in terms of percentage passing from one age to the next. Ideally, an item should reflect a fairly constant incremental function from one age level to the next. The most usable and valid item thus would have zero percentage passing at the youngest age level and 100 percent passing at the highest age level. Between these extremes there would be an irregular but steady incremental function. Items which met this criterion were considered to be valid, but to insure this fact a second criterion was used as well. A weight was devised based upon the ratio of mean ages of subjects passing an item and of subjects failing the item to the standard error of the difference of these ages. This weight affords a more rigorous index than percentage increases in passes.

This initial experimental trial differed from succeeding efforts in that children of known mental age were used. Further efforts at standardization of the scale used less selected populations and samples rather than mental-age groups determined in advance. Though helpful in initial placement of items, it is true that the selection procedure for subjects might include some bias in item performance. Such a bias should be corrected for in the preceding steps.

Indeed, children for whom obtained mental ages were already available were not used in the preliminary tryout for the preschool age group. Here chronological age groups were used. Some 500 preschool-age children were selected from birth registration data. Nearly all of these children came from a single community.

The Provisional Scales

The procedures described thus far yielded a sufficient number of items to allow two provisional scales to be made up. In order to assure sufficient items for the age levels from II through Superior Adult III with appropriate alternates to be included in each scale required 258 items. To yield the 129 items needed in Form L, 209 items were provisionally provided, while 199 items comprised the pool for Form M. As Terman and Merrill point out, this excess of items was none too large; indeed, more items might have allowed some better placement than actually occurred.

The final standardization was based upon a sample of 3,184 individuals. The procedures followed by Terman and Merrill including establishing both the basal and ceiling level of performance for each member of the sample. Each subject took both forms of the test, with the order counterbalanced. Not less than one day nor more than one week separated the testing for the two forms. Some seven graduate students, thoroughly trained in the procedures, were used for administration purposes. As complete uniformity in administration as possible was followed and in all instances the examiners recorded verbatim as completely as possible every response made to every item administered. This latter procedure allowed for scoring of items at given age levels with various criteria rather than a single criterion.

The Subjects

As previously stated, Terman and Merrill were intent upon standardization with a group of representative school children so that the norms would be appropriate in school settings. To assure representativeness in the sample, certain variables were closely controlled.

GEOGRAPHICAL DISTRIBUTION. For norms to be representative of all areas of the country, each geographical area must contain its appropriate number. To control on this variable, Terman and Merrill used seventeen communities in eleven states. The states, with different-size communities from them being used, were California, Nevada, New York, Colorado, Kansas, Virginia, Vermont, Texas, Minnesota, Indiana, and Kentucky. Two years of testing comprised this step, with the testing in the second year using information in regard to socioeconomic level as well as geographic distribution.

SOCIOECONOMIC STATUS. Some four measures of socioeconomic status were used during the first year of testing as a means to control for this variable. Their approximations by occupational class were fairly good during the first year, but balance of rural and urban cases was not. During the second year an effort was extended to increase the number of rural children within the sample. Even so, the rural sampling was not adequate. Added to this is the fact that where discrepancies occur in the sampling they favor upper occupational status.

SCHOOL SAMPLES. Terman and Merrill state that schools of average social status were selected from each community used. Just what this means, and how the school was designated, is not so clear. In any event, for the schools from which the norms were obtained all the children between ages 6 and 14 who were within one month of their birthdate were tested. There were 100 boys and 100 girls at each of these age levels included in the standardization procedure.

Problems existed when norming other age levels, however. Major problems were encountered in achieving a sample for norming at age 15 and above. As Terman and Merrill remark, the high schools of those days were very selective. Differences from state to state existed in compulsory school ages and this contributed to the problem as well. In larger communities, there was also the possibility of technical schools and vocational high schools which would siphon off certain types of youngsters from the academic high school. Within these limitations, there were to be fifty males and fifty females tested at each of the age levels from 15 through 18. Though there was an attempt to include representative cases who had dropped out of school as well as graduated, this step was poorly achieved. Overall, the advanced age group leaves much to be desired as a norming sample.

PRESCHOOL SUBJECTS. Selection of the samples to achieve norms for ages 2 through 5 was also filled with problems. To achieve as close as possible a continuation of the distribution for ages 6 through 14, the younger siblings of the school group were used. However, insufficient numbers of children were available from this source so other procedures were also followed. Included here were such things as birth records, school census, clinics and day nurseries, and the like. Problems in particular given communities were found from one area to another and from rural to urban settings. As a result, the representative nature of the preschool sample may be as questionable as the sample for the so-called adult norms.

NATIONALITY. The children who made up the samples in the norming of the 1937 Revision were all American born and of Caucasian extraction. Such a procedure has its effects on the kinds of norms obtained. Whether or not one criticizes this particular criterion depends upon the kinds of comparisons which are desirable. If all children are to be compared with a select group such as American-born white children then there is no quarrel. However, the norms will not be representative of all kinds of groups within the United States.

Overall, considering the problems in urban-rural selection, social-class distribution, representativeness of extreme age groups, and the use of only white children, one may question the utility of norms from the 1937 Stanford-Binet. Indeed there are some very real limitations to the scores, their interpretation, and the type of prediction to be made. The procedures followed in the revision, however, are highly defensible, and the flaws so often cited may be corrected with future work. One might assume from this that the 1960 Revision of the Stanford-Binet in point of fact corrects for these errors. However, since the 1960 Revision is actually not a revision at all but uses the 1937 Stanford-Binet as the basis for all decisions that are made, the problems are still present in the Binet as it is currently used. The psychometrist must decide whether the limitations are too severe for his use of the test or whether within these limitations he can utilize the scores for some helpful prediction for the individual.

The Final Scale

In assigning items to the age levels of the final scale, two problems were met. The first of these required eliminating the less satisfactory items. Once this was done the second step required so arranging items within age and from age to age that the mean mental age of each group corresponded with the mean chronological age. Thus there would be a mean IQ of 100, ideally, for each age level.

To achieve success on these two problems, each item in each test was rescored from the verbatim responses taken by the examiners at the time of testing. In the rescoring, responses both of a satisfactory and an unsatisfactory nature were written separately for each item. Almost a full year was used in this procedure of item assessment.

The next step then required demonstrating adequate placement of items through the percentage-passing concept. To control for sex differences, if any, each item was scored and the percentage passing computed for the sexes differentially. Comparison of item performance for each child across forms was also possible. Finally, the correlation of each item with total score was computed in order to assist in elimination of poor items.

The age scale will be accurately standardized only when items are located within the correct mental age level, and the appropriate weight or value of the item is assigned. Terman and Merrill point out that no rules to follow existed prior to their work. Under the circumstances, some error might not only be expected but was assured by the procedures. Despite this fact, the final scale yielded a placement that was the best devised to that time. It should be pointed out, however, that some six revisions were necessary to achieve adequate placement of items in Form L. Once this was done, Form M could be matched rather easily through the final placement of items in Form L.

Terman and Merrill also note that data regarding validity, sex differences, improvement with age, influence of schooling, and other such factors were not available to them at that time. Their concern with such matters is reflected in the fact that they did not simply dismiss the issues. Data were gathered and reported in a volume published in 1942 entitled *The Revision of the Stanford-Binet Scale: An Analysis of The Standardization Data* by Quinn McNemar. This volume is of such importance to the understanding of the Stanford-Binet Revisions and use of the test scores that it deserves considerable citation at this point.

Standardization Data

The care expressed in building Forms L and M of the 1937 Stanford Revision was followed up through the relatively complete analysis of the standardization data done by McNemar (1942). As with other aspects of the test, this step represented a significant extension of work over that done with any test prior to that time. The information contained in this volume of McNemar's is a significant contribution to the understanding of the test content, the norms, and prediction from those norms.

Age Placement

The initial chapter of this volume was written by Lewis M. Terman, and represents a repetition and some explication of the manual (Terman and Merrill, 1937). One of the matters considered by Terman in this chapter is the point in the age scale at which items are placed. The items were to be so arranged within the age scale that the mean IQ for each age level would be 100. Logically, each item should assume a 50 percent passing criterion at each of the ages at which it is placed. This criterion, as logical as it may be, does not work in the practical sense. As Terman reports, where a 50 percent criterion is used the mental ages of younger children will be overestimated and those of older children will be underestimated.

There is an added problem that evolves from the nature of mental growth. If we consider a continumn of development from birth to maturity, the units along the base line will not be equidistant from each other. The distance between mental age one and mental age two, for example, will be much larger than the distance between mental age 12 and mental age 13 (see Fig. 3-1). Whether or not, in fact, the differences are as great as they appear in the measurement procedures, the fact remains that observable differences are not equal at all age points. This decrease in unit differences with increased age must also affect the scatter performance on the test. Older children will show a wider scatter of performance than younger children will, primarily because the measurement distances are restricted. The inevitable result, as Terman makes clear, is that an item correctly located at the lower age level will show a higher percentage of passes for that age group than will a corresponding item correctly placed at an older age level.

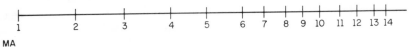

MA

Fig. 3-1. Hypothetical developmental distribution of mental ages.

This matter is somewhat further complicated by the relationship of a given item to other items both preceding and following it. What represents correct placement of an item will be reflected to some degree by the nature of the items surrounding it. Terman illustrates this by pointing out that the correct percentage of passes for age level XII depends to some degree at least on whether or not there is an age XI level and an age XIII level, each with appropriately placed items. In the original Stanford-Binet of 1916, ages 11 and 13 were not found. In the 1937 Revision there are ages 11 and 13. The result is that the items now appearing at age 12 for the 1937 Revision are influenced by the presence of these two age levels. But it is not merely a matter of what ages are selected for inclusion in the test. The make-up of items at a given year level, appropriately placed for that year level, influences to some degree what will be an appropriate makeup of items at the next succeeding year level. As a result of all these factors, a statement of percentage passing for any given item, though necessary, is hardly sufficient. There must be a considerable amount of empirical work done with given items, with these items in the context of other items at a given age level, and with comparisons of items between adjacent age levels.

Ideally, all of these problems could be solved and a test of such accurate make-up established that every item would work perfectly at its age level. There remains, however, as a restraint on this ideal, the fact that it is humanly impossible to devise enough items of exactly the correct difficulty for any given level in the context discussed above. As a result, the accuracy and validity of the measure is correspondingly reduced. What is of greater importance is the fact that Terman and Merrill worked so diligently to achieve as near the ideal criteria as possible. Not only were there several successive tryouts done in the field, but rescoring of items for placement at given age levels occurred as well. This step allowed different standards of passing or failing to adjust better the placement of the item. Terman points out that despite their great care there are still a small number of what he calls "relatively inferior tests" contained in the scale. The marvel is not that this occurred but that there are so few such items. With less care and concern for accuracy in measurement, the Stanford-Binet Revision would not have been the instrument which has so influenced the development of other tests.

There remains the problem of placement of items at the adult level. It is in this regard that perhaps the most fundamental errors in judgment were made by Terman and Merrill. Essentially, the assumption of Binet that mental growth ceases about age 16 was maintained. If this point represents the actual asymptotic function of mental growth, then the same devisor must be used for all individuals aged sixteen and above. There is a further confounding factor, since the slope of the mental growth curve is assumed to begin to flatten out prior to age 16. The standard for placement of items, it will be recalled, was to assure that the mean IQ for each age level was approximately 100. With the change in slope of the mental-growth curve and the asymptotic function at age 16, it was necessary to adjust the procedures followed for older age children. Terman and Merrill decided to make the adjustment by spreading the twelve months loss at age 16 over a three-year period. Thus, four months in CA would be dropped at the fourteenth year, four in the fifteenth, and four in the sixteenth. As a result, the maximum chronological age used in a devisor to achieve a ratio IQ (i.e., $\frac{MA}{CA} = IQ$) was now 15.

There is no quarrel with the procedure followed. The quarrel is with the assumption that mental growth ceases at age 16. Evidence available even at the time of the restandardization of the Stanford Revision indicated that this was too low an age figure. So long as the test is used only with children up to the age 14, perhaps the assumption is not in serious error. But there are problems if the test is used with older individuals, and particularly if there is some assumption that the so-called adult scales are accurate reflections of adult intellectual performance. In point of fact, these scales represent much more a kind of "top" for bright children of ages 11 through 14 than they do adult scales as such. This matter is of such importance that the psychometrist must bear it in mind in selecting the appropriate test for age groups over CA 15. Despite the limitations and the arguments cited here, Terman points out that the arrangement of tests at the upper age level does yield IQ distributions quite similar to those of lower age levels. This is an improvement, in and of itself over the 1916 Revision.

This raises another issue: Why choose an age scale in the first place? Would it not be easier to set up a test on the basis of a point scale and avoid some of these problems of what constitutes mental age? Particularly is this a valid question as one approaches whatever presumed asymptotic function for mental growth exists. At whatever age "adult maturity" is reached, an age scale is no longer appropriate. Having admitted that the point scale would be more easily standardized than the age scale, Terman nevertheless defends his procedure. Essentially his argument is that within those ages where age scales are appropriate, the examiner can determine item by item the progress of children more accurately and completely. This procedure can be extended then to some analysis of age level by age-level progress throughout the scatter. As defensible as this argument might seem, seldom is such a procedure actually followed by the examiner using the Stanford Revision. Discrete item-by-item analysis for the child is tenuous at best due to some of the strong characteristics upon which the test is based in the first place.

The level-by-level progress of the child is most reflected in terms of the total MA score achieved and less in what kind of performance occurred from one year level to another year level. Some form of pattern analysis even with those tests designed to yield such a pattern is difficult. With a test like the Stanford Revision of the Binet-Simon scales, it is indefensible.

And yet there is a very strong case to be made for the development of an age scale. This case revolves around the comparative qualities of mental age levels. The validity of the mental age is the crucial issue here, an issue still much questioned but for which some research is available indicating its acceptance. The issue becomes one of comparison of children of unlike chronological age who have achieved the same mental age. This issue, as related at least to classroom behavior, has been considered as follows:

> One facet of the problem is reflected in the validity of mental age as an expression of level of intelligence. If children of differing chronological ages obtain the same mental age, may they be expected to perform alike in the classroom. Again, little research has been conducted. Two studies, however, are directly pertinent to the question.
>
> Kolstoe (1954) matched two groups of children on mental age as determined by the Stanford-Binet. Each group had a mean MA of 11-3, but one group had a mean chronological age of 9-3 and the other a mean CA of 14-3. Thus, the mean IQ of the younger group was 127 and of the older group, 80. The groups differed, then, in CA and rate of growth but compared closely on level of intelligence. Kolstoe administered the Wechsler Intelligence Scale for Children and the Thurstones' Primary Mental Abilities Test. Seemingly, if the MA concept is invalid, the two groups, because of differences in experiences due to age differences and expression of mental traits, should be unalike on other measures of ability.
>
> Of the seventeen comparisons made (eleven subtests from the WISC and six from the PMA), four yielded statistically significant differ-

ences. Three of these (Comprehension and Coding from the WISC and Number from the PMA) favored the older group. The other (Digits from the WISC) favored the younger groups. The results, then, indicate that children matched carefully on MA perform alike on other and similar tasks reflecting the trait called intelligence.

A companion study, using the same sample, was conducted by Bliesmer (1954) and dealt more directly with classroom behaviors. The children were compared on several measures of reading. . . . Of the ten comparisons, half of them yielded statistically significant differences, each favoring the younger subgroup. Whatever invalidity in the MA exists, then, reflects against bright young subjects. Whether or not absolute differences are of importance is a matter for debate.

The two studies cited are insufficient to demonstrate conclusively the validity of the MA concept. Wechsler (1958, pp. 24–27) has presented his reasons for avoiding the concept, based upon limitations inherent in it. Since many tests, including Wechsler's, do not base norms upon MA's, the final acceptance or rejection of the concept will not invalidate intelligence tests. The central issue, however, bears on the use of any intelligence test, regardless of how scores are derived. Unless test scores are comparable at various ages and related systematically to behaviors emanating from intelligence, tests are of little value. For example, given the same task, brighter individuals should perform better than duller ones. Moreover, if differences in ability are controlled or removed, differences in task performance should not be found. The problem is complicated, of course, by motivational features. Still, too little effort has been expended on research which will illustrate the essential validity of intelligence tests. Until such research is available, opinion and argument will continue without empirical support. (Edwards and Scannell, 1968, pp. 99–100)

Distribution of IQ's

Beginning in Chapter 2, McNemar (1942) presents systematic data relating to major issues in the use of intelligence tests, and particularly the Stanford Revision. One matter of concern is the distribution of scores, and the particular distribution of intelligence quotients. McNemar has plotted the frequency distribution of IQ's for both Form L and Form M in four age groupings. The first of these encompasses the distributions of IQ's from ages 2½ through 5½, the second from ages 6 through 13, the third from ages 14 through 18, and the fourth, the composite of scores across all age units. The results indicate that the distribution for the first two age groups are fairly symmetrical. Though the distribution for the third age group (14 through 18) is reasonably normal, the spread is much less than with younger ages. This result is to be expected. The procedures followed in the standardization almost necessitate a restriction in range of IQ's for these upper age levels. McNemar makes the point that the total distribution is highly symmetrical but somewhat more peaked than expectations from the normal curve.

The departures from the normal distribution which are found are relatively small and are of such a minor nature that any interpretations of IQ's in terms of the normal distribution are undisturbed. Particularly, McNemar makes clear, the distributions are such that research utilizing the Stanford-Binet should be quite valid. Though the distributions are reasonably normal, equality of units certainly is not demonstrated, as McNemar points out. This brings up the issue of relative relationships among scores where absolute zero is undetermined. It is not possible to say that a child with an IQ of 140 is twice as bright as one with an IQ of 70, for example, since we do not know the distances involved even though the distribution of the scores obtained is normal. Again, some quite practical results are obtained in the use of scales even though knowledge of zero is lacking. Whatever criticism evolves for the Stanford-Binet in this regard applies equally to other tests of intelligence, and in point of fact, to any test of a psychological nature.

The statement has been long and widely accepted that the Stanford-Binet has a mean IQ of 100 with a standard deviation of 16 IQ points. Actually, this assumption is not really met. For example, even though some age groups are combined, the means all are above 100 and at least in the case of the youngest age group, the mean IQ is in excess of 106. In every instance as well, the standard deviations differ from 16. In actual fact the means for both forms exceeded 100 even when smoothed. Variability ranged from a low of 12.5 at age 6 to a high of 20.6 at age 2½ for Form L, and from 13.2 at age 6 to 20.7 at age 2½ on Form M. One outcome of such differences was incomparability of IQ's at different age levels. It was possible, for example, for a child taking Form L at age 6 to obtain an IQ of 113, while at age 2½ he had obtained an IQ of 121. Since each of these scores is one standard deviation above the mean for his age group, they represent the same score in the distribution.

Unless the psychometrist was careful in his evaluations it is easy to see how some apparently marked IQ changes occurred. Actually such changes may not have existed at all. This was probably the major reason for the adoption of the deviation IQ in the 1960 Stanford Revision, a departure which corrected for the problems cited here. Having corrected for that problem, however, other problems were thereby raised. This matter will be discussed further in the chapter dealing with the 1960 Revision.

Age-Grade Norms

One means of viewing the distributions cited in the above section, related but offering a somewhat different viewpoint as well, is by examining data for each grade and for age-grade groupings. For this purpose,

McNemar confines himself to children between ages 6 and 18 who were enrolled in school. Since norming occurred in a number of school systems in communities throughout the country, the analysis has certain limitations. Particularly since promotion policies will vary from one place to another, direct comparisons are somewhat in error. McNemar, therefore, cautions some reserve in generalizing this data to all communities and schools.

The age-grade distribution computed by McNemar shows an increasing range. There is also an increase in retardation as compared with acceleration. This result probably indicates a consistent promotion policy rather than any increase in retardation as such. Most schools apparently were more willing to retain a child in grade than to grade-skip. McNemar does make a point, however, that there seems to be greater acceleration by one grade than retardation by one grade.

The mean IQ for each age group was also plotted by grade, with results similar to those for age-grade norms. There is only a slight relationship between grade location and mean IQ. Since IQ is not related to age, even such a slight relationship is important. Either school curricula, at least in 1937, were so well selected that a child of average intelligence would be pretty well placed in grade or some bias was shared by item placement in the test with educational decisions. Considering the norming of the test, the latter seems a more likely explanation than the former. Indeed, McNemar concludes that the use of children within one month of birthdate may not give as adequate a picture of normal progress through school as would the use of children within one month of half-year birthdates. For example, instead of using children within plus or minus one month of seven years for norming purposes, children should be used within plus or minus one month of seven years six months, and so on.

Children who are accelerated by one grade averaged about eleven IQ points above the norm for the grade. As an average, those retarded by one grade tended to score about eleven points below their grade norm. An equal increment or decrement is found for two grades acceleration or retardation. Further extremes were not investigated since the numbers of children accelerated by three grades or more over their normal age group or retarded by that degree were not sufficient. McNemar makes the point that school progress of individuals does seem to be related to the matter of their intelligence, and may be dependent upon intellectual level. He cautions, however, that there is no greater predictive accuracy for individuals from this data than from any other source. The prediction, after all, is on the basis of groups of individuals of sufficient size, not by each individual himself. He makes it clear that the distributions do not allow prediction of the individual IQ from his age-grade location and infers that the reverse prediction will be just as inaccurate. Overall, within the age groups, younger children in the grade tend to have IQ's about average while those who are older in the grade tend to have IQ's below average.

The educational implications of such a finding may be of considerably greater importance. In considering the means by age, by grade, and by age-grade, McNemar states that the mental maturity of younger children is only slightly greater than that of older children in the same grade. Intellectually, all children in a given grade, on the average, have achieved about the same level of mental maturity as measured by the Stanford-Binet. One result of this is that children of different age within a grade contribute little to variation of mental age within that grade. The resulting homogeneity should assure greater teaching ease. Probably, according to McNemar, the grades are more homogenous in respect to mental level than if age were the sole criterion for promotion. Even so, whatever promotion policies were followed in the schools had not tended to reduce the variability in mental level within a grade over what might have been conceived if only chronological age were the basis.

McNemar has prepared a table indicating mental age ranges by grade and comments that these data reflect a picture of grading practices in the public schools of this country during the 1920's. The increasing variability from grade 1 through grade 12 for mental age calls for competence and versatility on the part of the teachers in reaching all such children. One significant point made by McNemar in this regard is that, despite the increase in the use of standardized ability and achievement tests prior to the collection of these data, very little effect had been exerted upon the actual school situation. There was as much heterogeneity in these data of the 1930's as had been true prior to the development of the group and individual tests from approximately 1915 to 1920. Though not a purpose of this book, McNemar does speculate on adequate provisions for individual differences in the schools. He concludes that ability grouping within a grade might seem the most feasible approach to the problem of acceleration and retardation. Various plans utilizing ability grouping have been tried educationally since that time, usually with little effectiveness.

Urban and Rural Comparisons

As mentioned earlier and reiterated by McNemar, the communities included in the norming procedures for the 1937 Revision were probably not representative as much as desired. Since this is the first attempt to include some nationwide sampling, the norms still represent a considerable improvement over prior test attempts. McNemar considered the data from the standpoint of urban, suburban, and rural communities. Differences between urban and suburban mean IQ's were minor, but rural groups scored lower at age level than either of the other two.

Interestingly, the smallest differences between rural and urban groups is in the age levels from 2 to 5½. As children enter and continue through school, differences between rural and urban norm groups tend to increase somewhat. This is probably a function more of educational facilities, teacher qualifications, and resources than it is some difference in ability by residential area.

Socioeconomic Variables

McNemar used a classifications scheme devised by Florence Goodenough for determining occupational status of individuals. Seven subgroups, ranging from professionals to day laborers, were provided in the classification. McNemar makes the point that this system is no better nor any worse than other procedures which were available. As in other studies, differences were found between occupational groups, particularly at the extremes. Children whose fathers were in the professions had an average IQ of about 115. Those children whose fathers were day laborers showed mean IQ's of about 96. Mean IQ's increased from the lowest occupational group to the highest for each of four age subgroups. The sole exception for this was in group five (semiskilled, minor clerical, and minor business) which showed higher mean IQ's at each of the age subgroup levels than for occupational group four (rural owners). The classification rural owners is probably misplaced in the occupational scheme of Goddenough. Thus groups 5 and 4 should actually be reversed.

Despite the differences found by occupational groups, there is still a considerable amount of overlap. McNemar makes the point that about ten percent of the children of day laborers, the lowest socioeconomic group, will have IQ's in excess of the mean of children of fathers who are professionals. At the same time, the overall performance of the children of the professional group is such that only about 10 percent of children in this classification have IQ's below the general average IQ of 100. Another interesting matter is the fact that standard deviations show little variation across occupational groups. There are no trends with age so that mean IQ's at the youngest age level for an occupational group are apt to be consistent with the highest age level.

Sibling Performances

Procedures followed in the norming allow comparisons among siblings which were not possible before. McNemar cites the uniqueness of the data here being due to four factors. First, there is less error of measurement in the sibling data because of the composite Form L and M IQ's which were achieved. Second, for either scale, scores are available for sibling pairs differing widely in age. Third, through a process of subdividing, correlations may be computed for different and related groups. For example, a preschool sibling may be compared with an older school-age sibling, or a school-age child may be compared with an older school-age brother or sister. Finally, the sibling samples, McNemar believes, are more representative of sibling relationships than had been reported in the past. The results across the various comparisons which are possible indicate correlation co-efficients ranging from .48 through .57. For the total number of sibling pairs available, a sample of 384 pairs, the obtained correlation coefficient is .53. Such a moderate correlation coefficient has been reported in other studies of sibling relationships. The fact that the relationships are of about the same value at the different age comparisons indicates that whatever factors are responsible for sibling resemblences in measured intelligence operate at all age levels.

Sex Differences

One issue in intelligence testing, discussed to some extent already, is the matter of item discrimination by sex. The major issue, of course, is whether or not all items tend to show a systematic sex difference. A related, somewhat secondary, but still important issue is whether specific kinds of items discriminate in favor of either sex. If there is an affirmative answer to either issue, certain decisions must be made relative to test content and/or subgroups for whom the test is relevant. McNemar approaches the issue by noting that the test constructor may operate on either one of two assumptions. First, he may assume that any sex differences that are found are indicators of true differences by sex in native ability. If this assumption is made, separate norms for boys and girls will be necessary to allow for the true difference.

The second possible assumption is that whatever differences are found are due to differences in experience, training, and interest, and not to differences in ability. If this assumption is made, all items which show a difference large enough to be considered significant will be removed from the test content. As McNemar remarks, Terman and Merrill agreed with the second of these assumptions and attempted to eliminate items which showed differences between the sexes. Limitations of the number of items available did not allow for the elimination of all such items. There was an attempt, as a result, to balance the occurrence of sex-differentiating items within the scale. Items occurring in the 1937 Revision which showed sex differences are cited in Chapter 2.

Having made the decision to include a certain number of sex-differentiating items, the issue becomes one of the degree to which this affects mean IQ's across the various age levels. McNemar prepared a table for such differences in IQ beginning at age 2 and continuing through age 18. Only at ages 2½ and 3½ were large enough IQ differences disclosed to indicate some problem. For subgroups combined for ages 2 through 5½ there is a slight superiority in mean scores for girls, for ages 6 through 14 and ages 15 through 18, the superiority rests slightly, very slightly, with boys. The differences in any event are too small to cause concern. It should be clear, however, that the test is so arranged that this result will be found. There is still the issue that certain kinds of behaviors of an intellectual nature may disclose true differences between males and females. This issue is avoided for the purposes of the scale by Terman and Merrill.

Item Differences for Sex

The determination as to significance between the sexes for a given item used the same criterion as established for item placement by year level: percentage passing. Critical ratios for differences in percent passing between the sexes were computed for each item. When this procedure was followed, several items were found favoring either sex.

Items which show differences large enough to reach significance tend to favor girls at preschool ages and boys at school ages. The meaning for this is not clear. McNemar comments on this confusion by affirming that highly similar items do not always yield consistent sex differences. By analysing each item for which sex differences are found, McNemar concludes that sex differences are a function of item content more than any differences in basic intellectual abilities called for by the item. Thus the issue remains exactly as it was before. Whether or not true sex differences exist for at least some kinds of intellectual behavior is unanswered by the content of the Stanford-Binet scale.

Reliability

A major and essential concern in any testing procedure is that of consistency in performance by the individual. Where the performance of the individual lacks consistency, the meaning of any given score is doubtful and must be attributed to chance. Statistical demonstration of reliability is necessary before any estimates of validity are possible. In standardized testing, reliability estimates, however computed, represent the available data about consistency and performance.

The Stanford revisions of the Binet-Simon scales represent something of a special case. Mental growth operates to increase the total amount of performance within increasing age. Scatter in performance patterns is the rule rather than the exception with increasing age. For example, a child of chronological age 12 who assumes the mean mental age for his group (that is, MA of 12) will show performance on more items than will a child of chronological age 9 who is also at the mean mental age for his group. Since scatter increases with chronological age, there should be a consequent increase in the standard error of measurement with mental age. But this increase is not only a function of age as such, but a function of performance as well. Documentation with literally thousands of cases with an age scale like the Stanford-Binet is too conclusive to warrant any question.

If one finds increasing scatter of performance with increasing MA, it would seem reasonable to find an increase of performance by high IQ groups within an age group. If this is true, the standard error of measurement for high IQ's should be greater than it is for lower IQ's. For a norming group of twelve-year-old children, for example, the standard error of measurement for IQ's 120 and above would be greater than for IQ's 80 and below. McNemar reports such a logical position, and demonstrates its existence by examples. Reliability estimates and standard errors of measurement must be computed and applied within the unique characteristics of the age scale and its distribution.

Estimating Reliability

Obviously then the make-up of the particular test will determine the reliability estimates which are possible. Since most tests do not have an alternate form, they depend either upon split half or test-retest reliability estimates, and most often the former rather than the latter. With those tests which do provide alternate forms, however, this reliability estimate is usually accepted as being more rigorous and stable than either of the others. The make-up of the Binet-Simon scales and the Revisions done by Terman at Stanford University are such that such an estimate with a split-half formula is not feasible. Much more reasonable, with the 1937 Revision, is utilization of the alternate-form procedure. Because of repetition of some items in both forms, the estimates are not as accurate or unbiased as they might be.

Within these limitations, McNemar points to two means by which reliability of IQ scores might be estimated. In either procedure it must be remembered that the intelligence quotient is a derived score: the score obtained with the Binet scales is a mental age. The characteristics of the mental age therefore affect the derivation of the ratio IQ and the consequent reliabilities which will attach to different age distributions.

The first procedure for estimating reliability proposed by McNemar requires subdividing IQ's into subgroups. Thus individuals whose composite IQ's fell between the interval 70 and 79 would constitute such a subgroup. The actual score on Form L and the actual score on Form M would be compared for each individual and the average difference between these scores obtained. With consequent statistical corrections, the resulting values are estimates of the reliability coefficient for the given IQ intervals. Such a reliability estimate for average differences was obtained for IQ groupings of 69 and below, 70–79, 80–89, and so on to 140 and above. The obtained coefficients tended to be greater for low IQ's than for higher, as was to be expected. In some instances, the size of the sample was quite small, however. As an estimate of population variance, a standard deviation of 16.6 was used in all cases. This standard deviation is the average of the standard deviations for Form L and Form M IQ distributions for almost three thousand cases. As cited earlier, in point of fact the standard deviations vary in some cases quite widely from this average SD.

The second method described and used by McNemar used arrays of variances. These were computed for Form L and Form M IQ's and directly compared. It was possible with this procedure to determine how accurately IQ on Form L, for example, could be predicted from the IQ on Form M. Given this information, an estimate of the equivalent correlation which represents a reliability coefficient could be made. Again, the estimates of realiability using variances tended to increase with lower IQ and to be highly comparable with those reliability estimates obtained with average differences. Such differences as were found, McNemar attributes to chance. As a result a smoothed distribution of reliabilities by IQ levels and the resulting standard error of measurement is reported for age levels 2½ to 5½, 6 to 13, and 14 to 18.

McNemar believes that these smoothed values are reasonably accurate estimates of reliability and errors of measurement. Both are reported because each plays a role in utilizing the test score. The reliability coefficient yields a measure of the relative accuracy with which groups of individuals may be ranked with the test. The standard error of measurement describes the amount of change that might be expected to occur by repeated testing of the individual, in units of the test itself. The psychometrist uses both kinds of information as a means of interpreting test scores. As has been mentioned, in the absence of consistency, test scores are meaningless. Such information as this is not cited for statistical sophistication, but for its absolute importance to any utilization of test scores, whether they be the Stanford-Binet or any other test.

Just as there may be error of measurement in the intelligence quotient so may there be error of measurement in the mental age. As a result, McNemar has computed standard error of measurement in months for mental-age scores. Related procedures to the estimate of standard error of measurement for IQ's were followed in this procedure with mental ages.

Spread of Scores

If one were able to build a perfect age scale, each individual measured by the test would pass all items at one year level and fail all items above that point. Thus there would be an exact score which represents his mental age. Such an ideal has not to this time been achieved, with the result that the estimate of an individual's intellectual level must be based upon some performance pattern over several adjacent year levels. For this reason we expect a child to pass all items at a given year level and then to pass a certain number of items at year levels above that point, decreasing in the number of such items passed until the ceiling age is reached at which no items are passed. Some amount of error is introduced in the fact that the ideal is not reached then. Complicating this fact is the additional fact that two children may achieve the same level score, MA, and yet not show the same kind of test performance. An example of differences in scatter for two children of equivalent mental age is given in Table 3-1. Such differences introduced further scores of error in the score obtained with the Stanford-Binet.

TABLE 3-1
HYPOTHETICAL PERFORMANCE PATTERNS (SCATTER)
FOR TWO CHILDREN OF EQUAL MA AND CA

Child 1				Child 2			
Year Level	Items Passed	Years	Months	Year Level	Items Passed	Years	Months
VI	6	6	0	VII	6	7	0
VII	5		10	VIII	3		6
VIII	5		10	IX	4		8
IX	3		6	X	1		2
X	3		6	XI	1		2
XI	2		4	XII	1		2
XII	1		2	XIII	1		2
XIII	1		2	XIV	1		2
XIV	0		0	AA	2		4
				SAI	0		0
		6	40			7	28

MA = 9 – 4   MA = 9 – 4

From Edwards and Scannell, 1968, p. 67.

Scatter must be expected, according to McNemar, because the scale is made up of items reflecting the percentage of an age group passing the item. The resulting curve from age to age for each item shows a rather gradual slope. Added to this is the fact that items are not perfectly intercorrelated. Given these two conditions, the results of our inadequacies in building the perfect test, we must expect some pattern of passes and failures for each individual over several age levels.

The score obtained by the Stanford Revision is intended to reflect a general ability. However, it seems reasonable that specific abilities make up such a general score and influence what that general value may be. If there are differences in performance on specific abilities, these will be reflected in the pattern of passes and failures. If there is a further probability, as McNemar notes, that group functions may also operate concurrently with specific ability, item performance must reflect these as well. Such specific and group factors may develop at different rates for the individual, depending on the state of mental growth at the time of testing. These latter factors will allow the opportunity for an individual to fail some items below his general level of performance and to pass some items above the general level of performance. Again, therefore, we must expect scatter on this ground alone.

At least two other factors make their contribution to the necessity for scatter in test performance. First of all, it is to be expected that a single item will show relative unreliability. Though the total of a number of items showing relative unreliability individually may yield a reliable test, each bit of unreliability does exert its influence on accuracy of measurement at a given time. There is of course the added problem that reliability of a single item varies for the same individual from one testing to another testing. This may be due in part to changes in mental function, but probably is not restricted just to that. Thus momentary considerations also influence reliability of a single item and its consequent work within the test from one point to another point. The already demonstrated increase in variability from lower to higher age levels is a final factor in the presence of scatter.

McNemar reports his attempts to deal with the presence of scatter on the basis of two approaches. The first of these deals with the function of the item as measuring general versus specific ability. The second approach attempts to determine the function of the individual in the amount of scatter obtained.

The "Pass-Fail" Criterion

Though several means of answering the question might be used, limitations in the data available restricted the procedures followed by McNemar. Specifically, he examined the pattern for passing and failing for those individuals who showed scatter of an abnormal nature. Individuals were used in the analysis who showed a spread of passing greatly above the mental-age level and cases where individuals showed a spread of failing far below the MA level. What constitutes extreme is an arbitrary decision, decided by McNemar by using approximately 25 percent of the cases available to him. In his opinion, such a percentage probably is too great to represent truly extreme variability. There were 709 subjects between the ages of 5 and 14 who showed a high degree of scatter in passing and 757 individuals with extreme failing scatter. For each of these individuals, particular items passed or failed were recorded. These items were then grouped into patterns, insofar as this was possible. The data were considered in terms of mental-age level, rather than chronological age. The resulting number of "patterns" was very large.

The resulting data were quite complex, and there was no known way to analyze it statistically. The conclusions drawn by McNemar, then, are based upon his examination on a somewhat subjective basis. One matter which seemed to occur with some consistency in the spread of performance in either direction dealt with recurring items. Certain items are used at different age levels with higher-scoring standards as one proceeds up the scale. If a child is administered an item near his mental-age level, which he passes at a higher criterion than necessary at that point he receives credit at higher age levels. This matter, in part, will help to account for extreme passes, then. In the same way, if he fails an item of a given scoring standard near his mental-age level, he has failed it at all ages below unless these were administered in finding a basal. Such a result in either direction introduces a possible specious effect on test performance.

McNemar holds that this feature will certainly not account for more than a portion of the extreme variations found. There did seem to be an associated factor in items which employ similar test situations, though the content of the item is different. For example, on Form L he reports some five items which are not the same test but are similar in nature and apparently lead to the spread of failures. These were picture absurdities, comprehension, verbal absurdities, digits, and memory for sentences. Though failure from one type of item to another in this case would not be as common as with the same items scored with different standards, there was still some consistency in inability to perform on several of these kinds of items where one was consistently missed. This fact raises the issue of inhibitory sources in performance. A point scale may be even more susceptible to such effects than an age scale. This issue is considered in terms of the Wechsler scales in later chapters. Fewer instances of such relatedness were found for those youngsters who tended to pass items far beyond the mental level achieved by them.

One might expect to find, where repeated items become a basis for increasing spread, that the vocabulary test is a chief offender. McNemar claims that this actually does not occur. Both vocabulary and repeating digits do recur as a test situation with higher scoring standards at many points in the scale. Performance on these items was not related to extending the variability, however, in the upward direction particularly. He accounts for this fact by stating that the vocabulary test is a reflection of the general function measured by the total test.

Overall, some explanation of this nature for the presence of scatter, particularly of an extreme nature, is inadequate. Certainly inability to apply data to different kinds of analyses is to a large degree responsible for this inadequacy. Given the approach taken by McNemar, attempting to explain scatter as a function of the scale seems less than helpful.

Scatter as a Function of Individual Performance

From the ideal viewpoint, the scatter obtained in any test performance should be a function of the individual more than it is a function of the test as such. The analyses attempted by McNemar for such an explanation of scatter are as unsatisfactory in their results as are the analyses done on the function of the scale itself. For one thing, he reports only negligible correlation coefficients (tetrachoric r's) between upward and downward spread of performance for a given mental-age level. Similarly, Pearson r's for variability scores from Form L to Form M are negligible to moderate only. Finally, correlation coefficients between variability and obtained IQ on Form L for a given MA group were negligible and all negative. The only possible conclusion one can draw is that McNemar was unable to explain the reason for kinds of scatter obtained with the 1937 Stanford Revision.

Validity

Item placement in an age scale is dependent upon the percentage of children passing the item at given age levels. Once information is available which indicates that younger children tend to fail and older children to easily pass the item, with a spread of percentages between these extremes, the item may be placed at the appropriate age level. McNemar makes the point that percentage passing is necessary though hardly sufficient information about the validity of the item. Validity in this sense applies to the correct placement of the item in the age scale.

The issue is a greater one, however, than merely determining difficulty of a given item. To build an intelligence test requires, first of all, that the test constructor determine what he believes intelligence to be. Having made this decision, he then selects items which reflect behaviorally this definition. Essentially, McNemar maintains, items should be selected which will satisfy some criterion of social utility.

Whatever the definition of intelligence assumed by the test constructor, it would seem reasonable that its expression is something that increases in quality and/or quantity during childhood at least. If intelligence does show development with age, it would seem reasonable that any item measuring the trait should show an increased percentage passing for successive age levels. Again, this does not assure that the item is valid. McNemar uses the example of the ability to throw a baseball a distance of twenty-five feet. As he says, there will be an increase in success with age during childhood but such an item would not be valid in an intelligence scale. There must be other criteria employed beyond the matter of percentage passing. Most frequently, test scores will be correlated with other tests already accepted, or with subjective ratings of the abilities of children by teachers or others who have contact with them, or of individual item with total score. Although these offer more usable information, they still do not assure the validity of the item as a measure of intelligence per se. In the 1937 Revision, the additional criterion used was to correlate the composite of L and M scores so that whatever items are retained will show some common factor, assumed to be general intelligence.

McNemar has reported data for each item included in each scale in terms of percentage passing the item across various age levels. There is the added factor of whether or not items included within any given age level should show a percentage increase in passing. Though one might assume that every item at a given year level should show the same percentage passing (say 60 percent), this criterion is too difficult to achieve ever to be realistic. But if items of different percentage passing must be included at each year level, how should they be arranged? McNemar makes it clear that there was no attempt to arrange the items within any age level in order of difficulty. He does not feel this to be any serious drawback for the utilization of the scales for the determination of general mental intellectual functioning of the child. Indeed, he makes the point that psychological reasons must frequently take precedence over statistical procedures in determining placement of items. One would assume then that some psychological reasoning, left unexplained by Terman and by McNemar, influences the placement of items within given year levels.

Whatever the reason for the placement of items followed by Terman and Merrill, the total effect should yield the best possible estimate of intellectual functioning (that is, mental age) of the child. As the result of this matter, however, criticisms were leveled at the placement of items, McNemar reports. For one thing, some clinicians believed that the order of items was incorrect in terms of difficulty. McNemar is aware that selected groups of individuals may not perform on the test as the norms group did. These represent exceptional cases rather than inadequacy in the norm itself. Indeed, he is aware that there are no substantive data reported by clinicians in this regard, only their impressions. As he also makes very plain this is an inadequate criterion at any time.

There is the added matter that the percentage passing will affect the variability of IQ's at each age level. In the 1937 Revision, variability of IQ differed widely from one level to another level. McNemar explains the differences in variation by age level as being due to the curves for percent passing. This matter is also considered at some length in the 1960 Revision by Pinneau.

The essential feature in item placement was to assure that the mean mental age was equal to the mean chronological age at every level. Shifting in items, in percentage passing, and in scoring standards were a considered part of this arrangement. Since convenience in administration and scoring also enter the placement of an item, this matter to some degree is a part of item placement as well. Considering the limitations in building any test, the item placement by Terman and Merrill in the 1937 Revision seems acceptable and defensible.

References

Edwards, A. J., and D. P. Scannell. *Educational Psychology: The Teaching-Learning Process.* Scranton, Pa.: Intext Educational Publishers, 1968.

McNemar, Q. *The Revision of the Stanford-Binet Scale.* Boston: Houghton, 1942.

Terman, L. M., and Maud A. Merrill. *Measuring Intelligence.* Boston: Houghton, 1937.

Wechsler, D. *The Measurement and Appraisal of Adult Intelligence.* Baltimore: Williams & Wilkins, 1958.

4

The 1960 Stanford Revision of the Binet-Simon Scales

Though called a revision, the 1960 edition of the Stanford-Binet is a modest change from prior revisions at best. Essentially, little has changed from the 1937 edition. A sample of about 4,500 children was used to combine Forms L and M, and to check placement of items from the 1937 Revision. The sample used was less representative than preceding samples had been so that limitations exist in the so-called revision. Perhaps the major change of the 1960 Revision is the employment of the deviation IQ. Though the use of the deviation IQ does avoid some problems associated with differing standard deviations at different age levels, clear superiority of deviation over ratio IQ's is still a matter of some debate. The attempt in the 1960 Revision was to strengthen the positive elements of the 1937 Revision and eliminate as much as possible some of the flaws. As Terman and Merrill make clear, a complete revision would have meant loss of considerable valuable information that could still be usable through a partial revision.

Terman and Merrill begin with a review of the history of the prior revisions. They point to the strong relation of Terman's work with the 1916 Revision to the intent of the original Binet-Simon scale. The 1916 Revision, then, employed the use of age levels, sampling of a variety of items which would reflect various mental functions and their interactions at work, and a score reflecting general intelligence as the outcome. Overall, the scale reflected the child's ability to adapt mentally to new problems. The decision was made by Terman to provide data for children between ages 3 and 16.

The use of age standards showed increasing difficulty of items from one level to the next. The performance of the child could then be compared to the performance of normal children of different age groups in order to determine for the individual his acceleration, retardation, or normality. The score yielded, as it had with the final two Binet-Simon scales, a mental age. The age-level score allows comparison in a way that no other score does, if the mental-age concept is valid. Thus the mental age obtained by the child can be compared directly to other children. If a child achieves a mental age of eight, regardless of his chronological age, the assumption is made that his mental level is that of the average eight-year-old child. Whether or not one agrees with the procedures and assumptions employed in the building of the 1916 Revision, these same notions remain to the present with the 1960 Revision.

Terman added a dimension to the 1916 Revision which had not been employed by Binet: the use of the IQ as a derived score. For purposes of expressing a rate score, the mental age was divided by the chronological age yielding the ratio IQ. In content Terman attempted to duplicate closely the materials of Binet but standardized on American children. The items used in the test were varied and heterogenous and reflected complex mental processes at work. There was no real attempt to determine what mental faculties might be sampled by any given item; instead, emphasis was placed on the combination of these faculties into some general score. In their discussion of the 1916 Revision as a part of the presentation of the 1960 Revision, however, Terman and Merrill make reference to the Binet structure which had posited direction, adaptation, and self-criticism as the elements entering intelligence. A discussion of this structure may be found in Edwards, 1971, Chapter 3.

Their discussion of the 1937 Revision of the Stanford-Binet scale highlights its importance as the essential Stanford Revision. The same features were found in the 1937 Revision as had been used in the 1916 Revision. The same kinds of items were employed, with a very frank admission of the heavy weight that verbal ability played in the items of the 1937 Revision. The strengths of the age scale are expressly denoted by Terman and Merrill in their discussion, and the total score as a measure of general intelligence.

Items were arranged at each age level to assure that the mean mental age should correspond to the mean chronological age. To achieve this outcome, test items must be selected which would be representative of the behaviors believed to be representative of intelligence at that age level, and a careful selection must be made of those individuals who would provide the norms. As before, the item selection depended primarily on an increase in percent passing for successive age levels, with the added requirement of sufficiently high biserial correlations with total score to indicate that the item reflected the purpose of the total scale. Subjects were selected within a month of their birthdays, equally divided as to sex, and representative on selected variables. A sample of just over 3,000 children was used to establish the norms for the 1937 Revision. Certain limitations were noted in the sample selection, with a consequent effect on the norms achieved.

Reliability estimates were based upon difference scores on the two forms for the standardizing sample. The scale proved to be more reliable for older than younger children and for lower than for higher intelligence quotients. Terman and Merrill maintain that the 1937 Revision had the particular strength that it allowed differentiations at those points where greatest diagnostic importance occurred. At this point they make a particularly important statement. The Stanford-Binet scales are age scales and yield a score that is a mental age. If IQ's are to be derived from the age unit and are to be compared from age level to age level, the relationship between the reliability of the scale and the magnitude of the IQ is most important. As they reveal (Terman and Merrill, 1960, p. 10), the relationships found were greater for lower than higher IQ's. The scattergram, in fact, is fan-shaped. They believe such a relationship must be present if there is to be constant meaning for the IQ from one age level to another.

Validity procedures also are reflected primarily in the means by which items were selected and placed at various year levels. Essentially, the criteria used were results in terms of mental age from the 1916 Revision, chronological age characteristics, and internal consistency of items.

Prior to presenting the information relevant to the 1960 Revision, Terman and Merrill summarize the 1937 Revision in this fashion:

> We have said that the 1937 Scale was an age scale making use of age standards of performance. It undertook to measure intelligence regarded as general ability. The many and varied aspects of this ability are demonstrated when a person undertakes to solve suitable problems that are not too easy and not too difficult. These problems were of known difficulty which had been determined by the performance of unselected samples at various age levels. They tested, without trying to disentangle, the various intellectual functions. The method was thus essentially Binet's method of testing "their combined function or capacity without any pretense of measuring the exact contribution of each to the total product" (Terman, 1916, p. 43). We have examined certain implications and certain limitations of Binet Scales. We shall now turn to a further consideration of what experience in the use of the 1937 Scale has to offer concerning the needs for revision. (Terman and Merrill, 1960, p. 12)

Characteristics of the Third Revision

The Binet scales had been devised for educational purposes: specifically, to identify children who would have difficulty succeeding in the regular academic curriculum of the Parisian schools. Binet had even made it clear that exceptional cases in terms of psychological and physical disabilities were excluded in the development of the scale. Since the Stanford Revisions bore so many characteristics of the original Binet-Simon scales, it is not surprising that their greatest utility was found in school settings, for academic prediction. However, between 1916 and 1960, both a greater concern about the utilization of ability for purposes of clinical diagnoses and development of some test for such settings had occurred. The more successful tests developed for clinical purposes had used subtests designed to reflect differential abilities as these might be important in the critical diagnoses.

This matter of subtest scores is first considered by Terman and Merrill in the discussion of the 1960 Revision. They point to the success of the 1937 scale in reflecting the general ability of the child. This strength at the same time must operate as a limitation for those individuals who wish to consider different aspects of intellectual ability for the individual. They point out that a number of classification schemes, either for the Stanford Revisions or for other tests, have had little or no justification from either the empirical or psychological point of view. As they state it, ". . . grouping tests together according to some logical classification scheme on the basis of some special ability which they appear to have in common has little psychological justification. *Too, such classifications as have been proposed have little in common, varying from one test user to another, and have often been proposed with no attempt at validation . . .*" (Terman and Merrill, 1960, p. 13, italics in original).

They attempt to specify this viewpoint by example, citing particularly the maze test. Several types of abilities probably enter performance on the maze test, they point out, including motor coordination, comprehension of verbal instructions, retention of the task, perceptual abilities, reasoning abilities, and perhaps several others. What combination of these might operate in the actual performance of the child will be impossible to determine. In the absence of this specific data necessary for the decision, any attempts by test authors or users to speak of such a task as reflecting a specific kind of ability is dangerous indeed. They point to discrepancies among individuals who attempt to classify tests on discrete bases by declaring that the maze test is considered by one individual as a test of reasoning ability and by another individual in a different scheme as a performance task—that is, a motor-ability task.

As a result of the difficulties associated with classifying tasks in discrete mental faculties, profiles based upon subtest performance by individuals have not been very successful. Too frequently test users, according to Terman and Merrill, attach psychological significance and make diagnoses from test profiles when the validity of these profiles is most questionable. To the present writer, their points are not only well taken but of considerable importance to testing, the accurate use of tests, and effective and efficient diagnosis and prediction.

Though differential diagnosis may not be possible with the tests currently available to us, this does not mean that clinicians may not gain information usable for their diagnostic purposes in the administration of the test. The well-trained, qualified clinician will observe a number of kinds of behaviors which do not enter the actual scoring of test items. This will allow for some qualitative analysis and at least tentative prediction and diagnosis by the clinician. Particularly do Terman and Merrill point to the examinee's work methods, how he approaches problems, his willingness to attempt difficult items with some intelligent efforts, his reaction to success and failure, and so on and on. To them, there are a number of personality traits that can be assessed at least subjectively in the standardized interview which reflects the testing session. Yet considerable care must be exercised in this direction as well. As they point out so aptly, the validity of the clinician is as important in determining the effectiveness and accuracy of testing as is the validity of the test itself.

Other Preliminary Considerations

A number of considerations enter decisions concerning the 1960 Revision. Nearly all of these were extensions of decisions already made in the prior revisions, sometimes with minor modifications. As a result, the issues discussed below are considered in greater detail in Chapter 3 of this book.

ITEM SELECTION. As had been true with preceding revisions, the percentage-passing criterion was employed as the essential procedure for selection of an item. Item location depended upon the combination of items yielding the correct relationship between mean MA and mean CA. Both these issues are discussed in considerable detail in Chapter 3.

VARIABILITY IN IQ. As previously pointed out, the curves plotted for percentage passing an item by age indicates an effect upon the variability of the IQ. If items are too easy or too difficult at any particular level, the resulting performance will affect the slope of the curve. Terman and Merrill point out that in the 1937 Revision differences in standard deviations from age level to age level were primarily due to this factor. Because there were too few items at age 6 which were of medium difficulty, the standard deviation was quite low. By contrast, a preponderance of items of medium difficulty at age 12 led to a standard deviation that was too high.

Where standard deviations vary from age level to age level, comparability is not possible. One error that results from greatly different standard deviations at different age levels is apparent changes in the functional performance of the child. The example which has been cited before applies here as well: a child may appear to change IQ if we look only at IQ values, when in the distribution the IQ's are actually at the same point. Thus he has an IQ of 120 at one point in time and an IQ of 110 at another point in time. If the standard deviation in the first case is 20 and in the second case is 10, his score reflects the same rank for both age distributions. In order to achieve comparability of IQ it is necessary to have stability of standard deviations from one age level to another age level. Simply having an average over all age levels which is violated in certain instances is not sufficient.

All this leads to a justification for the use of the deviation IQ in the 1960 Revision. Through statistical treatment, the variabilities of the 1937 Revision are controlled by giving all age levels a standard deviation of 16 and forcing the distributions to fit. It is important to remember that this is not a restandardization but a matter of statistical manipulation for the purposes of convenience. As a result some rather unusual things do occur. For example, on the 1960 Revision the child with a chronological age of seven years no months who obtains a mental age of seven years no months will have an IQ of 99. Similarly, the child of CA 9-0 and MA of 9-0 has an IQ of 97. By contrast, the child with the chronological age of 15-0 and a mental age of 15-0 has an IQ of 103. For scores around the mean, these departures do not appear to be greatly significant. They are magnified, however, at the extremes and if the psychometrist is not aware of this fact in the use of deviation IQ's with the Stanford-Binet he may draw some mistaken conclusions. Comparability of IQ from age level to age level is fine so long as it does not lead to predictive error. There is no assurance that this may not occur simply because deviation IQ's are used in the 1960 Revision.

TEST-RETEST RELIABILITY. Use of the 1937 Revision over a number of years had given information about test-retest correlation coefficients as well. These would act as another basis for determining the stability of the IQ, often over long periods of time. Terman and Merrill cite several studies indicating the stability of the IQ across age levels. The size of the correlations vary from moderate to high, depending in part upon the distance between testing as well as the time of initial testing.

Thus for children initially tested under chronological age 6 the correlations with increasing time tend to drop rather dramatically. Children who are first tested at age 6 or above tend to show much more stable test behavior over longer periods of time. This may mean that the kinds of items included in the preschool year levels in not congruent with that beginning about year 5 or 6. Certainly, there is some difference in the amount of verbal content found in items at years two through years four compared to later year levels. Beginning at age 6, particularly, verbal

behavior becomes more important and this may lead to the higher correlations across time. Since the pedictive relationship of Stanford-Binet
scores and school achievement also are greatly increased beginning at
age 6, this may further point to the verbal nature of the scale beginning
at that age.

Terman and Merrill make the point that studies indicating test-retest
reliability are important for issues such as the pattern of mental growth
over the lifetime of the individual, the shape of the growth curve, the
point at which ability no longer shows increment and thus is terminal, and
the like.

IQ CLASSIFICATION. Essentially the same classification scheme is used
for the 1960 Revision as had been used with the 1937 Scale. Terman and
Merrill make the strong point that classification terms used do not carry
implications of diagnostic significance. They are indicative of some cutoff
points which reflect significant numbers of individual achieving within
given score limits. For example, they point to the fact that some 2–3
percent of the standardization group in 1937 had IQ's below 69. They
used for this general grouping the classification "mentally defective." By
this term, they say, they meant to indicate mentally defective in terms of
what is average mentality on the scale. There is no necessary diagnostic
implication to the term otherwise.

Such a position represents a marked departure from past writings of
Terman and Merrill. Indeed, if the scores have no more meaning than
this it would seem reasonable to avoid the necessary time, money, and
energy of both the examiner and examinee in obtaining test scores.
Labels represent a shorthand which should signify behaviors that may be
identified and tested. Though labels do acquire social stigma over time
and must be periodically changed for that reason, there should be no
apology for a reasonably valid test performance which is predictive to
other kinds of behaviors outside the testing setting. One would assume
that the purpose of deriving scores is for this very purpose. Any less
purpose is much too expensive. In any event, the classification system,
with percentage of the population representing that grouping, is presented in Table 4-1.

PROBLEMS IN REVISION. The success of the 1937 Revision of the
Binet-Simon Scale raised a question both in terms of philosophy and
practice: When is a revision worthwhile? To answer this question, Terman and Merrill had to consider the advantages that might be obtained
by modernizing the test content, using more sophisticated methods of
building tests which had been developed in the thirty-odd years since the
1937 Revision, and significant issues needing answers in terms of limitations disclosed in the test since 1937. They point out at least two restrictions to undertaking any revision. The first of these involves the fact that,

TABLE 4-1

CLASSIFICATION SCHEME AND DISTRIBUTION OF THE 1937 STANFORD-BINET
STANDARDIZATION GROUP

IQ	Percent	Classification
160–169	0.03	
150–159	0.2	Very superior
140–149	1.1	
130–139	3.1	
120–129	8.2	Superior
110–119	18.1	High average
100–109	23.5	
90–99	23.0	Normal or average
80–89	14.5	Low average
70–79	5.6	Borderline defective
60–69	2.0	
50–59	0.4	
40–49	0.2	Mentally defective
30–39	0.03	

From Terman and Merrill, 1960, p. 18.

where a test has accumulated the significant data available with the 1937 Revision, such data will be negated in all probability by a revision. From this standpoint, utilization of the scale must begin anew. The second restriction involves the very practical matter of the sheer mental and physical labor involved in any standardizing of a test. They decided because of such restrictions to undertake a limited revision. The specified intent was to maintain utility to test users rather than to make those major changes which might reflect current theoretical and popular approaches to measuring ability.

The result of the revision is to retain those features characteristic of prior standardizations. The 1960 Revision, then, carries the same strengths that past users have found in the scale. At the same time it carries the same limitations. There is a matter of major importance at this point, however. The 1960 Revision is something of a misnomer; indeed, it is not a revision at all. As Terman and Merrill make clear, "... *Because of practical considerations we have not undertaken to restandardize the scales, but have undertaken to check existing standards against current empirical data ...*" (Terman and Merrill, 1960, p. 19, italics added). Utilizing information available from samples of youngsters tested during the 1950's, it was possible to match content, scoring standards, and resulting norms more suitably to children of the present decade than would be true with the 1937 Revision. Some material, then, was dropped because it was obsolete. In other instances, items were relocated at different age levels. In some other instances, different scoring standards were implemented.

One step taken by Terman and Merrill was to combine the two scales formerly available into a single scale. The subtests which appeared to be best for present-day purposes were taken from the two 1937 Scales to be used in the 1960 Revision. Gains from this procedure, they feel, included avoiding duplication of items at any age level, the presence of an alternate subtest at each age level, and the ability to choose items which showed the greatest discrimination values for the purposes of testing.The decision of which items to use was based primarily upon availability of scores of tests administered between 1950 and 1954. The performance of children in these samples was compared to those who had comprised the norms group for the 1937 Revision. Almost 4,500 test protocols were available at each age level from 2½ through 18 but complete data are not reported either in Terman and Merrill (1960) or in Pinneau (1961). There is the added, and in many respects damaging, consideration that those children for whom item difficulty in the 1960 Revision were used really do not constitute a representative sampling of youngsters. Terman and Merrill point out that they did attempt to avoid special selective factors, and believe that the sample is sufficiently representative to make the norms usable. The issue of the sample is of such importance that further consideration seems worthwhile.

THE SAMPLE. The availability of protocols seems to have been based upon the use of the test within routine testing programs in schools (Terman and Merrill, 1960, p. 21). Children normally are referred for testing because of educational problems, and this may represent something of a limit in the sample used for the purposes of restandardization. To avoid such problems, Terman and Merrill used tests from schools only where all the children either in the school or within a given grade had been tested with the 1937 Revision. Such data were available from schools in New Jersey, Minnesota, Iowa, New York, California, and Massachusetts. The number of students ranged from 91 in Massachusetts to 2,355 in California. Of the total sample of 4,498 children, approximately 50 percent are from one state alone. This further testifies to the inadequacy of sampling for representativeness. Terman and Merrill further make the point that they have excluded any tests given to children who had been referred to a psychological clinic. This fits in with the philosophy of Binet in building the original scales. Where tests are used for clinical purposes, such a procedure may represent a drawback. However, in school settings, for educational prediction, the procedure is defensible.

A preschool sample included some children tested in 1947 as well as a contemporary group. The school-age sample came from California, Massachusetts, and New Jersey. As an added source of information, two stratified samples were used. One sample was a group of 100 six-year-olds and the second sample was a group of 100 fifteen-year-olds, taken from two cities in California. They were selected on the basis of performance at the mean age of the 1937 standardization group. Occupational level of the father was the primary source of stratification, with the added item of grade placement for the fifteen-year-old group. All the children in both groups were tested with Form L and Form M, and this became a primary source of determining item placement and scoring standards for the Form LM which constituted the 1960 Revision. Comparisons could then be made with the performances of those children who constituted the sample from other states.

ITEM DIFFICULTY. Item placement is based upon the same criterion that had been employed in all prior Binet scales: item difficulty by age. The assumption is made that a valid item will show increasing and relatively smooth percentages passing from one age level to the next. This determination must be based upon percentage passing at successive *mental* ages. For this purpose, curves of percent passing were constructed for all the subtests with the 1950's sample and compared to the 1937 norms. Both chi-square probabilities and biserial correlation coefficients were computed for each item between the two samples. Table 4-2 is illustrative of the data reported for selected age levels. There are also attempts to show that no socioeconomic class differences occurred in performance, but only limited evidence is available on this matter. In terms of more current criticisms of intelligence tests, including the Binet, it is unfortunate that more precise data are not available. In any event, and as might be expected, there were shifts in item difficulty between the 1937 norming sample and that used in 1950 for the 1960 Revision. Because of these shifts some items were replaced in the scale, others were relocated in the scale, and still others were given new scoring standards.

SCALE CHANGES. As a result of the standardization, changes occurring in the 1960 Revision are of two types: content and structural. The primary changes in content resulted in eliminating subtests which were least satisfactory for the percentage-passing criterion. As mentioned earlier, items which had been repeated were also dropped in the Form LM. For items which were retained, relocation or rescoring might occur depending upon the performance of children tested in the 1950's. Certain changes in content were also taken to assure that there would be greater clarity in the administration of the item and to improve where possible the scoring, illustrations, and examples.

Of more direct importance, Terman and Merrill report, are the structural changes implemented in the 1960 Revision. Mean IQ's on the 1937 Revision had exceeded 100. To assure better location of items within the age scale, those items selected for the 1960 scale employed a procedure for correcting percentage passing by age for an item by the amount that the mean IQ at that CA level exceeded 100.

TABLE 4-2

COMPARATIVE PERFORMANCE DATA FOR ITEMS FROM SELECTED SUBTESTS IN THE
1937 AND 1960 REVISIONS

Item	1937%	1960%	Biserial Correlations 1937	Biserial Correlations 1960
Year III-6				
1. Comparison of balls	79	79	.82	.62
2. Patience: pictures	66	63	.54	.55
3. Discrimination: animal pictures	69	59	.66	.66
4. Response to pictures: level I	75	65	.60	.50
5. Sorting buttons	81	79	.66	.65
6. Comprehension I	72	60	.70	.62
Alt. Comparison of sticks	67	52	.81	.43
Year IX				
1. Paper cutting	64	57	.71	.62
2. Verbal absurdities II	48	50	.73	.83
3. Memory for designs I	50	44	.28	.60
4. Rhymes: new form	56	65	.52	.62
5. Making change	70	58	.62	.62
6. Repeating 4 digits: reversed	61	48	.58	.52
Alt. Rhymes: old form	59	51	.64	.69
SA II				
1. Vocabulary	22	13	.68	.91
2. Finding reasons III	34	27	.37	.72
3. Proverbs II	33	48	.61	.83
4. Ingenuity I	34	24	.43	.73
5. Essential differences	28	24	.56	.81
6. Repeating thought of passage I	26	37	.71	.82
Alt. Codes	38	41	.55	.82

From Terman and Merrill, 1960, pp. 343–344, 346.

There was also an adjustment of intelligence quotients for variations of an atypical nature. A further structural change extended tables of intelligence quotients to include CA groups 17 and 18, based upon the belief that mental age continues beyond age 16. For all ages, the matter of atypical variability has been corrected in the 1960 Revision. As will be recalled from the prior revisions, the standard deviation varied from age level to age level and sometimes to a large degree. For the 1960 Revision, deviation IQ's were computed thus correcting for this error.

Factor-Analytic Data

McNemar had attempted factor analysis of the items for the Stanford-Binet in 1937 and reported the emergence of one general common factor which would adequately explain performance (McNemar, 1942). Though certain group factors remained a possibility within the scale, these tended to be relatively minor in overall performance. Item selection for the 1960 Revision was made by Terman and Merrill on the basis of factor loadings which McNemar had reported for the 1937 Revision. The 1960 Revision, therefore, should represent even greater saturation of the general factor because more selectivity was possible between the two forms. For Average Adult level and above, Terman and Merrill report that there is a reduction in the number of memory items in the 1960 Revision in order to make the adult levels more consistent with the remainder of the test.

Standardization Data

Another feature contributing to the utility of the 1937 Revision, and a major strength in its own right, was the standardization material reported by McNemar (1942). Since the 1960 Revision is not a true revision, a similar book is not available for the current form of the Stanford-Binet. As a result, the McNemar volume remains as pertinent for use with the new test as it was for the old. It is true, however, that the function of the volume is limited to some degree by changes made in the 1960 Revision.

Though a book comparable to the McNemar volume is not available for the 1960 Revision, a supplementary source by Pinneau (1961) has been published. He reports that his purpose is to provide research data and the material necessary for a handbook for those professionally trained individuals who must evaluate performance of children and adults on such tests as the Stanford-Binet. A major source of data for this purpose is the Berkeley growth study (Bayley, 1933; Jones and Bayley, 1941; Bayley, 1949; Bayley, 1955). Particular emphasis is placed in this book of Pinneau's on the development of the deviation IQ and a justification for its inclusion in place of the ratio IQ reported in all prior forms of the Stanford revision.

The Deviation IQ

One widely noted feature of the 1937 Revision, and a feature cited earlier in these volumes, was the change in the size of the standard deviation at different age levels. These differences in variance open the possibility of mistaken judgment about changes of ability of a given child. There might appear to be, for example, a change when the child of age 6 achieves an IQ of 112; at age 9 an IQ of 116; and at age 12 and IQ of 120. The gain of approximately eight IQ points between ages 6 and 12 was spurious, since the standard deviations at the two respective year levels were 12 and 20. Both scores reflect the same rank in the distribution by age—that is, one standard deviation above the mean or the 84th percentile. To some degree, a change in the opposite direction was possible as well. Thus at age 2 the child might obtain an IQ of 121 while at age 6 he obtains an IQ of 112. It appears then that his IQ has dropped nine points when in fact the position again is the same in the two distributions.

Because of problems of this nature the deviation IQ appeared to Terman and Merrill to be a superior reporting score. It should be noted that Wechsler had begun the use of the deviation IQ in his point scales. Because of the stability feature of the deviation IQ particularly, Pinneau devised the table for the 1960 Revision, using a distribution at each year level with a mean of 100 and a standard deviation of 16. Since new data were not available, the data from the 1937 Revision were forced to fit such a distribution. With the deviation IQ, as Pinneau points out, an IQ maintains the same relative standing at any age level at which it is used. Thus if there is a change in the individual's deviation IQ, it must represent a change in the person himself, not a spurious test characteristic.

Pinneau says that the fluctuations in variance which occurred at the different age levels of the 1937 Revision were apparently due to variations in average item difficulty at different age levels (Pinneau, 1961, p. 46). It might appear that a feasible procedure then would be to make corrections only for those age levels which deviate widely from a standard deviation of 16. But, as Pinneau also observes, limiting the changes made only to such age levels would actually increase fluctuation of mean IQ's. This fact was demonstrated by data available from the Berkeley growth study in which the appropriate changes were made. By contrast, smoothed values may be determined and plotted for the standard deviation, and when this procedure is followed the ratio IQ's may then be transformed to deviation IQ's. This procedure lowered changes in means by approximately one-half. As a result of this procedure and its results, Pinneau illustrated the necessity for some standard score reporting such as deviation IQ.

It had been noted with prior versions of the scale that there was greater instability of scores for bright children than for dull ones. The assumption had been made by some psychometrists that this fact represented instability of the distribution of mental ages with increased age. The data available to Pinneau illustrated to him that it is, instead, a matter of construction in the scale. His analysis demonstrates that items at older mental ages achieve greater weight than those at younger mental ages. Added to this fact are those age changes which occurred in means and standard deviations for the ratio IQ. To some degree, Pinneau says, age variations which had existed in means where ratio IQ's were computed tended to accentuate the effects of variation with bright children. One strength of deviation IQ's, therefore, is to reduce considerably the insta-bility due to these changes in means by age, at least for bright children. Other sources of instability in test scores remain. Even so, Pinneau re-ports data indicating that the deviation IQ's are considerably more stable over age levels than the ratio IQ's were.

Pinneau asserts that the scores of an intelligence test serve two func-tions of critical importance. The first of these concerns determination of an individual's standing within a group of known characteristics, normally his own chronological age group. A second function, and one for which the ratio IQ was initially devised, is to indicate something about the ability level of the individual at a later point in life. This latter function serves as a predictive one, assuming stability of the IQ. Both of these functions are well met with the deviation IQ concept as it is included in the 1960 Revision, according to Pinneau. Certainly, the ability ranking of the indi-vidual within his own age group is considerably improved in the 1960 Revision. This stability may apply as well to future scores on the test, since there should be some prediction of the percentile rank of the individual across various ages. From this standpoint, then, the latter condition is met as well.

The evidence available to Pinneau also indicated that children who are bright at the younger age levels tend to grow faster mentally than those who are of lesser ability in the same age group. A bright four-year-old will grow faster mentally than any other four-year-old, and indeed, than any child except those younger of the same or higher ability. With increases in chronological age, then, the differences among bright and dull individuals will become wider and wider. Although there will be a tendency for comparable ranks to remain the same, and for the deviation IQ's to reflect less difference than is true in mental age, the difference between the very bright and the very dull child of the same age will be increasingly marked as they mature. This matter is of more than just statistical or philosophical interest. Decisions made about individuals on the basis of test scores are apt to be in error in directions different from those sometimes assumed. As a result, we are apt to underestimate the mental growth and consequent ability and achievement of a bright young child and to overestimate the mental growth and ability in achievement of the dull younger child.

The limitations placed by restrictions in the scale units available to us lead to error in many instances. There is relation in this to another kind of observation commonly accepted. Bloom (1964), for example, has pointed out the vast increases in intellectual ability of children in the very young years of life with some deceleration in this ability with increasing age and maturity. Certainly, test norms reflect the same principle, al-though the point at which maturity is reached varies from one test to another. The question is raised then: Are in fact mental-growth increments in the first few years of life much more significant than those which occur as the individual approaches maturity? Those wide differences which are observed and measured with tests available to us might lead to an oversimple acceptance of a "yes" answer. However, the differences in scale units between age groups may indeed be much smaller than has been accepted in the past. Thus the year of mental increment from age 12 to age 13 may be as wide as that from year 2 to year 3. The reason we are not able to demonstrate this may be in a limitation of the test, with the units available to us for expression of test performance. The issue remains one of considerable practical importance; at the same time, we must be concerned about maximum intellectual development of all children.

Practical Uses of Test Scores

Pinneau turns his attention next to the use of tests and their score expressions in practical situations of life. In his introduction, he points out that tests serve at least two functions. The first of these is to give some indication of how an individual stands relative to others of his own age and, given appropriate score expressions, the age group of which his performance may be considered typical. The second general use of intelligence-test scores is to allow prediction of performance by the individual at some future time. As he is careful to note, the accuracy of such prediction will depend on the age at which intelligence tests are administered and how great an interval of time occurs between administrations. Administrations closely related in time will show much higher predictive efficiency, for example, than those which may be separated by a number of years.

Pinneau then discusses the use of test scores in terms of the two functions cited above and most commonly expressed.

Use of the Deviation IQ and Mental Age

Scores have been, and are, expressed in a number of ways. It is not unusual in looking at a report from a psychometrist to find reported each of the following: the IQ, the mental age, the percentile rank, a band of percentile scores, and the range of both IQ's and MA's within which the score of the individual probably falls. Although one might assume that each of these expressions offers a different kind of information, in actuality each is related to all of the others and is merely a different way of giving the same information. Each of them is obtained from the actual performance of the child on the test administered, and the score expression in that test reflects the basis upon which all others are derived. Since a test such as the Stanford-Binet yields a score that is a mental age from which an IQ is derived, such scores are the more basic and meaningful of all scores commonly listed. Pinneau discusses both IQ and mental age as measures of ability. Particularly does he defend the use of the deviation IQ as compared with the ratio IQ since this represents the major change in score presentation in th 1960 Revision.

The Deviation IQ

The 1937 Revision of the Stanford-Binet Scale used ratio IQ's, computed on the basis of the formula

$$\frac{MA}{CA} \times 100 = IQ$$

The use of ratio IQ's for predictions about the individual was heavily dependent upon the variance for his age group. Pinneau makes the point clearly when he describes two representative samples of different ages each yielding mean IQ's of 100 but showing different standard deviations. If group one, for example, had a standard deviation of 10 while group two had a standard deviation of 20 IQ points, the following conditions would result.

> ... Sixteen percent of the subjects in the group with the larger variability will obtain scores above an IQ of 120. However, to include the top 16 percent of subjects in the other group, one will need to include all subjects obtaining an IQ of above 110. Thus, while the proportion of subjects above one standard deviation is the same in both groups, there is a different proportion above a given IQ score. (Pinneau, 1961, pp. 70–71)

In practical terms, this means that the ratio IQ would mean different things at different ages. Unless a psychometrist were aware of standard deviations at a given age level and employed these in comparing IQ's for an individual or between individuals, certain conclusions might be drawn which were not in fact plausible. To obtain comparability of IQ's, then, the 1960 Revision has employed the deviation IQ. Now a given IQ at one age obtains the same rank as the same IQ at a separate age. An IQ of 116 will be one standard deviation above the mean and at the 84th percentile at all age levels.

Assessing Achievement

Pinneau discusses the use of test scores in relation to several quite practical problems, both in and out of school. For one thing, he makes the point that parents tend to set expectations for their children based more often upon hope and desires than upon objective assessment. Parents need unbiased and reliable information as a means of determining what reasonable expectations to set for a given child. Parents establish goals for a given child on the basis of how an older sibling performed, or how one of the neighbor children is doing, or something of this nature. Whether or not such a comparison is realistic depends upon the relative intellectual competencies of the two individuals compared.

Pinneau urges the need for realistic assessment and expectations by parents as well as by others who meet the child. Whether the child is inferior, average, or superior in ability, the parent must accept the child with his peculiar strengths and limitations. One use of intelligence tests, then, is to supply parents with more accurate information upon which to draw conclusions. The literature contains a number of examples of case studies where parents have set too high expectations for children. The results have often been negative for child and parents. Pinneau makes the accurate point that, though such conditions must be avoided, it may be just as damaging to set too low expectations for a child by the parent. In his view, parents will be in a better position to set reasonable expectations given the kind of information that may be obtained with an individual intelligence test such as the Stanford-Binet.

There is just as great a need for accuracy within the school setting. On at least some occasions, teachers misinterpret the causes of certain behaviors. Almost all referrals to clinics for an intellectual assessment, for example, are restricted to those children who are not making normal school progress. In certain instances such children will be below average in ability, and perhaps achieving at a level which is congruent with their intellectual status. Under other circumstances, the lack of accomplishment in school may be explained on the basis of some emotional problem rather than an intellectual one. On still other occasions the child is quite bright, bored with the curriculum which he has encountered because he has already exceeded this independently, and thus is simply not performing because of a lack of challenge in the school program. All such problems need to be recognized as accurately as possible, Pinneau maintains, and certainly one contribution to such recognition and consequent amelioration is the use of the test. Indeed, in his estimation, children should be remeasured with individual tests periodically through their school careers.

Using the Mental Age

Though the deviation IQ has some very obvious strengths, it also contains a number of limitations. Its chief limitation lies in the fact it cannot be used for comparisons beyond relative standings. By contrast, the mental age offers a number of very practical uses beyond relative standing.

Pinneau specifically mentions two areas for which mental age has been shown to be helpful. One of these concerns the psychological correlates which have been demonstrated to be related to mental development as reflected in mental age. Within the school setting, for example, the mental-age level can be used to judge when a child is ready to begin a given learning task with a reasonable expectation for success. Under conditions of class size, availability of resources, and teacher competence, a child will have the greatest possibility of success in such a task as reading if he has obtained a mental age of around 6½ years. With a child who has a mental age, say, less than 6, either other instructional procedures must be provided or further readiness procedures should be employed until the child may be expected to be successful. Insofar as such outcomes may be demonstrated to be congruent with mental age, the utility of the score is assured.

The second practical value which Pinneau mentions for the use of mental age is the fact that the MA indicates the CA for which the obtained performance is the average score. This is the definition of mental age proposed by Terman and still widely accepted. However, a number of writers in the field have believed the statement is inaccurate to some degree. For example, the discussion by Thurstone of this issue in Part I of this series clarifies the arguments very well (Edwards, 1971, Chapter 7). In any event, Pinneau accepts the definition as proposed here and tries to illustrate its employment. The child may not be functioning very well in the particular setting in which he is found. An evaluation of him may indicate he may perform better in a group of either younger or older individuals. A comparison across age groups yields a kind of information, when accurate, that cannot be obtained by comparing the child's relative standing within his own age group. This possibility explains the retention of the mental-age concept as a score in the Stanford-Binet revisions, and probably assures its continuation in this and other scales in the future.

Pinneau has added a feature to the 1960 Revision which should aid in this latter kind of problem as well. In the 1937 Revision, Terman and Merrill pointed out that above the mental age of 13 there is little significance to the mental-age score. This was because such scores were not obtained on the basis of median performances of unselected groups for the chronological ages of fourteen and above. As has been mentioned before (see Part I), the so-called adult scales of the 1937 Revision really are mistitled to some degree since they are more "top" for bright twelve-, thirteen-, and fourteen-year-olds than they are adult scales. They were not standardized on this latter basis. But Pinneau has extended the mental-age concept from 13 to 18 years in the 1960 Revision by determining the average performance of age groups within those limits.

One use of the mental age which has been advocated educationally, and in some instances tried, is the use of grouping procedures based upon MA. Pinneau makes the point that such a grouping is short-lived at best, and has usually been termed a failure. The primary reason for this, of course, is that the young bright child is growing at a faster rate intellectually than the dull old child. Thus in September we might set up a group of children all of whom have mental ages of 9 but some of whom are as young as 7 and others of whom are as old as 13. Within just a few weeks and certainly by the end of the first semester, the younger children are already ahead of the older children intellectually and differences are becoming wider all the time. By the end of the year the differences within the group are so wide that little or nothing has been gained by the grouping procedure. To be successful, grouping by MA will call for frequent shifts in the composition of groups. Some such procedure as the ungraded classroom would seem to handle this problem much better than direct grouping on MA, a procedure advocated by Terman as early as 1919. Homogeneity on the basis of actual task performance may be more easily obtained than homogeneity on the basis of ability. This is true partially because of the fact that there is error in the measures that we use for determining mental age, or any other intellectual score expression, that is compounded in task performance.

Mental age also has a use with the untrained person, particularly the parent. Communication about the meaning of an IQ, the relative standing of the child in the group, is difficult for the untrained person to understand. To tell a parent that his child has an IQ of 132, stands at the 98th percentile, and has a score as good as or better than 98 children out of 100 in his own age group does little more than inform the parents that he has a bright child. Expectations set or comparisons to draw are much more difficult. However, if the child is given an equivalent mental age he can make some kinds of comparisons not otherwise possible and perhaps draw some conclusions which are more meaningful. Pinneau points out that most parents have a great deal more experience with children of different age levels than they do with children of the same ages. They are more apt to know something about typical behavior of children of different ages than of performances congruent with different levels of ability within the same age. Giving them information about how a child stands relative to an age group may be interpreted by them in a way not possible with the deviation IQ. Pinneau uses the following case study to illustrate this point.

> The merits of age comparisons are illustrated in a conference which the writer had with the mother of a four-year-old who obtained a deviation IQ of 147. In discussing with her the general level of performance on the tests, the writer indicated that at this age the child was very bright, that relative to others of his CA, he did as well as the top two or three of a representative sample of a thousand children.
>
> Naturally the mother was pleased to know that her son had done so well on the test. However, she immediately mentioned her concern and that of her husband, a mathematician, over the child not being able to do simple arithmetical problems. She gave as an example a problem as difficult as that which occurs at year IX in the Stanford-Binet—"If I were to buy four cents' worth of candy and should give the storekeeper ten cents, how much money would I get back? . . . It is obvious in this case that the parents, both of whom were professional people, had decidedly unrealistic ideas as to what should be expected of their son.
>
> It would have been a tedious task to detail to the mother the kinds of problems which a four year old with a DIQ of 147 could be expected to deal with effectively. It was fairly easy to get her to recognize that his performance was characteristic of that of a six-year-old who was ready to enter the first grade, and that solving the types of problems that she expected was beyond his level of ability and only to be reasonably expected of children eight or nine years of age who already had successfully experienced several years of elementary school. (Pinneau, 1961, p. 78)

Pinneau's point is well taken. There is a meaning to be attached to a mental age that simply is not possible with any other score expression on an intelligence test. The problem remains one of the validity of the mental-age concept. This issue has been widely debated but very little tested. Empirical evidence about the accuracy and adequacy of the mental age is greatly limited. Establishing the accurate experimental conditions to test the validity of the MA concept is of course a problem. For example, the older group must be accurately matched with the younger group at a point in time, and because of differences in mental growth will begin to show divergence within a short time after the original matching. Measures must be obtained rapidly for both predictor and criterion tests. Problems inherent in meeting such conditions have led to relatively little research, despite the importance of the issue. Chief among those studies demonstrating evidence relative to the validity of the mental-age concept are those of Bleismer (1954) and Kolstoe (1954). Of course, the issue of use of intelligence tests does not depend upon demonstration of the validity of the mental-age concept. However, if mental age may be used for comparative purposes it will substantially strengthen one kind of prediction for the individual, and thus is an issue that should be investigated further.

Stability of Scores

Pinneau points to the unalterable fact that growth in the individual is characterized by considerable amount of change. One problem in prediction is the fact that change is not consistent within the individual nor between individuals. As a result, the position of an individual within a group of known characteristics may change somewhat from time to time due to differential effects of "the growth spurt." This matter is as true of intelligence as it is of any other feature. It seems reasonable to expect that in the maturing of intelligence the individual will show some spurts and some plateaus. We do not know, at the time of a given measurement, whether the individual is in the midst of a growth spurt, about to begin a growth spurt, at the end of a growth spurt, or somewhere on a plateau.

For this reason some instability of scores will be found which are beyond control of the examiner and of the test constructor. Pinneau demonstrates some of this problem by pointing out that the changes that may occur in structure and function are not perfectly correlated with ability level, and this will lead to some variation in the relative standing of the individual in the group. A further effect of this matter, according to Pinneau, is an influence upon age variation in the size of the deviation IQ. One reason why correlation coefficients over long time periods are less stable than those over short time periods is due to this matter of variation from sources intrinsic to the individual. Unfortunately, having agreed that this is so, we are in no better position to specify the amount of change or variation which may occur for the individual from one time to another. Group fluctuation is more stable, because of some canceling factors, and therefore is more predictable. In any event, prediction, particularly of an individual nature, from ability scores must be expected to be in some degree of error. Those tests which demonstrate the least amount of error in such prediction are the ones which are most likely to be used in educational and clinical settings.

Prediction for Ability Scores

The correlation coefficients over time for scores are not perfect, though relatively high correlation coefficients may be found over fairly long time periods for groups (see for example, Bradway, Thompson, and Cravens, 1958). With the Stanford-Binet, this finding is particularly true where measures are taken first beginning about age 6 and correlated with later age administrations. Yet, as Pinneau points out, it would be most helpful if parents could be counseled about their children beginning very early in life, and particularly in the preschool years. But prediction from, say, age 4 to age 9 will not be nearly so good as that from age 9 to age 14. Pinneau submits that a major factor in this outcome is that the nature of mental ability may change as children mature and enter school. The kinds of abilities which are developing in the child prior to age 5, for example, may differ from those which develop after age 6. Perhaps much more pertinent and to the point, however, is the kind of content which must be included in preschool age tests. Because of the *functional* verbal level of the very young child, verbal tests are not as easy to devise at the young age level. As a result, there are many more instances of performance items in the Stanford-Binet scale up through age 5 than there are verbal items.

Beginning with age 6 and continuing and increasing from that point the verbal quality of the test is enhanced. As a result, prediction from the young age level will be relatively poor to the later age level. Since success in school is most heavily dependent upon verbal behavior, at least as schools and curricula are currently maintained, it is not unexpected that prediction of achievement from scores in the preschool years will be poorer than that after the child has achieved school age. One might wonder at the effects of including performance items throughout all age ranges for which the test is used, a matter which Wechsler has provided for in his scales. Such performance items, particularly if they serve as some measure of practical intelligence, might be used for prediction to a good many situations in life that are nonacademic in nature. Such predictions have importance in their own right. Thus we have returned to the fact that tests are most usable for the situations for which developed and for which the content is appropriate.

Despite the poor prediction of later school achievement and later test performance, Pinneau does make the very valuable point that test scores with young children have some importance in their own right. Frequently we need a functional measure for some decisions to be made at the present time concerning the child. All use of test scores is not restricted to future prediction, although there is implicit within the current functional decisions some prediction as well. Pinneau asserts that intelligence is one of those few psychological traits that have been studied sufficiently to allow some reasonably accurate reliability to be determined. As a result, prediction of an individual's rank from one time to another time is also possible.

Problems in prediction, arising both from the statistical matters pointed out earlier in this discussion and from more practical issues, have led Pinneau to establish a table giving an indication of the type of deviation which may be expected over periods of time between administrations (see Pinneau, 1961, appendix E, pp. 209–225). He remarks that the psychometrist who acquaints himself with such information is not apt to use scores from some prior administration for current prediction without a considerable amount of qualification. This is not to say that the deviation IQ is so unstable as to be totally invalid. This statement is by no means true. Indeed, as has been stated so many times before, one of the strengths of intelligence tests is the fact that we are aware of their limitations and therefore can use them in terms of their efficiency. This is true with the Stanford-Binet as it is with other tests, and is indicated in the kind of information which Pinneau can provide relative to the use of test scores from one time to another and the kind of change that can and does occur. The major use of such a table is to give an indication to the psychometrist as to the current need for a retest in order to get a more valid measure.

References

Bayley, Nancy. "Mental Growth During the First Three Years: A Developmental Study of Sixty-One Children by Repeated Tests," *Genetic Psychology Monographs*, Vol. 14 (1933), pp. 1–92.

Bayley, Nancy. "Consistency and Variability in the Growth of Intelligence from Birth to Eighteen Years," *Journal of Genetic Psychology*, Vol. 75 (1949). pp. 165–196.

Bayley, Nancy. "On the Growth of Intelligence," *American Psychologist*, Vol. 10 (1955), pp. 805–818.

Bliesmer, E. P. "A Comparison of Bright and Dull Children of Comparable Mental Ages with Respect to Various Reading Abilities," *Journal of Educational Psychology* Vol. 45 (1954), pp. 321–331.

Bloom, B. *Stability and Change in Human Characteristics.* New York: Wiley, 1964.

Bradway, Katherine P., C. W. Thompson, and R. B. Cravens. "Preschool I.Q.s after Twenty-Five Years," *Journal of Educational Psychology* Vol. 49 (1958), pp. 278–281.

Edwards, A. J. *Individual Mental Testing: Part I. History and Theories.* Scranton, Pa.: Intext Educational Publishers, 1971.

Jones, H. E., and Nancy Bayley. "The Berkeley Growth Study," *Child Development*, Vol. 12 (1941), pp. 167–173.

Kolstoe, O. P. "A Comparison of Mental Abilities of Bright and Dull Children of Comparable Mental Ages," *Journal of Educational Psychology*, Vol. 45 (1954), pp. 161–168.

McNemar, Q. *The Revision of the Stanford-Binet Scale.* Boston: Houghton, 1942.

Pinneau, S. *Changes in Intelligence Quotient: Infancy to Maturity.* Boston: Houghton, 1961.

Terman, L. M., and Maud A. Merrill. *Stanford-Binet Intelligence Scale. Manual for the Third Revision, Form L-M.* Boston: Houghton, 1960.

5

A Discussion of Age and Point Scales

The concept of a scale based upon level of mental development and expressed in year equivalents proved highly successful in the first two decades of this century. All psychologists did not accept the mental age as the appropriate score expression, however, due to limitations for many applied situations. Other measurement means were sought as alternatives to the mental age, alternatives applicable particularly to clinical needs for diagnosis. Following World War I, the use of point scales to measure aspects of intellectual functioning became increasingly popular.

The two approaches to measurement remain extant: the age scale exemplified in the Binet revisions and the point scale in the Wechsler tests. Differences between the two often are more apparent than real, and the final goal is the same. Because of logical and philosophical implications on test construction, comparisons and contrasts between the two as measurement approaches will be surveyed in this chapter.

The Point Scale and Its Strength

Where the Binet scales are age scales, the Wechsler scales have been of the type called *point scales*. Much of the rationale and development of point scales must be credited to Robert M. Yerkes, who had begun the development of the first such scale in 1913. As Yerkes points out in conjunction with that scale, he intended to measure intellectual ability by means of a single series of tests wherein credit could be allowed for qualitative aspects of an individual's responses. Yerkes credits E. B. Huey with the initial suggestions in this direction. One reason for devising such a scale was that Yerkes believed that an age scale, particularly of the Binet type, did not provide the kind of information needed for certain specific predictive situations. The age scale places items at a year level in terms of percentage passing without regard to relationships between such items nor with items at other year levels. In addition, as Yerkes demonstrates, each item is scored plus or minus, pass or fail. Though such general information might be usable for certain kinds of settings, Yerkes proposed that in clinical settings particularly the age scale approach is insufficient. The purpose from the very beginning, then, was to develop a different and hopefully better method rather than some modification of the Binet approach itself.

In initial attempts as early as 1913 Binet items were used, since some of their characteristics were already recognized and could be evaluated in terms of the newer idea of a point scale. The first steps undertaken by Yerkes and his associates was to try to determine the utility of a test which consisted of a single series of items with partial credits being given, using Binet items. If these initial steps proved satisfactory, then a more direct attempt at development of a complete point scale might be begun. Yerkes notes that criticisms of the age scale, and particularly the Binet test, had already occurred, both in the United States and in Europe. Some new method, usable in the specific clinical setting, was needed, recognized, and called for as early as 1910. It was to meet such a need that Yerkes began his first attempt.

The Point-Scale Method

Yerkes defines the point scale as following: "The Point Scale is an intelligence examination on the principle of a scale of tasks graduated by credit points . . ." (Yerkes and Foster, 1923, p. 7). Inherent in this definition is the principle that a series of tests will be used, each of which may be labeled and contain a number of items of the same type. As each item is administered, it will be afforded differential credit points depending upon the quality of the response given by the individual. These two features are the primary differences between a point scale and an age scale—although as will be clear from the following discussion, other differences have also been proposed. In the particular case of the Yerkes scales devised to 1925, the intent was to develop a test that could be administered to individuals with mental-age ranges from 3 through 16. In actual fact, the reliability of the instrument was greatest for ages 6 to 12, which should not be surprising considering the fact that it utilized Binet items. Score expressions used in the point scale devised by Yerkes range from 0 to 100, though a provision was made for expressing such scores as mental ages as well. As mentioned earlier, the primary basis for items was the Binet-Simon scale, although Yerkes states that other sources were used for item selection as well.

Yerkes makes one point in terms of the intent of the test that is crucial to any point scale. This deals with the fact that tests and items are selected which show a range through a considerable number of years. Thus a test will be included because it is usable not only with a six-year-old but with a twelve-year-old as well, and to the same degree. For such purposes, Yerkes particularly mentions the memory span and free-association tests. There is the possibility that performance will depend upon level of mental growth. Yerkes attempted to describe characteristic performances on tasks, and to make a discrimination in scoring wherever such differences were recognized. Grades of responses were needed, therefore, for the recognized stages of development. Yerkes points to the gradations identified and included in the scoring for various subtests used by him; for example, the free-association test has four grades, whereas a task calling for definition of concrete terms has two. The free-association test requires the child to say as many words as possible within a three-minute time period. To illustrate the gradation used in scoring, Yerkes allows one point credit for 30 to 44 words, two points for from 45 to 59 words, three points for from 60 to 74 words, and four points for 75 or more words. Just such gradations are used in several of the examinations on the assumption that they represent discriminable differences by age levels.

There is a further scoring difference which occurs in the point scale devised by Yerkes intended to discriminate individual differences more specifically than is possible with the Binet type scale. Thus subdivisions of tests may be credited separately with partial credits being given for certain subdivisions. A test which calls for the child to compare remembered objects may give one point for one item of difference and two points for two or more items of differences, for example. On the Binet type scale, the item would be either plus or minus, depending on whether or not the child reached the criterion specified for his age level.

Differences Between Point Scale and Age Scale

Yerkes indicates five differences between the point scale and the Binet scale which he believes to be of considerable significance and which denote the superiority of the point scale for at least certain purposes.

1. The entire point scale is administered to every child regardless of age. As Yerkes points out, to attempt to administer all of the Binet-Simon scales or the Stanford Revision of the scales is highly impractical. The examination is much too long, particularly for younger children. Establishing a basal and ceiling age seemed insufficient substitutes for adminis-

tering the entire test, at least to Yerkes. Particularly is this true when one considers that giving an entire test, as in the point scale, avoids any possibility of error in accurately determining basal and ceiling ages. Inaccuracy and consequent error are more apt to be found in those cases where greatest precision is needed: cases of mental deficiency, epilepsy, what Yerkes calls dementia praecox, and other forms of abnormality.

Yerkes points to one exception in the administration of the total test within the scale proposed in his book. Specifically the exception applies to the inability of the child to answer a single item on a given subtest. Specifically, he gives this example:

> If we are examining a four-year-old child who answers the question "What is a spoon?" by repeating "spoon" and who gives the same kind of reply for definitions of the other concrete words, there is obviously no necessity of asking for definitions of abstract terms. Such omissions are allowable only with very young children, and then only when the easier parts of the test have been failed entirely. (Yerkes and Foster, 1923, p. 8, footnote)

Discontinuing the test is thus based on a "floor," and only in exceptional cases. Ceiling effects are not so clear in the Yerkes example of the point scale, at least not as clear as they will be with later scales of a similar type.

2. The second advantage for the point scale over the age scale as cited by Yerkes is the fact that for any given test, numerical credit is allowed both for pass and fail and for various degrees of successes within limits of passing and failing. In this context Yerkes cites the fact that Terman advocated administering all parts of a subtest to gain additional information bearing on clinical matters. The difference between the age scale and the point scale is the total number of points allowed. For the Binet-type scale, for example, if three of five must be passed for credit, getting four of five or five of five will add nothing to the score of the individual, though it may be used for clinical evaluation. In the point scale, the child will get as many points as he actually passes items in the test itself. Thus he may get from one through five on a five-part item.

There is the added possibility of differential weighting in the point scale which is not allowable in the age scale. Yerkes states that in certain instances multiple points may be achieved by the individual while in others only a single point may be achieved. Weight, he says, may be given to those tasks which correlate most highly with selected criteria of intelligence such as age, academic success, and the like. Whether or not such point assignments are actually made in the point scale is an empirical matter determined independently of the scoring procedure as such. Apparently the argument has been widely accepted without much verification either in the Yerkes scales or other point scales that have followed.

3. Still another advantage of the point scale is the fact that all of the items of a single kind will be grouped under one test and given together. There had already been some questioning of items in the Stanford-Binet from this standpoint. In the Stanford-Binet, for example, digit span might be administered at a number of age levels. Would it not be more suitable to administer all the digit span at one time, some psychometrists had asked, to determine immediately the longest span available to the individual? Unfortunately, there were not very many instances where the items were common in type from year to year in the age scale. It was felt that one superiority of the point scale occurred because common items could be grouped and a sufficient variety of subtests of some extensive length made available. Whether or not one gains anything from grouping items of a similar type together is a fairly moot point. For example, some recent though limited evidence indicates that administering all digit-span items at one time may facilitate performance of young children but inhibit that of older ones (see Phye and Edwards, 1969). If this outcome is stable, not only for digit span but for other subtests where items are grouped together, the use to be made of such procedures in a point scale should show an additional type of weighting in order for expressed gains to be achieved. Again, this is an empirical question which has not been considered by many test constructors nor by researchers, unfortunately.

4. Another advantage cited by Yerkes for the point scale is the greater ease of altering its content as compared with that of the age scale. Using a percentage-passing concept brings difficulties in restandardization of items and consequent appropriate placement over periods of time. With the point scale, such restandardization would not be necessary, since the renorming will be much simpler and consequent changes in performance of a child may be evaluated more accurately.

5. Yerkes maintains that the greatest superiority for the point scale lies in the fact that it has research and diagnostic value that is not possible with an age scale. He asserts that the age scale has its greatest value with normal and retarded children (and particularly since these were the groups upon which the scales were first devised) but that the point scale has value with all kinds of children both normal and abnormal to whatever degree. For example, the point scale may be used with children who are blind and deaf in a way in which the Binet scale may not be without special adaptations. Yerkes shows how the point scale may be used when either one of two methods is followed. The first of these is to administer the point scale to a group of blind or of deaf children and compile a table of norms to be used for such specialized groups. The second possibility is to determine corrections which should be added to total score when certain subtests must be omitted for blind and/or deaf. This is the matter of prorating which occurs frequently in point scales. Yerkes makes this statement relevant to the point scale:

> Since the entire examination is given to each subject, since like questions are grouped together instead of being scattered throughout the examination in the order of difficulty, and since many abnormal cases tend to do particularly well or particularly poorly on some special kind of question, the point scale is preeminently fitted to reveal unusual patterns of response. (Yerkes and Foster, p. 12, 1923)

Such outcomes include what Yerkes refers to as unusual types of insanity, dealing with aged individuals, and so on. The point scale will allow, then, for certain kinds of peculiar patterns of performance between subtests. Though not so specifically stated at that time, it is apparent that the later pattern-analysis concept still widely used today was inherent in this argument of Yerkes. For example, he mentions the fact that unusual results in certain kinds of memory performance may be found to be typical of individuals suffering from a type of insanity. He speculates that manic patients would tend to give more words in three minutes than depressed patients would give and significantly more. Such examples open the door for a number of clinical uses with this kind of instrument.

Within this same context, Yerkes asserts that more exact mathematical treatment is possible with the point scale, since there is a finer discrimination of numerical scores than is true with the age scale. All kinds of statistical methods for treating results are possible that may not be so possible with the age scale. Whether or not this argument is a valid one may be questioned, since the arbitrary nature of zero and the size of the units along the scale are not assured simply by having finer individual mathematical units. Indeed, there may be some confounding and compounding of error if assumptions are made in this regard which are not in fact met.

Limitations of the Binet

Yerkes discusses the limitations of the Binet-type scale from the standpoint that mathematical methods may be applied only in terms of mental ages and not in terms of any particular test. As he says, the age scale suffers from the fact that each test is either passed or failed, which restricts the mathematical statements pertinent to measures of central tendency for each item within the test. There is less refinement in grading of scores on the age scale as a result of such limitations in the Binet.

Yerkes concludes this argument with the specific statement: " . . . thus we see that if we are interested in the special abilities of abnormal persons as measured by their performance on different tests, the point scale is more satisfactory than a year scale" (Yerkes and Foster, 1923, p. 14). He then goes on to discuss the relationships between the point scale as devised by him and the Stanford-Binet Revision. Since a child may remember specific items from a test, at least according to Yerkes, it is desirable to alternate kinds of examinations from one time to another. For this purpose he advocates the use of the point scale first, then six months or a year later the use of the Stanford Revision. He closes with this statement: "That the two examinations may be used thus without serious divergence in the results is shown in the fact that the correlation between results on the two scales has been found to be .87" (Yerkes and Foster, 1923, p. 14). There is no mention made of clinical significance in either instance in this particular case.

Comparisons of Binet and Point-Scale Method

In 1917 Yerkes presented a paper comparing age scales and point scales, a paper reprinted in his 1923 volume. He states first of all that scales for determining intellectual ability were very commonly used despite the fact that they were still crude and needed a considerable amount of improvement. He felt it important that instead of accepting test scores at their face values, constant study, modification, and if necessary replacement of tests continue. Only as this is done will validity and reliability continue to increase for whatever tests are chosen to be used. The study of human behavior, both theoretically and practically, had become an important issue by World War I, much too significant to ignore. Within this context, Yerkes proposed that evaluations of measures of intelligence be attempted so that critical conclusions might be drawn. This is the primary basis of his paper.

He next describes the two principle means of measurement, the point scale and the age scale. The point scale includes the variety of tests, each test bearing items of a comparable type, while the age scale tends to measure some unidentified factors. Beyond this there are two principal types of measurement of behavior. The first of these he refers to as the *scale or group test procedure*, while the second he calls the *single or specific functional measurement*. Both the age scale and the point scale fit under the first of these types. Scientifically and ideally, the second type, single or specific functional measurement, is superior. As tests approach this standard, they will be increasingly usable and valid. Of course, tests have been devised for specific and practical situations. As a result they have diverted somewhat from this ideal goal. Yet Yerkes maintains that increasingly the goal has been approached as new measures have been devised and particularly those tests which reflect graded, standardized, accurate, specific tests and methods. So long as the need persists, scales will continue to be developed. The accuracy of his statement is reflected in the fact that over half a century later we are still developing scales to assess human behavior and particularly that of intellectual behavior.

Yerkes raises the question, then, whether or not both the Binet and point-scale methods should be continued and refined beyond that point in time. Should, perhaps, one of them be dropped, or both dropped, and some new method of measurement devised? Tenatively he proposes that both methods be continued. Too many practical problems were being met to some satisfactory degree at least by the scales then available. At the same time he advocates that efforts should be extended toward developing reliable methods of measuring different kinds and degrees of human behavior. To achieve this end, he further advocates developing a scale that combines principles of the age scale and the point scale. Such a scale would include both qualitative and quantitative aspects of behavior. It should be modeled after the point scale by using selected and graded subtests. Standardization should be conducted in such a manner that subparts of the instruments could be used independently and thereby reflect specific functional tests. Yerkes advocates that by following such a procedure the advantages of what then existed as methods of measuring intelligence could be used and indeed added to.

Yerkes takes issue with a number of psychologists who had concluded that differences between the age scale and point scale were minor at best, and that the two scales yielded fundamentally the same information. This position he firmly rejects on the basis of several points of differences which he sees between the two approaches. Though somewhat repetitious of what has been said before, there is also an elaboration of some of these issues, so that we will reconsider them at this point.

Analysis of Age and Point Scales

The first difference mentioned by Yerkes is the one of selection of items and tests that make up the total scale. As he reminds us, the age scale as reflected in the Binet examination uses items in terms of percentage passing at different age levels. This determines not only the content of the test but the placement in age levels of each item. He concludes that such an approach implies that important forms of behavior must occur at various times during childhood, middle years, and adolescence. There is a dependence upon development, though this may not be accurately reflected in the way the scale is devised at all. By contrast, the point scale emphasizes the functions of intelligence which are to be measured and does not consider to any great degree the relation of such functions to stages of development. In the point scale, then, the assumption is made that all important forms of intellectual functioning are available in infancy or at least very early childhood, and that all of them develop at some reasonable rate throughout childhood and adolescence. Under this approach, there are certain fundamental tests which should appear in the scale at all age levels. Yerkes summarizes by saying that the age-scale approach emphasizes an assumption of "appearing function," while the point scale is more functional and makes the assumption of "developing functions."

He cites the viewpoint that genetic psychology has demonstrated that the important classes and types of behavior are available to the human by the end of the third year of life. Unfortunately, citations of research to this effect are not given by him. In any event, he accepts this viewpoint and operates on the assumption that whatever portions of intelligence develop after year 3 are simply further examples of the general type already available at that age. This assumption is of extreme importance not only to Yerkes scale but to any other point scale using the same kinds of subtests at all year levels. By contrast, as Yerkes makes clear, the variety of items used in the Binet from year level to year level reduce comparability of measurement on individuals of different ages. He maintains that this is true because different forms of behavior are measured by different kinds of items at the two year levels. When considering the six-year-old child who has passed items through year 9 and the ten-year-old child who has passed items through year 13, comparability is limited. With the point scale, by contrast, certain kinds of comparability are possible since both the nine- and thirteen-year-old child encounter the same items.

A second point of departure between the measuring procedures is the matter of standardization. Yerkes refers to the Binet scale as being internally standardized whereas the point scale is externally standardized. This returns us to the issue of selection of items and their replacement. The use of a percentage-passing concept for the placement of items leads to a scale which is inflexible, according to Yerkes, and therefore limited in its applications. While it may be highly accurate for a given group, it will be highly unreliable when applied to groups of individuals who differ markedly from the characteristics of the norm group. Yerkes maintains that due to this fact an internally standardized method for measuring human behavior is defective. By contrast, the point scale reflects an external means of standardization, since the tests are selected and arranged on the basis of abilities, not on the basis of performance by individuals.

The norms which were obtained with the point scale do not act as a limiting device in evaluating results. As groups other than that on which the point scale is standardized are used, the norms are simply expanded with consequent modification in the score reliability and validity. For any new group, with the point scale it is necessary only to administer the examination to a significant number of representative individuals. The method itself need not be revised, items need not be rearranged, and new items need not be substituted for old ones. From this standpoint, Yerkes believes the point scale to be more flexible and universally applicable than the age scale.

The third distinction between the two measuring methods concerns responses. In the age scale of the Binet type, a response is judged either right or wrong, and therefore an all-or-none criterion is used for each item. Yerkes maintains that this approach is less scientific, for the measurement is only a rough approximation of a quantity rather than being quantitative itself. By contrast, the point scale allows judgments which are of a qualitative nature. One is not restricted merely to passing or failing on an item; there may be differential amounts of credit given according to the quality or amount of response offered by the individual. A point scale then is distinctly quantitative in a fashion not true of the age scale. It includes a qualitative component as well. Neither of these quantitative or qualitative matters is truly approached by the age scale, according to Yerkes. He considers this to be a significant difference between the two methods of measurement, and indicative of the essentially scientific approach inherent in the point scale. Whether or not this goal is reached is a matter of some empirical importance, as previously pointed out. Merely increasing the numbers used in a scale with an arbitrary zero and unknown units is not particularly scientific.

Within the context of this third difference, Yerkes also points to differences in statistical treatment. He says that the Binet scale allows statistical treatment only in a restricted way. A point scale by contrast allows statistical treatment of a variety of significant features. Because one can manipulate scores statistically so well and so importantly with the point scale, Yerkes maintains that it has achieved added recognition and use. If the argument is valid, the point scale assumes a research importance which is not possible with the Binet scale. As a matter of fact, Yerkes makes the point that the Binet scale may be technologically useful but has very little research value. By contrast, the point scale possess both technological utility and research importance.

Some Problems in Tests

One strength cited earlier by Yerkes for the point scale is the fact that tests may receive differential weighting, depending upon their important relations with external criteria. One source of criticism of the point scale advocated by him was the fact that weights which he had assigned had no precise basis and seemed not to be based upon any definite scientific principle. Yerkes agrees that the criticisms are valid, although the same criticisms could be offered in the other scales. As he says, an age scale needs just as much evidence of sound and systematic weighting principles as does the point scale.

Still, Yerkes maintains that point-scale tests are not simply weighted in a completely haphazard fashion. By experience in examination, by computing correlation coefficients with measures of ability and certain external criteria, by assessing relationships between subtest scores, and the like, certain weightings were given in the Yerkes scale which would be superior to a truly arbitrary method. Indeed, with further developments in the scale, further refinement and institution of a scientific approach were to be carried out by him. What he advocates in its specific nature is a weighting based upon the relationship of a particular subtest with total score or with some measure of general intelligence. The greater the relationship between the subtests and this total score the greater the credit for that test. That there are some rather obvious dangers in such an approach should be apparent due to its circular nature. The matter of differential test weighting was thus not completely satisfied by 1923. An examination of current point scales will indicate that the issue is still not resolved.

A second problem in the building of tests is the matter of chronological age as compared with some more exact measure—what Yerkes refers to as physiological age. Yerkes takes a strong position against the use of chronological age as a comparative basis for mental age because of differences in rapidity of growth and maturation for individuals, for the sexes, and so on. Instead, he advocates that physiological age should be determined and the measures achieved with whatever kinds of tests compared to this rather than chronological age.

In summary, Yerkes presents a table (see Table 5-1) which demonstrates the significant differences between the Binet age scale and the Yerkes point scale. A number of the differences included in this table are more apparent than real.

TABLE 5-1
CHARACTERISTICS OF THE BINET AND POINT-SCALE METHODS OF MEASUREMENT

Binet Characteristics	Point-Scale Characteristics
(1) Multiple-group, age or year scale	Single graded-test scale
(2) Selection by relation of successes to age	Selection by function measured
(3) Varied, unrelated, ungraded tests	Each test so graded as to be available for wide range
(4) Internally standardized and inflexible	Externally standardized and flexible
(5) All-or-none judgments	More-or-less judgments
(6) Qualitative	Quantitative
(7) Measurements only slightly amenable to statistical treatment	Measurements wholly amenable to statistical treatment
(8) Tests weighted equally	Tests weighted unequally
(9) Implicit assumption, that of appearing functions	Implicit assumption, that of developing functions
(10) Measurements for different ages relatively incomparable	Measurement for different ages relatively comparable

From Yerkes and Foster, 1923, p. 156.

Analysis of the Stanford-Binet

Yerkes closes the article with an analysis of the Stanford-Binet scale. He begins by observing that a number of tests included within the Binet revision seemed to be heavily dependent upon education of the individual. Specifically, he includes in this category vocabulary, arithmetic reasoning, definitions of words, and explanation of fables. The major disadvantage to this approach, Yerkes believes, is its limitation for extension of the scale to adolescents and adults.

Yerkes attempts to group the Stanford-Binet items in terms of similarity of responses. The task he finds difficult and concludes that the Stanford Revision of 1916 reflects haphazardness in the distribution of a given test with consequent loss of scientific principles insofar as test placement is concerned. There seems to him to be no fundamental and functional principle for selecting tests for any particular group. Such a conclusion is not surprising. After all, the Binet was standardized on a different procedure, as Yerkes himself has clearly stated several times.

Still, Yerkes points out that neither the point scale nor the Binet scale is perfect, nor will either ever be. It is possible that from the work done with both, some new scales will be devised which will be superior. One of the future developments that he believed would occur was the use of graded tests where correlation coefficients have signified a high relationship with "varied measures of efficiency in living." He also points to the increased accurate standardization of tests of whatever type which will lead to more reliable norms as well as more varied ones. Ideally, such tests may be used in total or specific parts for more specific types of predictions of behavior. Finally, Yerkes says, scales will be developed which will use vertical instead of horizontal age lines. The scale will no longer reflect age, but the subtest within the scale as constituent parts will reflect ages. When the items of a subtest are sufficiently well graded, the examiner will know specifically what item to begin with for a child of a given age. This will lead to true vertical dimensions rather than horizontal ones. As is obvious, this state of affairs has not been reached, despite Yerkes' hopes.

An Early Example of the Point Scale Used by Wechsler

The possibility of measuring different functions and thereby offering differential diagnosis had been demonstrated with the point-scale technique. Wechsler accepted the possibilities inherent in the approach and published an article utilizing the technique with the Army Alpha subtests (Wechsler, 1932). Wechsler shows that tests may have value other than merely reporting a total score, and that this value had been exemplified

through the use of the Army Alpha both in clinical settings and in personnel work. The analysis of an individual's performance on individual subtests which make up a total examination could be used to reflect special
abilities or disabilities on the part of the individual. Insofar as the point
scale—any point scale—adequately defines and measures differential
functions, such a procedure is both plausible and significant. Wechsler
believed that several of the subtests of the Army Alpha could be used
within clinical settings for the type of differential diagnosis necessary for
decisions to be made about the individual.

One of the strengths noted by Wechsler in the Army Alpha as compared to the Stanford-Binet is the fact that equivalent kinds of material
are involved in all levels of performance. This again is a concept included
in the point scale. The subtests which make up the Army Alpha are more
closely related to specific abilities than the kinds of items which are placed
in the year levels of the Binet. The essential distinction pointed out by
Yerkes, for example, was the percentage-passing concept in selection of
Binet items as compared with items reflecting a designated function. It
is true, of course, that the Binet does not repeat types of items at each
year level as well, so that grouping is difficult even on this basis. Yerkes
and Foster (1923) had pointed out that their attempts at grouping Binet
items yielded about twenty-five different kinds of "subtests" with a very
limited number of items in most of them. Obviously such a procedure in
the Binet, then, would lead to problems and some test specifically designed to reflect the values of the point scale should be superior.

Certain measures of the Army Alpha Wechsler believed to be highly
useful for the purpose of differential diagnosis. Specifically he speaks of
the following kinds of subtests. One subtest in the Army Alpha, Test 8,
he believes to measure range of information. This test appears to be, in
its approach and content if not in its item presentation, a precursor of the
information subtest of the Bellevue, the WISC, and the WAIS. Arithmetical reasoning, in turn, is measured by two tests in the Army Alpha according to Wechsler, Tests 2 and 6.

The functioning of the individual in his environment becomes an
increasingly important concept in assessment of intelligence and its utilization, according to Wechsler, so that Test 3 of the Army Alpha assumes
significance. Wechsler maintains that such a test is a measure of comprehension of social relations. Again the linear relationship with later subtests devised for his own scale is evident. Language ability also becomes
a significant feature of adaptation of the individual, and Wechsler believed Test 4 of the Army Alpha reflected this trait. Finally, abstract
reasoning ability is reflected in two subtests of the Army Alpha, Tests 5
and 7, and are cited by him as usable for that purpose.

At this stage, then, one may note the kinds of functions which

Wechsler would include in a test setting, although these are by no means as complete as they became in his later development of scales. The attributes of the point scale are obviously superior, in Wechsler's view, for the purpose of assessing intellectual abilities and particularly in terms of the kinds of differential diagnosis which must be done in any behaviorally important situation.

Having cited the kinds of subtests from the Alpha which might reflect abilities of a discrete nature, Wechsler then discusses their use. He identifies the functions served by given subtests, and consequently their probable behavioral significance. The next step becomes a statistical one. It is only necessary to determine the score that an individual must make on any of these individual subtests in order to decide whether or not he may be rated as superior or inferior in respect to that particular ability or function. In the article cited here (Wechsler, 1932), a table is included which reports median scores for the individual subtests and total score limits for each subtest. He also supplies some evidence of the raw score deviation from the reported medians necessary for the individual to be considered superior or inferior on that particular subtest. In this context, the Bellevue scale is first developed.

References

Phye, G. D. and A. J. Edwards. "Immediate Memory Span: Implications for Individual Intelligence Testing," *The Professional Reviewer,* Vol. 7 (1970), pp. 1–2

Wechsler, D. "Analytic Use of the Army Alpha Examination," *Journal of Applied Psychology,* Vol. 16 (1932), pp. 254–256.

Yerkes, R. M. *A Point Scale for Measuring Mental Ability.* Baltimore: Warwick & York, 1913.

Yerkes, R. M. "The Binet Versus the Point Scale Method of Measuring Intelligence," *Journal of Applied Psychology* Vol. 1 (1917), pp. 110–122.

Yerkes, R. M. and Josephine C. Foster. *A Point Scale for Measuring Mental Ability: 1923 Revision.* Baltimore: Warwick & York, 1923.

6

The Wechsler-Bellevue Scales

Though Wechsler has contributed a number of specialized measuring devices in clinical and intellectual content, the principal tests for which he is responsible include the two Bellevue scales, the Wechsler Intelligence Scale for Children, the Wechsler Adult Intelligence Scale, and the now current Wechsler Primary and Preschool Scale of Intelligence. The content and nature of the currently used devices—the WISC, the WAIS and the WPPSI—demonstrate the essential characteristics included in the Bellevue scales. For this reason decisions made about the content, standardization, and score expressions of the Bellevue scales will serve as a principal point of departure.

In 1939, David Wechsler published the first edition of *The Measurement of Adult Intelligence*. This book described the development of the Wechsler-Bellevue scales and was a necessary corollary to the tests themselves. The tests and the corresponding manual proved so popular that in 1941 Wechsler published a second edition of *The Measurement of Adult Intelligence*, containing the same features but with the addition of some discussion of clinical features of the scale and the use of the instruments in diagnosis. Expanded data for certain subtests were also included. This second edition is the basis for the discussion of the Bellevue scales in this text.

The Need for and Role of an Adult Intelligence Scale

After an opening chapter dealing with the nature of intelligence as perceived by him (see Edwards, *Individual Mental Testing*, Part I, Chapter

8, 1971), Wechsler discusses the need for an adult intelligence test. Because schools had been the setting for the development and use of intelligence scales, almost all available instruments were designed for and included data from the examination of children. Wechsler states that this trend was the result of the relative ease with which children might be obtained as subjects. There is the added factor that it is easier to devise a test for children than it is adults, plus the fact that there are very obvious applications for children's tests that do not seem so obvious with an adult scale. This matter of application to very practical situations has served the test movement in at least two ways. The more obvious of these deals with academic achievement. Tests developed with children, particularly those of a Binet type, have shown substantial correlations with scholastic attainment. As Wechsler reminds us, the psychologist who has been trained well can make a fairly accurate differentiation between children of superior, average, and below-average ability with the administration of a test taking approximately an hour. Often this differentiation is more accurate than that of a teacher who may have observed such children over a time period of several months. Given such demonstrations of validity, intelligence tests should play a part in the academic setting, particularly in the initial admission of the child to the school setting. Whether or not such validity is indeed met has become an increasingly pointed question raised in recent years. In any event, the assumption was more readily accepted in the early days of development of such tests, with the result that a variety of tests designed to predict academic achievement was devised during the first quarter of the twentieth century.

Then there is a second area of considerable importance to the practical appliation of tests, as shown by Wechsler. This is the area of mental deficiency and its diagnosis. It was possible with the test devised by Binet and those who followed him to obtain some quantitative measure of degree of retardation. With the use of mental-age scores, the tests were applied directly to adults, not limited only to children. This utilization of a scale designed to measure abilities of children with adults becomes a major point of contention for Wechsler and one of the primary reasons for devising a scale normed on adults as such.

A breakthrough occurred with the development of the Army Alpha and Beta Tests during World War I. Wechsler points to the strength of the Alpha Test particularly as a thoroughly standardized group test. It contained the possibility of a rapid examination which would allow a fairly accurate classification of a large number of individuals. The major limitation was the fact that it did not allow individual diagnosis as such. Though further adult group tests were devised after World War I, little or no emphasis was placed on the development of individual intelligence tests devised for and normed on adults. The attempts to extend the Stanford-Binet with a small number of adults were shown to be inadequate, yet psychometrists continued to use the Binet with adults as though the norms were meaningful.

Wechsler says that the answer to the question of using a scale devised on children with adults is easy to find. There simply was nothing better at hand, and the test devised for children did meet a kind of need, no matter how imperfectly. If this argument sounds somewhat specious, consider the number of individuals in counseling today who defend certain tests because "there just isn't anything better at the present and we have a problem we have to deal with."

A final point made by Wechsler and a most convincing one, is that the continued use of tests helps to disclose limitations. Unfortunately, according to him, these were ignored by those who are most dedicated to the use of the Binet-type scale. There is some irony in this statement by Wechsler, since the same situations prevail in a number of clinicians who have great faith in the Wechsler scales despite distinct limitations which have been demonstrated.

When the above reasons are added to the fact that there are considerable difficulties in building and standardizing a new adult individual instrument, continued use of children's scales for adult purposes is not difficult to understand although it may be most difficult to accept.

Wechsler claims that such reasons have no scientific value. One must agree with him wholeheartedly on this. The deficiencies which he outlines subsequently in the children's scales consume a considerable basis for devising a more appropriate adult scale. Whether or not these deficiencies are in fact met by either Wechsler or others who devise an adult scale may be questioned. In any event, Wechsler does disclose some very pertinent deficiencies in the scales.

The first of these is that the children's scales are inappropriate for adults, since they have not been standardized on a sufficient number of cases. In most instances there are no adults used in the norming at all. To apply the tests to an adult for any diagnostic purpose seems sure to yield diagnostic error. The only justification would be if there is demonstration that whatever applies to children and their norms equally applies to adults. This argument has been questioned any number of times. Perhaps the inappropriateness just mentioned is best demonstrated by Wechsler's second point. As he says, much of the material that is included as content on the children's scale is inappropriate for use with adults. This is not merely a matter of difficulty level but one of interest and appeal. If the adult does not see the content of the test as being appropriate, his performance is apt to be less than optimum.

A third limitation in children's scales as applied to adults extends the matter of content beyond face validity. To score correctly on the children's scale very frequently requires a degree of accuracy that is divorced from other possible correct responses emphasizing comprehension.

Thus the child must respond with a precise answer in order to receive credit. This the child may do, particularly where some difficulty level established by norming on given age groups is followed. However, with the adult the single more precise response may not be as obvious nor as desirable. Thus the adult may give a correct response and yet be counted incorrect on the child's norms.

At the same time there is considerable emphasis placed upon speed in children's tests as compared to accuracy, according to Wechsler. Though Wechsler believes there is a significant correlation between speed and accuracy, the speed factor may be more significant with children as a means of estimating global ability than it is with adults. Particularly as an adult grows older, speed tests become more inappropriate. The role of speed in an adult scale of intelligence should be deemphasized then. This is a particularly interesting fact when one considers decisions about bonus points given for speeded performance in several scales of the WAIS. Though time limitations for minimum number of points are quite adequate in the adult scale, the influence of speed in obtaining high scores with any age group becomes a matter of question considering the argument offered here by Wechsler. Wechsler does allude to this matter as early as 1941 in the following way:

> When you tell a child, "put these blocks together as fast as you can," the chances are he will accept the instructions at their face value. One cannot be so sure of a similar acceptance in the case of the adult. He might be a type of individual characterizing the attitude, "look before you leap," or "first try to figure this thing out." In that case his attitude might only serve to get him a lower intelligence rating. On many performance tests the difference of a few seconds in the time taken to complete a set task often reduces a subject's score considerably. Facts like these do not, of course, imply that time scores cannot be used in testing adult intelligence, but they do show that their evaluation and interpretation may be considerably different from that which we place upon them in the case of children. (Wechsler, 1941, p. 18)

Where bonus points for speed performance in the subtest of the WAIS are given, the examinee is not informed of such time limitations. Perhaps this condition is explained by the quote above. Just what the considerably different evaluation and interpretation referred to by Wechsler may be with adults is not explained at this stage.

The most fundamental limitation, and by far the most valid cited by Wechsler, is the matter of the inapplicability of mental age scores for adult performance. Though mental age may have some quite pertinent meanings for children, it has none at all for an adult. Wechsler even maintains that the mental-age score of, say, 10 obtained by a child does not mean the same thing for an adult of thirty who obtains the same score. Thus he questions the essential validity of the MA concept, a matter much questioned but inadequately investigated even to this time. Whether or not comparisons of mental age may be made is less an issue in this context, however, than in whether or not the mental age score is applicable to adults at all. Since all tests, including those of Wechsler, reach a point of some ceiling of intellectual maturity, it would seem that beyond that point certainly mental age is questionable. For this reason alone, a test normed on adults and using a score expression appropriate to adult groups for comparative purposes is essential. Wechsler has succeeded in meeting this issue with the development of the Bellevue scales.

Content of the Bellevue Scales

The test constructor must consider two matters in the selection of items and subtests to include in a scale. There is, first of all, the matter of meeting certain statistical criteria. Additionally, there is a series of what Wechsler calls "general considerations" which act as restrictions and limitations in the decisions made.

General Considerations

The first of these considerations, and an essential one in the building of any intelligence test, is the test author's definition of intelligence, no matter how unspecifically this may be presented. Whatever notions permeate the test author's view toward the expression of intelligence must be reflected in the kinds of items and subtests which he will include in the test itself. Obviously, the content reflects certain assumed abilities and the psychometrist implicitly accepts these assumptions when using the test.

There are some quite specific matters which will restrict the choice of content as well. The first of these concerns the item content suitable for the scale characteristics. Items quite appropriate for an age scale may be inappropriate for a point scale, and vice versa. The continuous nature of the point scale will not allow inclusion of certain items which are most appropriate for a specific age group and its surrounding ages, particularly at the early ages. This asymptotic function of every test item is compounded by factors influencing difficulty levels to the point that eventually some novel quality enters the task not intended in a measure of the ability of the individual. Wechsler affirms that what is true of the item is true of a scale as well. There would be points beyond which a scale is simply not an appropriate nor effective measure of ability. In the case of the Bellevue scale this is true at age levels below seven. According to Wechsler, there is no suitable combination with the Bellevue which will discriminate below age 7 and still be valid for adult performance.

A second consideration which limits the kind and extent of item content is the matter of clinical diagnosis. Wechsler says that there are a considerable number of tests found in general measures of ability which are poor indicators of "intelligence" when used in clinical settings and compared to clinical experience. The percentage-passing concept so often used in the selection and placement of items is insufficient for many of the settings where intelligence tests may be used outside school. He gives as an example the fact that a similar percentage of adults succeed in repeating eight digits forward as succeed in solving the ingenuity problem of the 1937 Stanford-Binet. The fact that percentages are the same does not indicate that the two are equally valid measures of ability. Wechsler states that in fifteen years of testing individuals he has not found a single person of inferior ability who passed the ingenuity problem but he has found a large number of mentally defective adults who will pass the digit task. Rather than an isolated instance, Wechsler believes such outcomes are very common and can be demonstrated over and over again with a large number of clinicians.

All in all, then, there must be some practical criterion of the validity of an item and a test if any prediction is to be made. Too seldom has such a pragmatic position been taken by test constructors. Wechsler says that all too frequently merely statistical and a priori reasons are used for inclusion of items in tests. As important as these may be, they leave a considerable area of error possible in outcomes from the test scores. He makes the cogent point: ". . . the only way one can know whether a test item is a really 'good' measure of intelligence is by actually trying it out" (Wechsler, 1941, p. 77). This matter of tryout is demonstrated with a number of items, apparently equally good in content on a priori grounds, when the Bellevue scales were constructed. He takes a most strong position that any final decisions about the validity of a test should be pragmatic. Reliability is an essential feature, but it must be supplemented by the demonstrated validity of actual, accurate usage. As Wechsler further asserts, the ideal situation would call for such pragmatic criteria for every item as well as for the test as a whole. As ideal as this would be, he admits that no test has achieved it, not even his. However, he does believe that the Wechsler scales come closer to meeting such a pragmatic ideal than any other adult scale devised to that time.

Final Procedures Used

Within the context of the matters discussed above, Weschler describes the procedures used in making a final choice of tests to include in the Bellevue scales. Specifically, these procedures were:

1. Intelligence tests commonly used were analyzed for content. The types of functions supposedly measured by the test as described by the author were noted, and the characteristics of the norming

group were determined. Reliability measures reported for the test were examined.

2. The validity of each of these tests was then examined with the emphasis placed on correlation coefficients reported for other recognized tests of ability but more importantly with certain subjective ratings of intelligence. Such subjective ratings included teachers' estimates, estimates of business executives where tests had been used in industry, and, specifically for the Army Alpha and Beta, ratings by Army officers.

3. A rating of the test for clinical purposes was attempted not only by Wechsler but by a number of other clinicians as well. Ratings assigned to tests by various individuals could then be checked in terms of certain types of interjudge agreements.

4. Groups of known ability level, as measured by recognized tests, were used as the basis of tryouts for what seemed likely kinds of tests to include the scale. Wechsler reports that two years were devoted to this step alone. Groups of twenty to fifty individuals were used for the purpose of determining whether or not different kinds of subtests reflected the kind of ability measured by other recognized tests.

This last step eventually led to the selection of twelve subtests, eleven of which were included in the Bellevue scales. The specific subtests chosen are given in Table 6-1. It will be noted that the vocabulary test is listed as an alternate. This occurred, Wechsler reports, because the vocabulary test was not added until a large number of individuals had already been examined, and sufficient statistical data were not available at that time to include it as one of the subtests.

TABLE 6-1
SUBTESTS SELECTED FOR INCLUSION
IN THE WECHSLER-BELLEVUE SCALES I AND II

 1. An Information Test
 2. A General Comprehension Test
 3. A Combined Memory Span Test for Digits Forward and Backward
 4. A Similarities Test
 5. An Arithmetical Reasoning Test
 6. A Picture Arrangement Test
 7. A Picture Completion Test
 8. A Block Design Test
 9. An Object Assembly Test
10. A Digit Symbol Test
Alternate—A Vocabulary Test

From Wechsler, 1941, p. 79.

The ten subtests and the alternate may be combined in four different ways, according to Wechsler. These will yield separate but interrelated intelligence scales. The first combination is intended for persons age 16 to 60 and includes the ten tests but with the allowance of using as few as seven, depending upon the suitability of the subtests for the individuals. The second combination is what Weclsler refers to as an *adolescent scale*, intended for individuals between ages 10 and 16, and using the same subtests but with separate standardization. Each combination uses all ten tests, or at least may use all ten tests, with vocabulary as an alternate.

The other two combinations subdivide the ten subtests on the basis of a Performance scale, which includes tests 6 through 10, and a Verbal scale, including tests one through five with the vocabulary as the alternate. It should be noted the primary emphasis is placed upon the use of all subtests in combination as the best estimate of the individual's ability to function in the environment. The subdivision in the performance for Verbal and Performance scales with separate scores was considered an added convenience, not a substitute. As noted in Part I of this series, there has been an unfortunate tendency, as pointed out by Wechsler, to utilize Verbal and Performance scale IQ's and neglect the Full scale IQ.

Description of Rationale for the Varied Subtests

For each of the subtests included in the scale, based upon the data collected over the two-year period of experimentation, Wechsler attempts to define the types of abilities measured and the rationale for inclusion in an adult scale.

INFORMATION TEST. Psychometrists have attempted to determine a subject's range of information for many years, Wechsler points out, and such examinations had frequently been used by psychiatrists to estimate the intellectual ability of an individual prior to the introduction of standardized tests. By contrast, psychologists and test constructors had tended to ignore such information when devising measures of ability. The group test allowed the possibility of utilization of such a subtest, as illustrated in the Army Alpha. Though one might quarrel that amount of information which an individual possesses depends upon his background and educational level, Wechsler maintains that this is not a serious invalidation of the use of the subtest. The kind of knowledge which the individual must possess in order to succeed at the test becomes a criterion. Wechsler maintains that if the type of question used to determine range of information is well chosen, performance by the adult will be a relatively accurate indication of his intellectual ability.

Wechsler began with about seventy-five questions intended to elicit range of information data. These were grouped into sets of twenty-five to thirty and administered to individuals of previously determined ability.

The final twenty-five items included in the information test were chosen on the basis of success and failure within these subgroups. The question was felt to be both usable and valid if it showed increasing frequency of success with higher intellectual ability determined by a recognized test. Wechsler asserts that the information test proved to be one of the most satisfactory in the battery, since it shows small declines with age and correlates with total score with a coefficient of .67. Considering some of his comments about limitations in percentage passing with age, the results are at least interesting.

The questions are ordered for the information test in terms of approximation to difficulty level. Wechsler tells us that in certain other parts of the country the order may be determined to be somewhat inaccurate. By and large, however, the order of presentation should be fairly standard.

COMPREHENSION TEST. Comprehension items have been used in most ability tests, and Wechsler agrees that their popularity is justified. The results apply particularly to the clinical setting because of utility in diagnosis of certain clinical conditions. Although he offers no data, Wechsler maintains that the kind of response made by the individual may be used by the clinician to diagnose certain personality aberrations. Additionally the responses given by the individual reflect a good bit about his social and cultural background.

Wechsler began with a list of thirty questions intended to reflect the adequacy of the individual's responses to comprehension of social relationships. In final form, the subtests included twelve of these questions, chosen upon the same procedures that influenced the final form of the information subtest. Although there is some duplication of these questions with the Stanford Revision of the Binet and with the Army Alpha, Wechsler maintains such duplication is of little importance. From his clinical experience, comprehension questions show less practice effects than most other kinds of items. He points out that most individuals will persist in a given response even if some other response to a social comprehension situation is suggested.

Wechsler speculates upon the functions which the comprehension subtest might measure. It might seem to be a test of common sense, and was so designated in the Army Alpha. Basically, Wechsler says that success depends upon the individual possessing a certain amount of quite practical information and some generalized ability to use his past experiences. The questions in the final form of the comprehension test seem to him to reflect the kinds of questions which most adults have encountered at one time or another and for which some response must be made in social situations. Several of these comprehension questions are quite unsuited to children because they lack such experiences. Wechsler reports that the comprehension subtest correlates .66 with total score for those between ages 20 and 34 and .68 with total score for those between ages 35 and 49.

ARITHMETICAL REASONING TEST. The inclusion of an arithmetic test is best justified on the basis that a certain amount of mental alertness is necessary for successful solution. To Wechsler arithmetical reasoning is a good indicator of global ability. It also is included in such scales as the Bellevue because it is fairly easy to devise and standardize as well. The chief limitation, and one that is frequently cited by critics of tests, is the influence of education and occupation on the performance of the individual. While those who work consistently with numbers will tend to be proficient at such tasks, other individuals who have less contact with the use of numbers will often be penalized in performance. Wechsler adds that another shortcoming of an arithmetical reasoning test is the influence of attentional factors and temporary emotional states on the performance.

One of the chief defenses of the inclusion of such a subtest is the fact that it has face validity with adults. Wechsler maintains that most adults look upon arithmetic questions as being quite worthy tasks for an adult. The problems included in the subtest of the Bellevue used commonpl~ situations and quite practical calculations. Reading is unnecessary, except for the last two items which may be read by the examiner, and therefore verbalization is largely avoided. At least at the time of revising of this subtest, any person who had acquired education to the seventh-grade level could perform on the items.

The correlations reported with total score are .63 for the age group 20 through 34 and .67 for the age group 35 through 49. Performance on this particular subtest does not deteriorate as rapidly as the performance scale subtests or the memory scale subtest. At the same time performance on arithmetical reasoning does not show the consistency of vocabulary, general information, or general comprehension.

MEMORY SPAN. The memory-span-for-digits test has a common history in nearly all intelligence tests, as Wechsler points out. The original Binet scale used a memory-span test and the various revisions have continued the practice. As a measure of retention, it has proved popular both in testing and experimental settings to the present date. One of its appeals lies in the fact that its administration is quite easy, scoring is quick and exact, and it reflects rather directly the short-term memory function of the individual tested. Despite these positive points, the memory-span test shows the lowest correlation with total score and correlates rather poorly with other subtests. Wechsler believes that this poor corrleation is due to the fact that the ability reflected in memory span contains only a small portion of the g factor proposed by Spearman. He cites research by Spearman and others indicating that memory span is relatively independent of the general factor.

Because of its limitations, Wechsler considered eliminating the subtest from the battery but finally decided to include it for two reasons. First of all, memory span is a quite good measure of ability for low ability levels. The individual who performs quite poorly on short spans will in most instances be found to be retarded. The exception to this is in certain cases of organic diseases. The second reason for inclusion is that difficulties encountered by the individual in repetition of digits either forward or backward may be of some diagnostic significance in the clinical setting. This will be particularly true for memory defects which are symptomatic of organic conditions. With older individuals, rapid decline in memory span may indicate such organic conditions.

Wechsler included digits forward and backward in a single test in order to extend the range of the test. The role accorded to memory span in terms of total score is reduced over what it would be had the two tests been administered separately.Wechsler reports a correlation coefficient of .51 for memory span and total score.

SIMILARITIES TEST. Wechsler claims that this subtest is the best of the entire scale. Some twelve items are included, selected from over twenty initial items.

There are several merits for the subtest as reported by Wechsler. For one thing, it is easy to administer and seems to be interesting to adults. It also seems to contain a considerable amount of the general factor which should be reflected in total score. Finally, the responses made by the individual may be examined for qualitative features of the logical character of his thinking. Thus one may examine the response for superficial as compared to essential qualities, and the distinction will indicate something about the general intellectual functioning of the individual. Wechsler states that it is surprising how large a percentage of adults are quite superficial in the type of response which they make. Because of such differences, differences in scoring weights are allowed. Thus essential likenesses will receive two points while superficial ones will receive only one point. He defends this procedure in the following manner: "This qualitative difference in response is of value not only because it furnishes a more discriminating scoring method, but because it is often suggestive both of the evenness and level of the subject's intellectual functioning . . ." (Wechsler, 1941, p. 89). Within this context, some adults will show mostly one credit responses and thereby indicate an evenness of intellectual ability correlated, Wechsler believes, with the kind of work for which a high grade of intellect is not necessary. By contrast, other individuals will show a varied proportion of zero, one, and two credits and even within this erraticism show the possibility of a high grade of intellectual work. Obviously the individual who consistently receives two credits would be the kind of individual who might be expected to conduct the highest level of intellectual work.

Wechsler reports that the similarity subtest correlates .73 with total score.

PICTURE-ARRANGEMENT TEST. The picture-arrangement task is a cartoon-type test in which the subject arranges pictures in a correct order. Though of considerable interest to persons taking the test, it has not been one commonly used in either individual or group tests. The Wechsler-Bellevue scales contain eleven such sets. Initially, over twenty cartoons had been assembled. The final selection was based upon interest value, scoring ease, and discrimination. Wechsler admits that such criteria are quite difficult to meet, and the task as it appeared in the 1939 Bellevue scale is somewhat unsatisfactory. The problem, he feels, is not in terms of the item selected or the time spent but limitations that are common to any picture arrangement test.

Despite these limitations, Wechsler feels that the picture-arrangement test has very definite merits. Possibly the chief kind of information obtained with such a test is the ability of the individual to comprehend a total situation and respond to its totality. Unless a person gets the idea of the story inherent in the series of pictures, it is not possible for him to assemble them in a reasonable order. Added to this strength is the fact that the items included in the Bellevue scales reflect quite practical situations of a very human nature. Persons who respond well on this test are able to use their general intelligence in a variety of other social situations for adaptation. Whatever comprehension is involved in the picture-arrangement test apparently differs somewhat systematically from that in the comprehension subtest as such, since correlations are of a low to moderate magnitude for the age groups used in norming.

For certain of the items in the picture-arrangement test, some credit will be given even where the order is not correct. This is true for those longer series, involving five or six pictures, where the order given by the subject is sensible even though not quite correct. The credit allowed on this basis is derived from performance of some two-hundred subjects and the frequency with which such imperfect arrangements were made by these individuals.

As Wechsler points out, the picture-arrangement test does not correlate very well with other tests of the scale and tends to deteriorate with age. The matter of low intercorrelations with other subtests is not a serious one if the subtests are intended to measure somewhat different aspects of general ability. The more pertinent question would then be the degree to which the subtest correlates with the total score. For the picture-arrangement test, the correlation coefficient is .51, the same amount of correlation found for memory for digits. The same suspicion should be reserved for picture arrangement as an adequate measure of general ability as is applied to digit repetition. It should be noted that higher correlation coefficients for picture arrangement with total score are reported for the WAIS.

PICTURE-COMPLETION TEST. Picture completion is here used to signify the identification of a missing portion of a picture. The task has been popular both with individual tests like the Binet and a number of group tests as a measure of some performance quality. Wechsler makes the cogent point that suitable items for this kind of test are difficult to find, particularly since too-familiar obejcts increase the ease of performance and unfamiliar ones reduce the ease of performance. Some fifteen items were included in the picture completion test of the Bellevue scales, selected from a total of about thirty-five such items. Discrimination value —the percentage-passing concept—was the basic for selection for inclusion in the subtest. Over all, Wechsler is pleased with the subtest, as it turns out to be one of the best of the performance scales. Particularly is it suitable for those with low intelligence to help identify deficiencies of a general nature. Wechsler believes that the test involves a high degree of perceptual and conceptual abilities in performance, particularly involving visual recognition and identification. The specific performance requires the individual to identify the totality of every object, the essential features of the object, and the portion which is essential to the form or function of the object.

Although fifteen seconds were allowed for each item, Wechsler maintains that this is not a timed test since the limit is more than sufficient for all individuals who can perform adequately at the task. He presents evidence to support this claim by pointing out that increasing time limits per item to thirty seconds had very little effect on total score for the subtest. Within the Performance scale, the picture-completion test maintains better performance with increasing age than most of the other Performance scale subtests. Perhaps the major limitation is in the fact that those of high ability show a ceiling effect, and thus differentiation of high average and above ability levels is not very accurate with the subtest. The subtest shows a correlation coefficient of .61 with total score.

BLOCK DESIGN. The block-design task, based upon Kohs' work, is a significant test in the performance scale, showing a correlation with total score of .73. Overall, it shares common variance with most of the verbal tests and correlates better with comprehension, information, and vocabulary than some of the other verbal subtests do. Thus it apparently measures much of what is measured by so-called verbal tasks. Wechsler believes that the mental performance involved with the block-design test requires both esthetic and analytic ability. There are some seven figures used in the subtest, increasing in complexity.

Wechsler maintains that performance on the block design is particularly suited to qualitative analysis. Observation of the subject as he performs on the task can yield a considerable amount of information to the skilled psychometrist. One may observe whether the individual approaches the task in its totality or breaks it into its elements; those who tend to break the pattern into its component parts perform better than those who try to take the total picture into account. Additionally, reactions of an emotional nature and various kinds of attitudes on the part of the individual performing on the task can be observed by the pschometrist and used for inferential purposes. Certain of the nonintellective traits, those of a temperamental nature mentioned by Wechsler in other writings, may be observed in the performance of the individual.

Particularly does the subtest have value for diagnostic purposes in Wechsler's estimation. An individual with mental deterioration or one who is becoming senile will have particular difficulty with this subtest, frequently being unable to complete even the simplest of the designs. Wechsler believes this to be due to a lack of ability to synthesize on the part of those who have brain disease, or mental deterioration, or senility. Perhaps included in this behavior is the inability of the individual to make appropriate shifts in thought. As would be expected from some of the foregoing comments, performance deteriorates with increasing age. Wechsler states that with persons over forty, performance is progressively worse as they age. Indeed, he offers this as a portion of the proof needed to demonstrate a decline of intellectual ability with age. This argument is all the more acceptable when one considers the relationship of block design performance to general ability. Given appropriate norms, it is possible as well to estimate the amount of deterioration that is occurring for the individual with age.

DIGIT-SYMBOL TEST. This test requires substitution of symbols of a somewhat novel form for numbers. The task had been quite popular in different kinds of psychological tasks including a number of intelligence scales. Both speed and accuracy are concerned in the score, with the individual who can be both accurate and rapid achieving the highest possible score. Wechsler expresses some concern about the effects of motor performance on the intellectual expression involved. Evidence gathered by him indicates that the motor factor was less important than he thought it might be originally for most instances, though in other instances it turned out to be more important than he had hoped. For example, the illiterate who has little practice with paper-and-pencil tasks will perform quite poorly on this test regardless of his intellectual ability. For such indiviuals the task should not be used, according to Wechsler.

With older individuals, even where literate, the problem exists with motor set and motor speed. So long as performance losses with age are correlated with general ability to learn and perform, this is an inconsequential matter. Evidence was needed then by Wechsler on the independence of motor speed from ability as such. He examined the available data to determine the possible influence of motor speed on performance and found a decline in performance after age 25 and particularly after age 40. However, this decline in performance on the digit-symbol test was roughly proportional to the ability of the individual at a younger age and as reflected in his total score. As a result, the subtest was retained in the scale and is believed to offer information of a helpful nature in terms of both general ability and diagnostic features.

One diagnostic outcome noted by Wechsler is the fact that a neurotic and unstable individual will tend to do poorly on a test like the digit-symbol test. This may be due to an inability to concentrate and apply himself for more than a few seconds at a time. This becomes compounded with some emotional reactions to any task that requires persistence on his part. Wechsler maintains that this poor performance by the neurotic individual is more a matter of decreased mental efficiency than it is some impairment of intellectual ability. The correlation of digit symbol with total score was .67 for the age group 20 through 34 and .70 for the age group 35 through 49. Digit symbol, as previously mentioned, shows rapid decline with age.

OBJECT ASSEMBLY. Formboards are used in the object assembly task, employing very common objects. There is a figure of a whole person, the mannikin, a head in profile, and a hand. These are cut into pieces and presented in a fashion requiring an individual to be able to realize their configuration in order to successfully assemble them in the time limit given. Wechsler admits that he had considerable hesitation about including this kind of task in the scale. Those formboards which had been used with children were obviously unsuited for adults, and further show little discrimination value with adult age groups. For prediction, the form boards leave a great deal to be desired. Utilizing forms like the hand and profile did increase their value, but not to a degree sufficient to cause them to be used with assurance. Practice looms very large in the use of formboards of the type included in this subtest. As a result, retest scores are not to be trusted.

Yet Wechsler decided to leave the subtest in the scale because of other features which he believed compensate for these very serious limitations. For one thing, the contribution to total score is sufficient to justify its inclusion at the same time that correlation with other subtests is low. Most of the reduction of intertest correlation coefficients is due to the imappropriateness of the test for a somewhat small and probably specialized group of persons. Performance on the subtest shows stable and rapid increases to about age 13 and steady performance after age 30. The age group 15 to 30, by contrast, shows extremely erratic performance for a considerable number of individuals. Wechsler accounts for this on the basis of momentary changes of attention and interest within that age group.

But the major justification for including the object assembly test in the scale lies in its qualitative aspects. Again, observational data about the approach of the individual to the task and his consequent performance is a significant tool in the hand of a competent psychometrist. It is essential that the individual recognize what the total completed picture will be in order to be successful. For example, the mental defective will simply start trying to fit pieces together by a trial-and-error method. The brighter individual will realize that he has some figure of a known nature and begin fitting the pieces together on the basis of the total pattern. Between these extremes there are some other responses which reflect either less than perfect realization of how the pieces fit to form the total or the sudden realization of the total figure after performance has begun.

Correlation with total score shows increases with age, being .41 for the age group 20 through 34 and .51 for the age group 35 through 49. Wechsler says that older people perform more like children than do young adults. He implies that there is some particular ability shared commonly as a part of this age matter. No evidence is offered on this point.

VOCABULARY TEST. The place of a vocabulary scale in a test of intelligence is perhaps the most widely accepted matter of any bearing on the measurement of ability. It would be difficult to find any test that is labeled a test of intelligence which does not include a vocabulary measure in some form. Indeed, some tests are nothing more than tests of vocabulary. Wechsler defends the inclusion of a vocabulary test on the basis that such a subtest is an excellent measure of general ability, not restricted to the educational level of the person. Apparently individuals even with little schooling can build excellent vocabularies if they possess a high degree of learning ability, and can add to the fund of verbal information and ideas in their day-to-day activities and social contacts.

It is true, Wechsler maintains, that the number of words a man acquires is influenced by the kinds of opportunities presented to him both culturally and educationally. Using a vocabulary test with a person who is illiterate or who comes from another culture will be unfair. Because of such limitations, Wechsler originally omitted the vocabulary test from his battery. When work had progressed to a sufficient level, he realized the error of this decision. Except for a limited number of special cases, he concluded that the amount of education and the other possible limitations which exist are much less influential on the effective range of a person's vocabulary than he and other psychologists had believed. Indeed, he says that available information indicates that illiterates and those who come from other cultures with only a moderate amount of English will be penalized less by vocabulary tasks than by some other kinds of tasks which are seemingly not so language-oriented in nature. The work had proceeded to such a level that the vocabulary test could be included only as an alternate in the Wechsler-Bellevue scale. Obviously, it achieves a major status in the WISC and the WAIS. The correlation coefficient of vocabulary score with total score on the Bellevue for some four hundred subjects is reported by Wechsler to be .85. This high correlation is often found in other intelligence scales as well.

Wechsler used a standard school dictionary for the purpose of choosing the words included by him in the vocabulary list. The procedure followed is interesting, and described as follows:

> The list was arrived at by choosing one hundred words at random in the following manner: beginning with an odd page, we selected every top word but one in the left-hand column of every fifth page and continued the process until we had listed one hundred words. These one hundred words were arranged in rough order of difficulty, devised into two lists of fifty each, and given to experimental groups of known intelligence level. By this method the words which seemed to discriminate poorly between different intelligence levels, were quickly eliminated. After some further experimentation the two lists were consolidated into one of sixty, then of fifty words, and finally cut down to the present list of forty-two. The order of difficulty, at least for the individuals in the New York City area, is fairly consistent, except that there are always certain words which were especially easy or hard for some individuals. (Wechsler, 1941, p. 101).

In the selection process, Wechsler adds, highly technical, obsolete or esoteric words were excluded. The procedure, then, allowed for some kind of random selection of words of a fairly common nature, ordered in the list on the basis of a percentage-passing criterion.

As is indicated by the size of the correlation coefficient with total score, the vocabulary task is an excellent estimate of general ability. But Wechsler maintains that it serves a greater role than this in testing. It has qualitative possibilities of importance to the clinical as well as to the educational setting. When an individual defines a word he gives much more than the meaning of this word. Wechsler believes that the definition offered by the individual can give us some information about the quality and character of the thinking process of the person. Although it will require some analysis by the psychometrist of the response, the return from such analysis will be worthwhile. Of course, the definition offered may also yield information about the cultural background of the individual. A retarded subject who comes from a home with a high educational level may be able to define certain relatively uncommon words and fail on certain others which may be more generally known.

But the most important quality of the vocabulary task for clinical purposes is the matter of the thinking process of the individual as reflected in his definitions. Wechsler says this is particularly true of the individual where language disturbance represents the formal basis upon which diagnosis may be made. With the schizophrenic, the definitions given for words are apt to be somewhat bizarre in terms of the content of ideas and peculiarities of expression. He gives some examples of words as defined by schizophrenics to indicate this rather bizarre and peculiar verbal behavior. The responses given are not inaccurate, but they may be quite unusual in their content and expression. He points out that the schizophrenic may also show marked perseveration in his vocabulary, be quite redundant in the definitions he offers, and frequently incoherent in the kind of content presented for a given definition.

The quantitative score of a vocabulary test includes only those items which are correct, and so the vocabulary score of a schizophrenic may be quite high. The suggestion of schizophrenia is not in the number of items correct but in the quality of the responses given.

Certain items in the vocabulary test allowed either one or one-half credit, others either one credit or none at all. Thus differential credits for quality of response were included from the first scale in the vocabulary test and have been maintained. It is interesting to note that performance on a vocabulary test remains high with increasing age. There is, however, some decline with age just as is true with other intellectual abilities.

The Norming Sample

In the preliminary discussion to describing the population used to standardize this test, Wechsler points to the need for representativeness in the samples chosen. No matter how good an intelligence test may be intrinsically, its utilization, including any diagnostic values that it may have, depends upon the relationship of the group from which norms were established and the individual with whom the diagnosis is to be made. Wechsler makes the added point that statistical control is hardly sufficient. Beyond meeting a statistical criterion, the quality of the norms sample and individuals with whom the test is to be used must be known and fully described. Such knowledge, as he says, is very difficult to obtain and evaluate, and there is much left to be desired in the selection of the sample for the Wechsler-Bellevue scales. Because of such limitations,

Wechsler describes those factors for which he attempted control for both statistical and qualitative purposes.

Factors Controlled in the Bellevue Standardization

Four central factors were selected by Wechsler for purposes of control: age, education level, sex differences, and social factors. Each of these is discussed in some detail in the manual.

AGE. The development of a scale exclusively for adults, and normed on such a group, brings up issues of age not encountered in prior tests. Obviously age is a significant influence in the norms of tests for children, and separate samples for the various age groups have been employed in all the best tests, including the Binet and its Stanford Revisions. Wechsler makes the point that separate norms for different ages among adult groups has not been usually the case, however. Instead, individuals from some basic and usually adolescent age level have been used as the base for all other adult groups. Thus if the test constructor assumes that mental growth ceases around age 17, all individuals older than 17 would use the norms for the group seventeen years of age. This homogenous compilation Wechsler believes to be in serious error, as he has illustrated both with his test and with research. He remarks most aptly that to use the norms for an individual of age 17 to determine the level of performance of an individual of age 60 is unwarranted and a source of serious error. As a result, the Wechsler-Bellevue scales included age norms for all groups up to age 60.

EDUCATION LEVEL. The matter of educational level is of even greater significance for an adult scale than it may be for children. Wechsler adduces that systematic and high relationships are found between educational attainment and performance on intelligence tests with all kinds of scales. He reports that in most instances the correlation coefficient will range from .60 to .80. For the Wechsler-Bellevue scales, the correlation between intelligence test performance and educational level is .64. A reasonable inference which might be drawn from this fact is that education influences performance on the intelligence test, and indeed this has been a major criticism of such tests. Wechsler believes that such an explanation is simplistic.

Obtaining a high correlation coefficient between educational attainment and performance on an intelligence test does not indicate cause-and-effect relationships. Although there is the possibility that the high level of education does lead to better scores on intelligence tests directly, there are other possibilities proposed by Wechsler and worthy of some serious consideration. For example, it is possible that the individual who attains a high level of education is simply brighter than most of his peers. This would be the reverse of the argument conventionally presented. Wechsler says this is particularly true and most obvious in the case of the mental defective.

There is another alternative that some other factor influences both the level of educational attainment and performance on the intelligence test. Certainly, Wechsler points out that intelligence-test performance is influenced by the amount of schooling which the individual has had. But he believes that educational level should be considered in some larger context than just the kind of formal education achieved in the classroom. Some individuals of quite limited amounts of formal education still perform quite well on intelligence tests. If the content of the test is selected to represent general kinds of situations rather than specific formal ones, this should be particularly true. As a result, the word "education" must include the ability to take advantage of life experiences from whatever source, and not just the situation of the formal structured classroom.

However it operates rigorous control for this educational factor is difficult. Wechsler says that ideally it might be done by standardizing the tests on groups differentiated according to the amount of formal education obtained. The norms would then be available for the individual in terms of, say, the highest grade completed. Such a procedure would be monumental in its undertaking. As a result it is not feasible, and some other approximations must be used. For the age group 10 to 16 included in the Bellevue scale, for example, Wechsler says this problem is met by selecting the age groups in such a way that the average educational level is approximately equal to that of the average individual in the total population. With adults, such a procedure is less plausible and possible.

Indeed, with adults, occupational status becomes a more satisfactory means of controlling than did educational level as such. As a result, occupational level was used in selection of the adult samples in the Bellevue scales. Wechsler found a systematic relationship between the educational attainment of groups so chosen and U.S. Census figures. He shows that there is a rather remarkable correspondence between the level of educational attainment for the country as a whole and that of the sample used by him for standardizing the Bellevue. The correspondence is such that he maintains that the sampling which is based primarily upon occupational level of individuals in our society will reflect fairly accurately the educational level of such groups and thereby control for differences in educational achievement.

SEX DIFFERENCES. On certain kinds of tasks, girls will be superior to boys in performance, while on other kinds of tasks the opposite results will be found. The number of such tests actually occurring in intelligence scales tend to be relatively small. When total score is taken into consideration, Wechsler notes, differences between males and females tend to cancel. In terms of the Bellevue scales no subtests were retained which showed a significant difference in total scores between males and females. At the same time, women tend to score somewhat higher on total score at almost every year level. This, with other information available to him, leads Wechsler to suspect that women may show a measurable superiority to men insofar as general ability is concerned. He makes a very interesting statement: "We have more than a 'sneaking suspicion' that the female of the species is not only more deadly, but also more intelligent than the male" (Wechsler, 1941, p. 109).

SOCIAL FACTORS. The final variable included for control by Wechsler really reflects a set or group of conditions. Specifically, Wechsler includes in this category examples of "race," social status, and economic status. Ideally, again, he points out that standardization should occur for each of these categories in order to make the intelligence scale most useful. More practically, Wechsler believes that it is not possible to norm on these specific variables, particularly in view of the lack of agreement on the definition and consequences of these subfactors. That this position is not a satisfactory one has been illustrated by the increasing arguments leveled against the standardization of intelligence tests and the fact that these subfactors are so ignored. Probably the chief argument against tests today lies in this very matter. In any event, Wechsler avoided the problem with the Bellevue scales by stating explicitly that the norms could not be used for the black population of the United States. Whether or not any psychometrist has taken the statement seriously is another matter. He does admit to having tested a number of black individuals, but these were not included in the standardization. Standardization of the Bellevue scales was upon white adults only. The reason for not including the performances of blacks in the norms given by Wechsler is that he felt such mixed norms would need special explanations and reservations.

The problems involved in separate standardization with resulting sufficient reliability dictated to Wechsler the necessity for relying upon the performance of white individuals as the norming group. Outside of non-English speaking individuals, he believed such norms are applicable to all citizens of this country. To indicate something of the complexity of this matter, there is today a considerable body of literature indicating that spoken English is not the same even for persons born and raised in this culture. The kind of English spoken by a child from one kind of home differs quite systematically from that spoken by the child from a different kind of home. These differences will tend to be exagerated as adult status is reached, and many individuals have criticized not only tests but educational efforts of all sorts on the basis that the "English" is inappropriate for certain subgroups. This whole matter apparently was not perceived by Wechsler in the 1940's nor by anyone else for that matter. In any event, Wechsler stresses that his arguments seem to make a virtue out of necessity and that in the long run the only possible justification for the norming done on whites alone is that he believes that he has a fair cross section of what may be called "American intelligence."

Perhaps of equal concern in the matter of standardization is the locale from which the standardizing samples came. Nearly all of the subjects used by Wechsler in the standardization of the Bellevue came from New York City and New York State. Certain matching attempts with the total population were followed, so that he believed that representation was achieved. He admits, however, that the total sample probably is more representative of New York State than it is of the rest of the country. Since the mean on the Army Alpha for the white population of New York State was about the average of that of the nation as a whole, Wechsler assumes that the mean scores will not differ from the various age groups between his sample in the United States. As he points out, further studies will be needed to determine the legitimacy of the assumption. Included in such an analysis would be the matter of variability as well.

The Sampling Procedures

The adult sample included in the standardization of the Bellevue scales included individuals from what Wechsler describes as "all walks of life" (Wechsler, 1941, p. 110). As many individuals in this general category who volunteered were included in the testing as long as they were not mentally or physically ill and had at least some basic understanding of spoken and written English. The sample included something over 1,800 adults ranging from age 17 to 80. From this group, individuals were included in the norming based upon the occupational distribution of the adult population in the United States. The United States census for 1930 was used as the source for this occupational labeling, but obviously a number of categories included there were not applicable to a sample primarily from the city of New York. As a result, certain kinds of estimates and substitutions were used. The chief basis for this substitution was to use individuals from urban occupational groups which had an approximate mean intelligence rating for the occupations listed nationwide. As an example of this, Wechsler reports that barbers, bakers, and teamsters could be substituted for farmers (p. 111), since the mean intelligence ratings were the same. He reports that some other such substitutions were made. All in all, percentages for various occupational groups show a reasonable correspondence between the norms sample and the census data. Admittedly, kinds of substitutions and locale of individual subjects acceptable in the 1930's would no longer be acceptable today.

Social status of the individuals used in the norming is a separate matter for consideration. Wechsler reports that individuals were included from almost every social and economic class to be found in the city of New York. It is true, however, that special groups tended to furnish an unusually large number of individuals. That somewhat specialized nature of the sample can be quickly indicated by reference to Table 6-2. One of the

TABLE 6-2
SOURCES OF ADULT SAMPLING IN THE BELLEVUE SCALES, AGES 16 TO 69

Source	N
Home of subjects (mostly housewives)	130
Political, social, and fraternal organizations	126
Commercial establishments	14
Federal project workers, hospital workers, including professional, clerical, skilled, unskilled and domestic workers	255
Hospital wards and clinics (nonmental cases)	176
Transient Bureau (all types who happen to be passing through the city and are in need of temporary aid)	67
Summer resort (Coney Island Beach)	58
Adult vocational schools	234
Day high schools	48
Old-age institutions	73
Total	1,181

From Wechsler, 1941, p. 114.

problems, of course, is that no central source is available as it is for children where schools are easily available for standardization. In selecting and norming a test for adults, the test maker must sample much more widely. Some of the groups used in the Bellevue sampling are questionable largely because of their effects on norms. The relevance of such groups for special diagnostic purposes may also be questioned. The problems inherent in finding an appropriate adult representative sample should soften criticism, however, and Wechsler is to be commended for listing the sources of his sample. As is to be expected, some of the limitations in the sampling procedure followed with the Bellevue have been corrected in the later Wechsler Adult Intelligence Scale.

Following this procedure yielded very few individuals who would allow for a floor in the norms, the defective group. An attempt to approximate the number of individuals in the general population was followed by using patients at the Bellevue Psychiatric Hospital and those committed to some New York State institutions. Wechsler assumed that about 3 percent of the total population is defective, and included approximately this number in the final standardization.

Selecting a sample of children was much simpler, because of the availability of schools within New York City. The procedures followed were quite similar to those used in the standardization of the Stanford-Binet. Largely, so-called representative or average schools were used without the population consisting of predominately a single racial or social group. In addition, the school population was believed to be fairly average in ability, neither significantly above nor below the performance of children in New York City schools as a whole. All children in a school were not used, so that by the end of the year approximately 1,300 children between ages 6 and 17 were available. These had been tested at different times, in different schools of course, and by different examiners. An additional 200 children were obtained in Yonkers and New Jersey schools, giving a total sample of about 1,500. The final selection for inclusion in the norming sample was a set of children in the New York public schools. About 2 percent of the final children sampled consisted of low-grade defectives not in school.

Standardization Results

The Bellevue scales are point scales (see Chapter 5). As a result, the total score obtained for the individual is some summation of credits obtained on individual items and subtests. The decision to use the point-scale system required certain theoretical assumptions and bases being considered and answered. One of the issues which must be met is to determine what portion of the total shall be assigned to any given subtest. The simplest way to meet this problem is by weighting all subtests equally. This procedure has been frequently followed, but it has some obvious problems associated with it. As an alternative, then, some predetermined system of scoring can be employed which will assign the value of each subtest to total score. Regardless of the number of items in the subtest, the weight will be fixed. Wechsler makes clear that the employment of this procedure requires that the test author evaluate the subtests and their proportionate contribution to the total measure of the individual's intellectual level. Obviously, this would be a most difficult procedure to follow.

A statistical alternative pointed out by Wechsler is one of utilizing multiple correlation coefficients. There is a considerable amount of work required in this procedure, and particularly when we consider the lack of computers in the 1930's available for the purpose, so that Wechsler did not employ this procedure. Even if the labor were not so onerous, the results, he believes, do not justify the outcome. Perhaps a much more practical criterion to follow is the quality of the test and subtests to measure the behavior desired. In Wechsler's view, this requires evaluation of the test in terms of clinical experience. If the test does the job clinically, then decisions may be made about subtest weights on more practical grounds.

Score Expressions

Initially, Wechsler made the assumption that the separate subtests of the Bellevue scale had equal importance. As a result, each subtest contributed the same weight to total score regardless of the number of items found in the subtest. This procedure allows adding or omitting subtests from the scale without altering the nature of the norms. For example, a given subtest may be omitted and the remainder of the subtests prorated to obtain essentially the same total score. Where each test is equated to every other test and scores are expressed as z scores (standard deviation units), additions and omissions allow the employment of prorating procedures.

The age group 20 through 34 was used as the basis of standardization. For this age group the raw scores of each subtest were ranked in a distribution and statistical constants computed. Based upon performance on the subtest for this age group, Wechsler determined that a scale of about 20 points would best fit the data of all subtests. Within this range, a mean scale score of 10 was established with a standard deviation of 3 scale-score points. The raw-score distributions of each subtest were fitted to this scale-score system and thus all subtests showed identical means and approximately equal variations. One other step was then required. A table was drawn up in which the equivalents of original scores were given in terms of equal portions of the SD units. These scores were used to obtain the norms and were used in the Bellevue, as they are in the current Wechsler scales, as a means of determining the individual's rating on the scale.

In the Wechsler scales, then, all subtests are given equal weight regardless of number of items. The raw score on each subtest is transformed through the use of tables to a standard score based upon a mean of 10, a standard deviation of 3, and a range of 20 scale-score points.

Significance of Results

Certain results obtained by Wechsler assume significance because they reflect data not previously obtained with a test specifically designed for use with adult age groups. One of the things which the data yield is an increase and then subsequent decrease of total score for the various tests with increasing age. With the Full scale, for example, there is an increase in calculated mean from age 7½ through age 22½ with a subsequent decline to age 57½. Approximately the same results are found for both Verbal scale and Performance scale, though the point of inflection varies slightly from that for Full scale. When means and standard deviations are smoothed, an asymptotic function is reached around age 18 and maintained through age 22 for the Full scale. Insofar as the test is an adequate measure of performance, this would seem to indicate that mental growth continues to about the mid-20's and then begins a slow but gradual decline into old age.

At the younger age levels reported, performance is relatively poor with fairly high standard deviations. As Wechsler observes, this means that the Bellevue scales really were not appropriate for children of younger age levels. The critical cutoff point was about age 10. When the WISC was devised from the Wechsler-Bellevue II, then, it was necessary to add items and standardize for children under age 10. For the original Bellevue scales, at least, Wechsler advocates that the scale should not be used until the child is at least ten years old.

Changes in variability with age are a second matter of some interest in the data with adults. Wechsler computed the ratio of the means to the standard deviations, the coefficient of variation, and reports these for each age group 10 through 60. As children grow older from ages 10 through 18 or so, there is a decrease in variability. This finding supports other tests and research. Beginning about age 18, however, there is an increase in variability with increase in age up to age 60. This also agrees with prior research. Wechsler notes that the decrease in variability with increasing age in children may be a matter of education and background, a matter considered in prior research anf reported in Part I of this series. The matter of increases in variability with age in adulthood is more of a problem. As Wechsler sees it, when individuals grow older one effect of death should be to eliminate extreme deviates so that there should be a subsequent decrease in variability with age. Apparently this factor is not working as would be expected, however. Other explanations are not so readily available and Wechsler leaves the problem for future research.

When IQ's are used in place of weighted-scale scores, the coefficients of variation are very similar for all age groups from 10 through 60. Wechsler maintains that this result indicates that the method he uses for calculating the IQ considers both the change of test score with age and differences in variability of subtests scored at different ages. Since the coefficients of variation for both the Verbal and Performance scales are highly similar, their combination into a Full scale seems justified. Indeed, as Wechsler has maintained elsewhere, the measure of both verbal and performance ability for the individual should make a Full Scale score a particularly meaningful one. That relatively lesser emphasis has been put on Full Scale scores by psychometrists is no fault of the test itself.

Validity

Wechsler points out that the essential criterion of any test score is that of validity. The question becomes one of how one may be sure that a given test is a good measure of intelligence. To him, the only honest reply is through experience. When a test is used in the clinical setting, and it is found to do the job needed in that setting, it may be considered a valid measure. No quarrel may be taken with this position. Yet there are certain kinds of statistical criteria which can and should be employed as well. Wechsler finds it regrettable that ultimate decisions of validity are based only on empirical judgments. His point is well taken, particularly when some form of validity of a congruent or concurrent nature is used to the exclusion of other predictive forms. His discussion of such statistical criteria is of considerable substance.

The usual procedure for validating a new test has been to set as a criterion some well-established test which has been accepted as a "good" measure of the trait in question and then appraise the validity of the new one on the basis of the degree to which it correlates with the already established test. The significance of this correlation will depend entirely upon the original criterion, and it is therefore the criterion itself, rather than the new test, which needs examination. In practice the general tendency has been to accept tests already in use as being more or less established measures of the traits in question, but for the most part these criteria themselves have never been validated. The situation in the case of intelligence tests is not so bad as in other fields of testing, but even here the absence of validated criteria imposes serious limitations on the conclusion that the tests really measure intelligence. The various revisions of the Binet Scales, which, in spite of all criticism, we accept as among our best single measures of intelligence, are no exceptions. Their final validation rests primarily on the fact that they have worked well in practice, and not because of any compelling statistical correlations.

As evidence we need only recall some of the early arguments in their favor. Thus, one of the reasons which Binet gave for devising his tests was that teachers could not very well be trusted to estimate the true intelligence of their pupils. But several years later Terman and others came along and gave as one of the proofs of the excellence of their revisions of this scale the fact that IQ ratings correlated very highly with school progress. In other words, teachers' judgments which were first condemned were now used as supporting criteria for the validity of the tests. This obviously begs the question, but the dilemma involved is almost inevitable.

The trouble is not with the teachers' ratings. The same circularity is involved when ratings of any judges are set up as a criterion. In the case of the Alpha test, the estimates used at the beginning were those of Army officers; in the case of certain tests offered in industry, the estimates were of supervisors and executives. But these estimates were no more valid than those of the teachers. The tests were urged upon the army and industry because it was pointed out the estimates of officers and personnel managers could not always be relied on; then the tests were "sold" to them because they correlated well with practical judgments. From what we have just said, it appears that every new intelligence test, unless it is merely intended as an alternate for an old one, must itself be validated anew. Such validation is especially necessary if, as in our case, we start with the view the generally accepted criterion is not as valid as supposed. The Bellevue Scales were devised because of the belief that the Binet Scales were not sufficiently "good" measures of intelligence for adults. Otherwise, indeed, we should not have gone to the trouble of devising our test. But we do not thereby deny the desirability of showing a correlation between them and other tests of intelligence. (Wechsler, 1941, pp. 130–131).

Indeed, the questions raised by Wechsler about the Binet are as suitable for the Bellevue scales as they were for the Binet.

In line with the statistical data desired, the Bellevue IQ's obtained for an age group between 14 and 16 were correlated with the Stanford-Binet IQ's ($N = 75$), yielding a coefficient of .82. Thus the two tests seem to share a considerable amount of variation and thereby apparently to be measuring somewhat the same thing.

Other concurrent estimates of validity were computed. Among these were the correlations between Bellevue scores and teacher estimates and a resulting correlation coefficient of about .50 was found. This corresponds very well with other such studies. The study done by Belinsky, Israel, and Wechsler and discussed in Part I of this series is also offered as validity data. It will be recalled that this is a judgment of the efficiency of the Bellevue and Binet IQ's and correlated with psychiatric recommendations for institutionalization or noninstitutionalization of presumed retardates. In addition, Wechsler reports a number of individual cases comparing performance on the Binet and the Bellevue and indicating some superiority for Bellevue scores.

All in all, the validity data leave much to be desired. This is not unusual since most new tests (as the Bellevue was then) have not been available long enough for sufficient validity data to be amassed. With our current use of the WISC and WAIS, considerably more validity studies have been conducted and will be considered in Part III of this series.

Reliability

Reliability estimates reported for subtests and for scales are satisfactory. The correlation coefficients reported for test-retest situations, ranging in time from one month to one year, are good. Other evidences of reliability are not reported.

Other Issues in the Bellevue

The remainder of this edition of the *Measurement of Adult Intelligence* deals with such matters as classifying intelligence, and defining and interpreting the role of mental deficiency and deterioration. Of considerable significance is a chapter dealing with diagnostic and clinical features of the Bellevue scales. Of great practical significance is a chapter on limitations and special merits of the scale.

References

Edwards, A. J. *Individual Mental Testing. Part I: History and Theories.* Scranton, Pa.: Intext Educational Publishers, 1971.

Wechsler, D. *The Measurement of Adult Intelligence.* Baltimore: Williams & Wilkins, 1939.

Wechsler, D. *The Measurement of Adult Intelligence.* 2nd ed. Baltimore: Williams & Wilkins, 1941.

7

Clinical Uses of the Bellevue Scale

During World War II the Bellevue scales received a rather extensive application in the military setting. As a result of data gathered under these conditions, Wechsler published a third edition of *The Measurement of Adult Intelligence* in 1944. In his preface to this third edition, Wechsler points out that most of the changes are concerned with certain clinical applications and the matter of mental deterioration. Procedures for determining subtest performance differences which might have significance for various clinical conditions had been improved and are reported in this third edition. The importance of these matters for subtest analysis with the Wechsler Adult Intelligence Scale and Wechsler Intelligence Scale for Children makes it worthwhile to review this particular content of the third edition at this stage.

Classifying Intelligence

One aspect of decisions about clinical symptoms, and particularly those referring to deficiency and retardation, lies in the expressed intelligence of the individual. The use of an intelligence scale, designed to differentiate among individuals and the level of functioning available for a given person, is one important bit of information necessary to the clinician. A central problem which enters into the utilization of such a scale, then, requires that a system of classifying levels of ability result from the scores and be both reliable and valid for the criterior.

Wechsler outlines some of the problems in classifying intelligence, since the measures are not as precise and objective as those of physical phenomena. He uses the analogy of the spectrum of colors in the rainbow. General intelligence, he says, is a continuum just as the colors of the rainbow are a continuum, and there is no precise interruption from one level to another level. This matter has been recognized since Binet first attempted to distinguish degrees of retardation and to differentiate the level of ability he called moron from that of the normal child. In the same way, and with some extension, Wechsler points to the levels of defective, borderline, dull-normal, average, superior, genius, and so on. These are not clearly differentiable levels from the immediately preceding level. The extremes, of course, can be recognized and distinguished easily. Most frequently the problem in intelligence testing, whether in the clinic or the school, is concerned with adjacent classifications, not extreme ones. Wechsler makes the added point that it is convention and custom which determine the labels assigned to the various degrees of ability, and even the number of such degrees identified. Labels may change from generation to generation; attitudes toward levels probably remain relatively unchanged.

A significant contribution of psychology, according to Wechsler, is the precision given to concepts about intelligent behavior. Terminology has changed very little. But by introducing quantitative methods, psychologists were able to afford reliability in a way that was not previously possible. He states that there have not been any particularly new configurations in intelligent behavior added by psychologists (at least to 1944), simply greater precision for those concepts already available. The devising of tests which yield quantitative measures has been a significant forward step in this process.

The practical outcomes of such precise classification schemes are not so obvious to most individuals, Wechsler states. Primarily, this lack of practical value is a reflection of the dependence on valid data. In terms of classifying mental ability, the score obtained on a test designed to measure intelligence becomes the primary means of measurement and decision making. Most tests, including the Bellevue scale, yield as the measure of brightness an intelligence quotient. This score must demonstrate constancy, an issue previously discussed, and when it does so a decision about classifications within this measure is necessary. Such meaning, in past instances, had been more idiosyncratic than Wechsler had felt necessary.

Within this viewpoint he criticizes the scheme used by Terman. For example, Wechsler points out that in the classification scheme devised by Terman the second digit of every class is a zero. Thus scores below 70 are given the classification feeble-mindedness, those between 80 and 90 dullness, and so on. The basis for this decision is not at all clear; in fact, other classification systems have not used zeros for the limiting class level. Kuhlman, for example, considered all IQ's below 75 as mentally defective and IQ's between 85 and 94 as dull. There is some disparity within the system used by Terman. Instead of some rather arbitrary cutoff point, Wechsler decided to use a classification system which would define intelligence levels in terms of the frequency with which they occur statistically in a population reflecting a normal distribution of the trait.

The Wechsler Classification System

In the 1944 edition of *Measurement of Adult Intelligence,* Wechsler established intervals for classification purposes on the basis of multiples of probable error as these departed from the mean. The term *mental defective* was applied to the individual whose score on the Bellevue scale was at least three probable errors below the mean. On a percentage basis, this would include just over 2 percent of the total population. Those individuals who obtained IQ's on the Bellevue scale between −2 probable errors and −3 probable errors were labeled *borderline,* and this included almost 7 percent of the total population. By contrast, an equal number of individuals in the general population would obtain scores between +2 PE and +3 PE, and the label used here by Wechsler is superior. Table 7-1 includes the classification scheme both in terms of probable error limits and IQ limits with the appropriate percentages quoted.

TABLE 7-1
BASES FOR CLASSIFICATION OF INTELLIGENCE LEVELS

Classification	Probable Error Limits	IQ Limits	Percent Included
Defective	−3 PE and below	65 and below	2.2
Borderline	−2 PE to −3 PE	66 – 79	6.7
Dull normal	−1 PE to −2 PE	80 – 90	16.1
Average	−1 PE to +1 PE	91 – 110	50.0
Bright normal	+1 PE to +2 PE	111 – 119	16.1
Superior	+2 PE to +3 PE	120 – 127	6.7
Very superior	+3 PE and over	128 and over	2.2

Adapted from Wechsler, 1944, p. 40.

The divisions decided upon by Wechsler, he feels, are not wholly arbitrary, at least not nearly to the extent that other classifications systems had been. In defense of this position, he points out that estimates which had been made in this country of the probable incidence of mental deficiency had averaged up to 3 percent of the total population. If between 2 and 3 percent of the general population may indeed be expected to be mentally deficient, the cutoff point and probable error decided upon by Wechsler seems most appropriate. Evidence about other points in the classification scheme is not as well established.

Wechsler decided to use the increasing multiples of probable error for these classifications, as a kind of a best estimate of the actual percentage of the population which would be diagnosed within these categories independently of the measure. The accuracy of such a procedure is debatable. The result, in any event, is a symmetrical distribution of some seven categories with 50 percent of the population being considered average in ability, and the remainder of the population being distributed into three categories below and above this average group.

Although not totally satisfied with the labels used within the scheme, Wechsler leaves open the possibility that future experience and data can lead to whatever changes are necessary within the classification. At least he has attempted to lend some order to what had been some degree of chaos before. A degree of change, it should be noted, does occur in the classification scheme used with the Wechsler Adult Intelligence Scale.

Of even greater interest, perhaps, is the fact that each classification beginning with borderline and proceding up the scale from that point begins with a quantity ending in a zero. Terman, for some reason, was turned around. One of the strengths which Wechsler saw for the statistical procedure followed by him was the comparison of scores from one scale to another.

This method of classifying intelligence, quite aside from interpretive matters, relies upon a statistical concept of intelligence. Though not the first such scheme to attempt this procedure, Wechsler maintains that it is more rigorously developed, with some assumptions stated more precisely. Of chief importance, he feels, is that there is no attempt to give an absolute definition of what intelligence "really" is. The IQ, in the Wechsler scale, acts as a ranking device telling how much below or above the average any individual may be as compared with persons in the norming group. Again, in the Wechsler scales, the norm group consists of individuals of the same age for whom specified factors are controlled. This raises the question: If the individual is being compared with the average person of his age group, what is the average? Wechsler makes a very clear statement that he does not know what the average really represents. In the point scale represented by the Bellevue, it is a numerical score; a performance on the test. In a mental-age scale, it is of course the MA equivalent. Wechsler says that the numerical score representing the average on the point scale is as meaningful as the mental-age equivalent, though psychologists prior to that time had believed in a meaning for mental ages which he felt unacceptable. In this light, a discussion of rejection of the mental-age concept by Wechsler and the reasons for it is given in the Chapter on David Wechsler in Part I of this series (Edwards, 1971).

A further step toward defense of a statistical concept of intelligence is taken by Wechsler through a comparison of the work of Galton. He states that Galton defined genius in his study of superiority in the English people through a statistical position. Actually Galton defined the genius as the individual who achieves a position, because of the quality of his contribution to society, of one man in a million. This basis for defining intellectual level in terms of performance Wechsler believes will lead to a more scientific classification of ability. In an analogous fashion, the Wechsler schema then allows a statement of the occurrence of the given classification within the general population. The very superior individual will be one in fifty, the superior individual one in about fifteen, and the average individual one in two. Wechsler avoids labels like genius, since he feels the intelligence-test score cannot identify the quality of production which would lead to the accurate use of the term. One can only agree with his position on this. Whether or not a definitive position is reached by a statistical denotation of the number of times a score will occur in a general population is still debatable.

Wechsler recognizes some of the problems in this statistical concept of intelligence by stressing the difficulty some individuals have in understanding and accepting such a concept. To many individuals this will lead to somewhat impractical and at times relatively absurd outcomes. But, he says, these absurd outcomes are not so much the result of the concept of a statistical nature as the fact the concept is not completely understood and therefore used knowingly. Essentially the classification scheme is dependent upon the characteristics of the group upon which it is derived. For those groups which are inappropriate, the statistical concept is obviously mistaken. He used as an example of this the matter of social status. If social class influences score which given subgroups obtain on a test such as the Wechsler scales, then the norms obtained on any particular social group could not be used with any other. The norms group would yield scores inappropriate to the group with which the test is to be used. At least if one attempts to use the test on an inappropriate group, terms used in the classification system such as "average," "deficient," "very superior," and the like would lack statistical meaning. Current arguments about the use of intelligence tests with certain subgroups in this country are of just this very nature. It would appear by Wechsler's own argument that the test devised by him may be quite inappropriate for certain subgroups in this country. This he would not deny; indeed, he admits that a test such as his standardized on a white sample is inappropriate for a black sample. At least it must be considered inappropriate until both samples are demonstrated to be alike.

Wechsler makes the strong point that the statistical concept of intelligence does contain a very fundamental implication which must be accepted. Intelligence, in this concept, is defined in terms of relative position of an individual within a group of known characteristics. It can be used appropriately only in this sense, and when used otherwise reduces the classification system to inaccuracy.

Comments About the IQ

Using the IQ as the basis of classification of mental levels forces us to keep in mind that a measure of intelligence is a ranking system. Any given score must be interpreted in terms of its relative relationship to other scores. In certain practical situations, Wechsler says, we do use test results as though the scores represented absolute quantities. Particularly is this true when some ability measure is used to estimate mental efficiency. Where some lower limit, however arbitrarily established, is set for some application, we have essentially a measure of necessary aptitude for efficient performance. One may say that the minimum IQ necessary for admission to a given program must be such and such a level. This changes the meaning of the relative nature of IQ's, but under certain circumstances may appear to be necessary.

Wechsler includes in the Appendix a table of efficiency quotients by which weighted scores are compared to the average individual in the age range 20 to 24. This age group was chosen since it represents the point at which performance is best on the Bellevue scale. A similar table is still found with the Wechsler Adult Intelligence Scale but with the age group used as the base the group between ages 25 and 34.

Wechsler believes that the IQ is the best single measure of intelligence, since it does reflect a relative measure. However, he quickly cautions that it is not the most complete measure, nor is it the only measure of ability. Intelligence is a quite complicated matter and cannot be defined by any single number. Too many other factors enter into the obtaining of the number itself and the test content. These nonintellective factors, discussed in Part I of this series, are not reflected directly in the measures and therefore cannot be completely accounted for in the score obtained. As a result, observations of a subject's behavior during the examination become an important source of information for interpretative purposes. The past history of the individual and his reactions to the environment will also be a significant source of information in most instances where decisions must be made.

Included in this past history will be such matters as the social background of the individual, his emotional stability, the vocational and economic adjustments which he has made in his adult life. Wechsler comments that " . . . the kind of life one lives is itself a pretty good test of a person's intelligence . . ." (Wechsler, 1944, p. 47). With this information about the past history of the individual, a more pertinent interpretation of the test result may be made. This past history assumes particular importance when the score obtained on the test differs to some significant degree with the past history of the individual. Classification by means of the test will probably be in error.

Wechsler observes that the inexperienced examiner is apt to underestimate the importance of the past history just as physicians sometimes tend to overemphasize it. There is some balance, then, between the actual life history of the individual as accurately reported and the psychometric pattern observed in the testing setting. One of the problems of those not sufficiently trained in psychometrics is this very difficulty. Wechsler notes, for example, that teachers who are accustomed to the administration and interpretation of group test results are apt to disregard much of the important information from a life history. This matter is extended and compounded with the school psychologist who administers a large number of tests but obtains little more than the IQ and reports it to the teacher. The same kind of mistakes may quite well be made by such an individual. The college professor who writes books about individual mental testing is also apt to fall into the same trap. These individuals are all considered to engage in what Wechsler refers to as apersonal psychometrics. He maintains that the competent psychologist has a much greater role than he is frequently accorded, and maybe even than he is willing to assume. The techniques, including the individual test, are a means of diagnosis and not an end or answer in themselves. He reaffirms that the ability of the psychologist to interpret the IQ once it is obtained is even more important than to obtain an accurate IQ in the first place. In a footnote, he makes the following quite pertinent observation:

> The interpretation of psychometric results, in our opinion, is or should be the job of the psychologist who administers them. Even the familiar IQ as we have seen, is a rather complicated quantity. It is not reasonable to throw the onus of the interpretation upon the average doctor, teacher, judge and social worker to whom reports containing IQ's eventually go. Unfortunately the common practice of sending numerical data to schools, social agencies, and courts has in many instances served to deprive the psychologist of that function. The net result has been that the doctor, teacher, judge, and social worker frequently take it upon themselves to do the interpretation. This is in part due to the fact that persons in administrative positions in time acquire a belief in their own expertness on a great many different subjects. In part, however, it is due to the fact that psychologists themselves have too often been remiss in the way that they present their results. A psychological report which contains two or three different IQ's accompanied by a mass of technical analysis, is hardly what the lay person wants or can digest. In practical situations nobody is particularly interested in the particular score which a subject obtains on a particular test. What he wants to know is what that IQ means in terms of general or specific ability for adjustment. (Wechsler, 1944, p. 48)

This statement is an apt one not only for the role of the psychologist but for his training as well.

Those factors which influence scores and consequently the classification of levels of intelligence need to be evaluated by the psychologist as much as possible. This is particularly true, according to Wechsler, with that group which is defined as deficient. As he declares, and as all serious past efforts have agreed, a label like mental defective should not be used lightly nor inappropriately. Stigma does result from such a label and, as Wechsler warns, the decision to use the label may even lead to permanent institutionalization of the individual. With a child, the use of a label like mental deficiency brings up the question of whether or not education is a possibility and, what may be at least as important, what kind of treatment and training will be undertaken. A label like mental deficiency includes not only the psychological concept but also social, medical, and legal concepts. One is not restricted in his use of the classification system only to the bare essentials of the test schema. In most instances the labeling generalizes to many other aspects of the individual's life. Thus the matter of classification is a most serious one. For this reason, as much precision and accuracy in the labeling technique as possible is necessary and the maximum amount of reliable and valid information to be obtained from the test is necessary as well. This ties into the issue of deficiency and deterioration and the clinical significance of test scores.

Mental Deficiency

Given a statistical definition of intelligence, test performance may be correlated with behavioral outcomes to offer more precise definitions of various levels of intellectual brightness. Historically there has been a considerable emphasis upon the degrees of mental lack, since such individuals represent a serious source of social problems. One may consider deficiency only in terms of the approximate 2 percent, as defined by Wechsler, of the population obtaining IQ's at least three probable errors below the average for the population. The lack of precision in cutoff points must include as well the problem of borderline and, to some degree, dull-normal individuals. There is, again in the statistical definition of Wechsler, some 25 percent of the general population which shows a degree of intellectual deficiency sufficient to be of concern. Mental deficiency needs a more rigorous definition than had been possible in the past, and Wechsler attempts to state this definition.

There is a somewhat related though different problem as well. With increasing age in the adult population, it will be noted that individuals show functioning which is less efficient and, indeed, may reach a level of nearly complete defectiveness in the condition known as senility. Concern about the matter of mental deterioration with increasing age is as important in an adult population as is the definition of the concept of mental deficiency. Prior to the development of the Bellevue scales, little research was possible although considerable philosophy and theory had been offered. The Bellevue scales offered the opportunity to describe more accurately the course of intellectual performance over age, the point at which decline is most marked, and the types of performance in which deterioration may be most easily detected. These matters remain a consequence in the use of the Wechsler Adult scale today, but the essential issues were described and discussed by Wechsler in the third edition of the *Measurement of Adult Intelligence.*

Defining Mental Deficiency

As mentioned, the matter of mental deficiency was of concern to society long before the first tests were devised. Certainly the major impetus for the development of the Binet scales was the matter of describing children who would be unable to benefit from normal academic programs due to a developmental lack in mental ability. With this impetus, concern developed about other social functions of the individual who lacks sufficient mental competence. Wechsler notes that there have been two aspects of this problem that have evolved from the beginning of the twentieth century. First is the need to define in at least an abstract manner what is meant by mental deficiency. Arising from this definition is the necessity for describing the outcome of deficiency behaviorally. The role of the psychologist has been to extend the definition of mental defect from the quantitative methods to a description of behavioral outcomes for the individual. The abstract definitions that have been so popular could, through the use of standardized intelligence tests, be supplemented, refined, and made more rigorous through the use of the score for precise description of the condition.

Of course, being able to define mental deficiency in terms of score did not solve the problem of accurate classification at all. What cutoff points should be assigned to degrees of deficiency remains. The same problem operates here, then, as operated in a general classification scheme for all levels of ability. In the statistical concept preferred by Wechsler, the mental defective can be described only as an individual who achieves a test score such that his rank within the norms group places him at a given percentile rank or in a given percentage group. If this were the total possible, the outcome would be subject to argument indeed. But, as Wechsler makes clear, there are other things that can be said about the individual to whom the label defective is assigned. Of some importance to the label are the behaviors which the individual can or cannot show. For example, what kinds of tasks can he perform on, what are the possibilities of successful academic work at various levels, what are the possibilities of learning a skill which may be used for vocational independence, and so on? Such matters Wechsler points out as significant and useful but of themselves insufficient for a *psychometric* classification. Indeed, the usual psychometric definition is the IQ or MA obtained by the individual on the scale used. This returns us then to the statistical definition.

Wechsler maintains that the statistical definition of deficiency advocated by him differs from psychometric definitions in several ways. The chief one of these, according to him, is the fact that no precise IQ or mental age is given which will classify an individual as mentally defective. Though this may seem confusing, the argument is quite acceptable. Wechsler decided to use the classification defective, for example, only with individuals who obtained scores at least three probable errors below the mean. This corresponded to about 2 percent of a normal distribution and correlated well with observed and empirical data about the degree of retardation occurring in the nation as a whole. Although it is true that this corresponds to an IQ of 65 and below on the Bellevue scale, that is a matter only of the range of scores possible with the scale itself. It would be possible to build a test, for example, in which the cutoff point designated (minus 3 PE or below) would be at IQ 50 or even at IQ 75. The exact value of the IQ is relatively unimportant in this matter of classification. What is needed is a standardized test. Beyond that point, the issue of whether or not the individual is mentally defective will depend on other factors.

The first of these other factors derives from the fact that Wechsler prefers some biological definition of intelligence which includes both nonintellective and intellective factors. The second factor is the statistical definition of relative ability which he advocates. The third is the fact that he rejects an idea that mental deficiency is of itself a unitary trait. This latter point as Wechsler gives it in his discussion of mental deficiency deserves some elaboration.

The mentally defective individual is not an individual who suffers from a disease but one whose intellectual lack places him in a social grouping of those who are unable to cope with the environment. Because the individual is unable to deal with his environment, it may be necessary to provide special educational procedures at best or institutionalization at worst. The mental defective is an individual who is unable to care for himself. This does not mean that he does not have available to him a number of abilities. Indeed, he does have such abilities available to him, but is unable to use them effectively in the environment. Wechsler comments that the actions of the defective will appear at times to be both senseless and inadequate, and under certain conditions may even be quite perverse and antisocial. Inconsistency in actions is much more common for his behavior than consistency. Thus inappropriate behavior will not be found at all times and to the same degree, but in varying quantities under quite diverse situations. The same thing may be said about perversity or inadequacy or any of the other behavioral forms. Wechsler raises the question as to whether or not mental deficiency, as defined in these kinds of actions, is merely a matter of lack of intellectual ability or whether it also includes some other more global aspects of the individual's development.

He answers the question by stating that except for the very lowest degrees of intelligence it is necessary to consider factors other than intellectual inability as such in order to diagnose mental deficiency. This would be particularly true of marginal individuals who fall in the category of dull-normal and borderline or moron. For such individuals the obtained IQ alone will not be sufficient to classify accurately all individuals as deficient. He cites instances in which individuals obtained IQ's, say, above 70 and yet who showed defective behavior while other individuals obtaining IQ's of 60 or below might still show a considerable history of adequate adjustment to the environment. Several cases are presented by him illustrating inconsistency between behavior and test performance. Wechsler makes the point, as he has in other writings, that there are individuals who may test at a deficient level who do adapt and adjust to the environment quite well. Certainly on the basis of common sense, and probably on the basis of law, such individuals cannot be considered deficient and should not be treated as such. For individuals who depend totally on test performance and the consequent score, however, such individuals will be treated as deficient. This returns us to the idea that he has proposed earlier that the psychologist needs much more information than just the test IQ in order to make an adequate classification of the individual. In Wechsler's terminology, the more apersonal psychometrics that are used the more apt are false conclusions to be drawn.

Indeed, Wechsler maintains that there are several kinds of mental deficiency, a matter discussed more fully in Part I of this series. Briefly, he advocates that there are both intellectual and social defectives and probably emotional or moral defectives as well. The intellectual defective may be rather accurately diagnosed by the better tests available to us. The social defective will be best disclosed by his life history. The emotional defective cannot be so easily or precisely identified by either or both sources. Clinical experience leads Wechsler to believe that such a group is found in our society, and the psychologist must be alert to the possibilities and must be competent to diagnose them. As Wechsler also has noted earlier, the various types do show some degree of systematic relationship but the correlation coefficient is not high enough to use one category as diagnostic of either of the others. This should mean that the emotional defective, then, may not appear defective on the basis either of psychometric tests nor of life history, and therefore needs some other basis of discrimination for classification purposes. At the same time a certain amount of error is inherent either in diagnosing the intellectual deficient with tests alone or the social defective with life history alone.

Mental Deterioration

The matter of accurate diagnosis must include something beyond the essential quantitative data available. This opens the matter of clinical diagnosis from performance (and life history), a matter which has achieved increasing importance with the use of the Wechsler scales. Before considering this matter of clinical diagnosis, however, the area of deterioration in adult groups with increasing age deserves attention.

Wechsler gives a somewhat more precise behavioral definition of mental deterioration then he was able to give for mental deficiency. The term "mental" he uses in the sense of intellectual abilities, the kinds of things measured by the subtests of the Bellevue scale. "Deterioration" is reflected in the fact that the individual is no longer able to perform intellectual tasks with the same speed, accuracy, and efficiency as previously. There is in the matter of mental deterioration a comparison between score performance at one point and that at another point in the life of the individual. It would surprise no one that the individual at age 25 is able to perform better on specific kinds of tasks than he can at age 50. Although there might be certain kinds of behaviors where he is more efficient at the older age, this is a matter less of intellectual ability than it is a matter of repetition within a specific category. When given tasks of an intellectual nature somewhat unrehearsed by him, the fifty-year-old will not be able to perform as well as he did at twenty-five. The matter now becomes one of how much loss occurs, the point in age at which it accelerates most rapidly, and the probable effective causes for the loss.

In this context, Wechsler says that mental deterioration may be considered under two categories: the first concerns loss associated with increase in age and the second concerns loss consequent to organic conditions of the brain. For all individuals the former condition holds and may be considered of a normal, natural type. For some individuals, and perhaps for all individuals who live long enough, the latter condition also holds and may be considered pathological in nature.

Wechsler states that although the distinction may be convenient, there is very little psychological difference between the two except in terms of the rate at which deterioration occurs. There is the added matter in terms of physical conditions of the mental functions which may be involved. For most elderly people, according to Wechsler, the deterioration found is quite similar to that found with organic brain disease. The extreme mental deterioration that may occur during senility is a terminal condition which had its beginnings fairly early in life and which continued slowly but quite steadily with age and became most apparent at the point when senility was reached.

This brings up yet another issue which Wechsler attempts to deal with. Is the term "mental deterioration" to be reserved only for conditions in which there is extreme loss of ability, as in senility, or is it to be used as a term which will apply to all decline from its manifestation first in the twenties until the more marked outcomes are observed? The answer to this question again may be merely a matter of convenience. It appears that Wechsler considers the entire spectrum to be of some significance however in terms of the discussion which follows.

During childhood and continuing to the maturation of intellectual abilities, there is an increasing function for all individuals, although not at the same rate. At some point, apparent intellectual maturity is achieved and some stabilization and gradual decline of ability then follows. The incremental function, of course, reflects the childhood and adolescence of the individual and has been well described in other contexts. Some point of maturation, though debatable as to age, is generally recognized by psychologists. The decline following some asymptotic function of intellectual development is not so clearly known, has not been as well studied as intellectual increases, and therefore must be described in a more general fashion.

Wechsler maintains that all human capacities begin to show a decline at some point in the life of the individual, and in most instances before the age of 30 or 35. For most human capacities, the maximum point and the beginning of decline is somewhere in the early twenties. He notes that once decline begins, it tends to be linear from about age 30 up to about age 60 for most individuals. Beyond age 60 the decline will be much more rapid. Wechsler maintains that intellectual abilities will show greater decline with age than physical abilities. This is in opposition to much common belief, and even beliefs held by many psychologists. He also observes that the slopes of the curves will be dependent to some degree upon the nature of the test used. Thus the exact age point at which decline begins, the rate at which it continues, and the point at which it becomes most accelerated may vary depending upon the measure. With those kinds of tests most commonly considered to measure intelligence, as such, however, little variation from the general function if not the exact point should be found.

There is the added matter of different kinds of intellectual abilities.

Information on specific subtest performance had not been available before the development of the Bellevue scales, and even within this context sample problems limited the amount of information Wechsler had available to him. However, based upon the information which he did have, he reports that any given ability shows an essentially linear function from about age 20 or 25 up to age 60 or 65. There were some differences in the age at which initial decline began and the age at which the rate of decline differed from one subtest to another subtest. He draws the conclusion, therefore, that different mental abilities will tend to show somewhat different rates of decline.

Wechsler considers this to be a fortunate event psychometrically since it will alow differences between subtest performance to be used for determining whether or not mental deterioration in any given ability has begun, and the degree to which it has progressed. This establishes an essential basis again for diagnosis, at least for one category of behavior. It should be noted at this point that the statements made apply to data available with the Bellevue scales up to 1944. Somewhat more careful statements are made by Wechsler in the fourth edition of his work published in 1958 (Wechsler, *The Measurement and Appraisal of Adult Intelligence*, 1958). This matter will be returned to in a succeeding chapter. One may conclude at this point that mental decline is a normal function of the organism, that it begins fairly early in life, and that it may not be arrested. Indeed, the only possible alternative is an acceleration in mental deterioration.

Within this context, however, the question may be raised as to how literally a term like "deterioration" should be used for an individual who is thirty-five years of age. One may accept the position that such decline has already begun and agree with Wechsler, at the same time, that to speak of deterioration in such an individual is stretching the point somewhat. Indeed, he maintains that we should reserve the term "deterioration" only to such loss in ability as is significantly greater than that due to the age factor alone; that is, that which may be considered normal losses.

This suggests that some estimate of the normal loss of ability for an individual who is considered average may be compared with an estimate of the variability for all ages of the normal population. Given information of this type, it should then be possible to quantitatively specify what is meant by deterioration.

To measure mental deterioration will require three separate but interrelated kinds of information. First, we must be able to measure with some degree of precision and accuracy the present functioning ability of the individual. Second, it will be necessary to have some evaluation, if not a measure, of previous level of functioning. Third, any differences that occur between the first and second of these measures must be expressed in quantitative form so that the difference may be assessed meaningfully. Up until 1944, Wechsler reminds us , these steps had not been taken. The Bellevue provided an opportunity to gather such data.

The development of the Bellevue scale did allow for measuring the current functioning of the individual at whatever adult age. The problem of prior functioning, however, could not be met simply because such measures were not usually available. As a result, other sources of information had to be used to estimate as reliably as possible the previous functioning of the individual. It should be noted that use of the Bellevue scale at various ages of the individual following 1944 would supply the very kind of information needed for more accurate assessment.

In the absence of the data, however, Wechsler found it necessary to depend on certain kinds of information from the life history of the individual. He speaks of such things, for example, as whether or not the individual is a high school graduate, whether or not he has been in some responsible position vocationally and/or socially over a period of years, his social prestige in the community, and so on and so on. This kind of information would at least offer some estimate of ability for the individual. However, such information is so unreliable that there must be a considerable divergence between current functioning and the estimate based upon this life history information in order to make a diagnosis of deterioration at all. As Wechsler notes, where such a divergence is so great, no psychometric evaluation is needed anyway. A common-sense observation of the individual would disclose the fact that he has deteriorated considerably.

The psychometric examination of the Bellevue type, then, has the inherent merit that it can disclose quite small differences in ability which will have utility for clinical diagnosis that would not otherwise be possible. When this condition is met, it should be possible to recognize deterioration in the functioning of the individual long before it is so obvious that it cannot be missed. Until such precise information across testings at differing times in the life of the individual are available, other approximations which may be used to diagnose deterioration are necessary. For this purpose, stable characteristics of certain subtests in the scale may be used, Wechsler believes.

As indicated earlier, all subtests do not show the same rate of decline. Some subtests show slower decline with age than others. For example, performance on the general-information test is more apt to remain fairly constant over long time periods than the performance on the substitution test, for whatever reasons. Since this is true for groups of individuals, some estimate of prior function may be obtained in the absence of psychometric data. According to Wechsler, if the kinds of intellectual abilities which do not decline very much with age are the ones which are least affected by deterioration, then the score that any individual attains on these tests should reflect something about original ability. With several such tests within a scale, an estimate of mental deterioration and past functioning level may be made from the present ability level of the individual. The procedure is one of comparing mean scores obtained by an individual on those tests which are relatively unimpaired across age levels with mean scores obtained on tests which are relatively very much impaired across age levels. The corresponding ratio may be used to determine the degree, if any, of deterioration for the individual. This procedure Wechsler refers to as the *differential test score method* of measuring mental deterioration.

In applying the procedure, there is a comparison of performance between those tests for which decline is slight over age (called by Wechsler "hold") and the performance on those subtests which show more marked decline with age (called by Wechsler "don't hold"). All subtests are not used in this procedure. Indeed, Wechsler maintains that the type of ability measured by the test must be considered as well. There must at least be some functional similarity between those tests which are going to be compared. Unless there is functional similarity, he states that test combinations may be made which will be spurious even though significant.

For this reason it is not possible to simply compare the performance on the Verbal with the performance on the Performance scale. To do so would penalize individuals who have fairly good verbal ability. Since differences in verbal and performance abilities increase with age, those with good verbal capacity would appear to deteriorate with age while those with good performance capacity would not appear to deteriorate nearly so much. In the latter condition, the differences between verbal and performance scales grow less and less with age. This would necessitate the outcome that Wechsler describes. Within the hold and don't-hold categories, then, there are approximately equal numbers of both verbal and performance tests.

The exact procedure followed is to obtain the sum of the weighted scores on the hold tests and compare this with the sum of the weighted scores on the don't-hold subtests. More strictly, the sum of scores on the first four of the hold tests is compared with the sum of scores on the first four of the don't-hold tests. The resulting comparison can be given either in terms of ratio or difference between sums.

The next step is to answer the age-old question "how much of a difference makes a difference?" With the particular score patterns adapted to this procedure for determining deterioration, how much difference must be found to decide that the individual has either a significant deterioration or at least a large enough deterioration to be of some diagnostic significance? To answer this question requires a return to statistical definitions as Wechsler has used for classification of ability and for determining mental deficiency. Unfortunately, the number of individuals in a society such as ours at various age levels with a significant degree of mental deterioration has not yet been determined. Even less data is available on the degree of deterioration that might be considered large enough for diagnostic significance. Wechsler is required to overcome this problem by some approximation of such numbers. He does this by computing the mean scores of each of the subtests at successive age periods. For those subtests included within the hold and don't-hold categories, it is possible to obtain a total weighted score that may be expected for each of these subbatteries. It is then possible to determine what is normal or average deterioration at each of the given age levels to which the subbatteries will be applied. This Wechsler has done and has tabled for those who wish to follow the procedure. It should be noted that these tables are not found in the 1958 revision of his text primarily because subsequent study has not supported the procedure for accurate clinical diagnosis. Wechsler does believe that his experience demonstrates the procedure's usefulness particularly when confined within certain limitations.

With the procedures followed in 1944, Wechsler defines deterioration in the following manner. "An individual may be said to show signs of possible deterioration if he shows a greater than 10 percent loss, and of definite deterioration if a loss greater than 20 percent than that allowed for by the normal decline with age ..." (Wechsler, 1944, p. 66). The basis upon which the 10 percent and the 20 percent were determined is not given by Wechsler. This seems to be a rule of thumb adopted by him without other particular support. As he points out, the greater the loss, obviously the greater the probability that true deterioration has set in. In any event, an index may be computed by summing the scale-score values on the hold tests and subtracting from that the sum of scale scores on the don't-hold tests, then dividing by the sum for the whole test. The resulting percentage must be compared to what will be normal decline in order to see whether the remaining decline is significantly large enough to be considered of diagnostic value.

Wechsler believes the procedure may be applied to conditions such as schizophrenia, again where the appropriate subbatteries of subtests are used. There is the added point that certain functions seem to occur with great frequency in the deterioration of mentally ill persons regardless of the disease itself. He specifically mentions alcholics, paretics, seniles and schizophrenics as sharing in common poor performance on digits backward, hard associations, reproducing designs, and digit symbol. Reasons for the performance differ from one group to the other. The reasons which he gives, as Wechsler is candid enough to point out, are not the reasons which are given by other authorities, however.

Regardless of the agreement or lack of it among authorities, Wechsler says that an interesting question does arise. What is the nature of the deteriorative process? Despite the fact that special disabilities will occur as a result of injury or insult, the agreement among disabilities for different kinds of injuries indicate the possibility of a generalized nature in deterioration. Wechsler points out that the brain acts as a whole. An impairment in one place must affect to some degree the functioning of the whole organ. Although there may be differing amounts of disorganization across abilities, this is secondary in importance to him. Agreement is of such a nature that it appears that the subtests used are not particularly important if they are sensitive to intellectual functioning. This returns to the idea he has proposed earlier of some agreement in abilities measured.

Wechsler concludes that mental deterioration is revealed best by measuring the response speed of the individual, how well he learns, and how well he can preceive new relationships particularly if they are spatial in origin. These are the kinds of abilities which he believes are reflected in the subtests assigned to the subbatteries of "hold" and "don't hold." As such, the conclusion is based upon a circular argument. It should be repeated at this point that resulting research did not support the basis for determining mental deterioration that Wechsler had hoped it would. In any event, he asserts that it is not the form of the test but the function of the test, the ability that must be displayed in answering items which determines the diagnostic value of the subtest.

The rather prolonged discussion of this matter of determining mental deterioration is not included as a definitive procedure but in part to illustrate the clinical validity which Wechsler has espoused and which he believes must supplement all empirical efforts. Indeed, empiricism casts some doubt on even this level of clinical diagnosis. Yet, as mentioned in terms of the 1958 edition of Wechsler's text, he still maintains some clinical uses and gives reasons which will be cited at a later time for his position. A second reason for the inclusion of this discussion, then, is not to present a procedure which should be followed by the psychometrist but to illustrate something about the procedures followed by Wechsler, based upon some implicit assumptions, true or false, which lead to the kind of clinical diagnosis still commonly followed with the Wechsler scale. This matter of clinical diagnosis specifically with the Bellevue scale becomes of importance then.

Diagnostic and Clinical Features of the Bellevue Scale

Wechsler begins his discussion of the diagnostic and clinical features of the Bellevue scale by pointing out that the *primary* purpose of an intelligence test is to offer to the psychometrist a valid and reliable measure of an individual's global intellectual capacity. As obvious as this may seem, this outcome is not so often noted with the Wechsler scales as it should be. Wechsler adds that there are some secondary features which should also be obtained as a result of the use of a well-standardized individual test. Something more than IQ or even an MA should be obtained from the test results, he believes. There is always a certain amount of information which may be noted in the observational part of the test about the individual's reaction to the testing mode, any particular abilities or disabilities which are obvious enough to be described, even perhaps some personality features of the individual which are available and should be used by the psychometrist for the best interest of the examinee. However, as he also notes, until the time of the availability of the Bellevue scale such information was based on the individual examiner's clinical experience and wisdom. He also makes the point that this will undoubtedly remain true to some degree at least even with the use of the Bellevue scales. The belief may be extended to results obtained for the WAIS, WISC, and WPPSI.

It should be possible, as Wechsler notes, to improve upon the subjective basis for deriving information about the individual. This could be done if a scale included subtests with distinct merits for each and certain diagnostic possibilities which may be demonstrated empirically from the test itself. The purpose of the discussion Wechsler undertakes here is to try to indicate what features of the Bellevue scale seem to have some clinical and diagnostic value.

Since the scale contains both a verbal and performance subscale, it would seem obvious that the first possible value would lie in this division. The verbal scale, insofar as it taps primarily verbal facility, should indicate something about the individual's ability to use words and to deal with symbols. Insofar as the performance scale is "nonverbal," it should indicate something about the individual's ability to manipulate objects and to deal with visual patterns. Wechsler maintains that a division on the basis of verbal and performance subscales is warranted because of different kinds of abilities which exist and have been demonstrated and which enter into a number of occupational aptitudes for adults. He points out that clerical workers and teachers, for example, will do much better on verbal tests than they do on the performance scale. By contrast, manual workers and mechanics will tend to do better on performance type tasks than they will on verbal tasks. There should be some information of utilization in forecasting vocational aptitude, then, for the two kinds of scales on the Bellevue.

But discrepancies between Verbal and Performance scale scores have much greater importance than vocational prediction, Wechsler believes. Particularly if the differences between Verbal and Performance scale scores are large, there may be some clinical significance due to correlations with types of mental pathology.

Again the problem arises as to how much difference is necessary to indicate a possibility of pathological significance. Wechsler points out that for those individuals who obtain IQ's around the average, a variation of up to ten points between Verbal and Performance subscale IQ's is normal. As one departs from the normal range, discrepancies may be expected to be larger. For example, Wechsler uses the instance of individuals of very high intelligence. As he is aware, they will tend to do better on verbal than performance tasks with the result that differences should be much larger in order to achieve any diagnostic significance. Increased age also shows some departures between Verbal and Performance scores as there is a decline in functioning due to age. There can be various kinds of group differences, various kinds of cultural differences, and so on. As a result, Wechsler makes the significant point that differences between an individual's Verbal and Performance subtest scores should be interpreted clinically only after appropriate consideration has been given to all kinds of factors that may contribute to such a difference. This should mean that there would be relatively few instances where scale-score differences are of importance unless they are extremely large.

A second feature of the Bellevue scale which Wechsler believes to be of some clinical significance is the fact that different abilities are measured by the subtests and certain comparisons may be made between these different subtests at all levels of intellectual functioning. This points in the direction of pattern analysis, which has achieved a significant role in the use of the Wechsler scale. The reason such analysis can be carried out, Wechsler maintains, is the fact that the same type of material is used throughout the Bellevue scale and the individual subtests of the scales have been equated. The equation, of course, is on the basis of equal weights being assigned to all subtests established. As a result, individual subtest scores may be compared in order to see whether or not test patterns of some clinical significance result.

The procedure to be followed in this analysis is to determine the mean expectancy for any given subtest for the individual and see whether or not his actual performance on a subtest deviates significantly from that. If an individual has a total score of 50 on the Verbal scale, the mean expected score for each subtest would be ten. His actual performance on each of the subtests can be compared to see whether or not the scale scores obtained depart significantly from that mean expected value. His age becomes a matter of concern and Wechsler has tabled the means and standard deviations of subtests for the different age groups for both Verbal and Performance scales. Again, we return to the question of what constitutes a significantly different score from the subtest to the mean expectancy.

Tables, at the time of the publication of the 1944 edition, had not yet been computed for this purpose. For this reason, Wechsler advocates the use of a rule of thumb. For those who have a full scale IQ between 80 and 110 Wechsler advocates dividing the mean subtest score by four. He uses as an example an individual who makes a Full Scale score of 56. For the ten subtests in the total test this would mean a mean expectancy of 5.6 points. Dividing this value by four yields a value of 1.4 points. Thus any individual subtest score that deviates more than 1½ points from the mean would be considered significant by him. Obviously the higher the score of the individual the greater the departure from the mean must be in order to achieve significance.

It should be noted that the decision about departure fron normal is an individual matter. The total test functioning is an important component in any decisions about clinical significance, then. This point has been too often overlooked by individuals who have attempted the use of pattern analysis but have taken general rather than individual means in departures as the basis for this.

Once the analysis of the performance of the individual on the total score had determined what departure per subtest will be significant, it becomes plausible to examine the pattern of performance for the individual to determine particular departures and suggest clinical significance. Wechsler advocates for this purpose a procedure which employs the use of signs. A "sign" is a low test score which has been determined as characteristic of a particular type type of condition or disfunction. He reminds us that if an individual shows a sign of a particular organic involvement he does not necessarily have the condition. There are, after all, other conditions or even the absence of such conditions where the sign might be present. But he feels the necessary first step is to find out the number of subtests where there is a relatively low or relatively high deviation from the norm for the individual.

If the system of determining signs and using them is to be worthwhile, it is necessary that there be some demonstrable relationships between the signs themselves and the various clinical conditions to be diagnosed. In 1944 the kind of statistical work which would be necessary to demonstrate such relationships had only begun. As a result, comments on specific patterns and organic conditions of whatever kind will not be attempted in this discussion. Wechsler does propose the degree of deviation from the mean subtest score necessary for signs to be significant, and this deviation has been maintained. For that reason, the quantitative basis of assigning signs is given in Table 7-2.

TABLE 7-2
QUANTITATIVE BASES FOR SIGN SIGNIFICANCE

+	Deviation of from 1.5 to 2.5 units *above* the mean subtest score
+ +	Deviation of 3 or more units *above* the mean subtest score
−	Deviation of from 1.5 to 2.5 units *below* the mean subtest score
− −	Deviation of 3 or more units *below* the mean subtest score
0	Deviation of +1.5 to −1.5 units from the mean subtest score

From Wechsler, 1944, p. 153. All deviations are in terms of weighted score units.

Wechsler discusses the conditions and patterns in test performance which his clinical experience indicates may be tested. A number of case studies are also reported in support of this position. Comments on the procedures and validity of the outcomes will be reserved for a later chapter.

References

Edwards, A. J. *Individual Mental Testing: Part I. History and Theories.* Scranton, Pa.: Intext Educational Publishers, 1971.

Wechsler, D. *The Measurement of Adult Intelligence.* 3rd ed. Baltimore: Williams & Wilkins, 1944.

Wechsler, D. *The Measurement and Appraisal of Adult Intelligence.* Baltimore: Williams & Wilkins, 1958.

8

The Current Wechsler Scales: The WISC and WPPSI

The Bellevue scales experienced considerable success, particularly among clinicians, both as a means of estimating intellectual level and for specific clinical problems. This success led Wechsler to further developments of the adult scale, devising a childrens' scale to complement the adult scale, and very recently to the developing of a preschool age instrument. Chronologically, the intelligence scale for children appeared first in 1949, the adult intelligence scale currently in vogue was published in 1955, and the preschool scale was published in 1968. The characteristics of the two children's tests will be considered in this chapter.

The Intelligence Scale for Children

In 1946, Wechsler published a second form of the Bellevue scale. This form, with similar but differing content to the Wechsler-Bellevue I, was standardized on 1,000 male adults between ages 18 and 40. The rationale behind the instrument was the same as that for Form I of the Wechsler-Bellevue, and the same kind of clinical implications discussed in the prior chapter were applicable to the second form. However, Form II of the Bellevue lost its identity because it became the basis of a scale intended for measuring the ability of children. The content of the Wechsler Intelligence Scale for Children is taken largely from the Wechsler-Bellevue Form II, with some items in each subtest added at the easier end in order to provide a floor for the younger child.

Despite this overlap of materials, Wechsler states that the WISC is quite distinct from the Bellevue scale. Certainly a foremost difference is the fact that the WISC is independently standardized. The WISC is intended for the testing of children from ages 5 through 15. Wechsler warns, however, that knowledge of the Bellevue scale does not automatically insure competence with the new WISC. There are differences in directions for presenting the tasks, and there are differences in terms of scoring standards, weights assigned, and bonus points for individual items. For this reason, careful study by even the most experienced psychometrist would be necessary for proficiency with the WISC.

Standardization of the WISC

Wechsler devoted some five years to devising and standardizing the intelligence scale for children, including time spent in developing the Wechsler-Bellevue II. One hundred boys and one hundred girls were used as the sample at each of the age levels from age 5 through age 15. Children were selected on the basis of proximity to mid-year age. With only a few exceptions, each child was within 1½ months of his midyear. Thus for a child seven years of age to be included within this sample he must have achieved an age somewhere between seven years, four months, and fifteen days and seven years, seven months, and fifteen days. This choice, arbitrary as it is, introduces some differences in scores between the Stanford-Binet and the WISC. Whether or not such differences are significant is a matter of some debate, but certain differences pointed by psychometrists in performance may be explained on some such superficial basis as this.

The exception to very strigent enforcement of these age limitations is for those cases which constituted the mentally deficient sample. Even here, Wechsler reports, nearly every child was within two months of the midyear.

The sample then consists of 2,200 cases—1,100 boys and 1,100 girls. Though many more children were actually tested with the WISC, this final number includes all of those who satisfied other sampling requirements for standardization purposes. One limitation in the sample is the fact that it is restricted to white children only.

SOURCES OF VARIATION CONTROLLED IN THE SAMPLE. To control for sources of variation in scores which would invalidate application to children in the United States generally, Wechsler used representative numbers for geographical areas of the United States, urban-rural distribution, and parental occupation as a socioeconomic factor.

The first of these factors, geographic distribution in the United States, was met through dividing the country into four areas. The percentage of the United States population in each of these geographic areas was then matched rather carefully with the percentage of children chosen in the total sample.

In a similar vein, distribution of the population in terms of urban and rural residence according to the 1940 census is reflected in the sample used to standardize the WISC.

Finally, Wechsler attempted to achieve representative features in the norms group by controlling for occupation. The fathers of the children included in the standardizing group were occupationally similar to all employed white males in the United States. Wechsler consolidated some fourteen categories in the U.S. Census into nine categories as the basis for selection of the standardizing sample.

SAMPLE SELECTION. Wechsler reports that some eighty-five communities were used as the basis for standardization. Though apparently most if not all of the testing was done in schools, the communities and schools used are not described. All children in the school were not tested, since Wechsler states that samples for given schools were drawn in such a manner that the whim of an examiner or school official would not influence the inclusion or exclusion of a given child.

In contrast to this sparse description of the selection of children for standardization, the portion of the sample representing mentally deficient children is much more adequately described. There were a total of fifty-five individuals who were included as deficient. Most of these came from the Illinois State School in Lincoln, the Letchworth Village School in New York, and the Wayne County Training School in Michigan. In addition, Wechsler reports that "a few selected cases" were taken from special classes in two public schools. No other identification of this sample is given. In each instance, the children used were restricted to obtained IQ's between 50 and 70. Any child who was believed to be deficient because of accident or postnatal disease was excluded.

The information provided by Wechsler in the Manual for the WISC (1949) is supplemented somewhat by Seashore, Wesman, and Doppelt (1950). They give added information on the proportion of rural and urban children expected and obtained in each of the geographic areas and the occupation of the fathers of the children by occupational area as well. All in all they conclude that the sampling procedure is adequate, leading to representativeness in the score distribution. They also point out that the number of children in various types of families is not representative. For example, rural families tended to be somewhat larger than urban families, and laboring parents have more children than white-collar workers. To include this factor in selection of the sample would have led to such problems as to render it infeasible.

Following a discussion of the deviations in intelligent quotients, scale-score values, and relationships among scores, Seashore, Wesman, and Doppelt present evidence about the relationship of intelligence quotient to the factors controlled in the standardizing sample. Wechsler had decided to establish a distribution at each age level with a mean IQ of 100 and a standard deviation of 15 IQ points. One necessary function is the demonstration that the mean and standard deviation for Verbal, Performance, and Full scales actually meet this condition both for the total sample and for boys and girls at each age level. As Seashore et al., point out, the position is met exactly for the total sample of 2,200 youngsters.

Within the samples of boys and girls, however, there are some discrepancies most of which are very small. Within the Verbal scale, boys show a mean IQ on the Verbal scale at age 9½ of 99.2. The highest obtained mean IQ was 102.4, at both ages 12½ and 15½. The lowest obtained standard deviation for the Verbal scale for boys is at year 15½, with an SD of 13.5 points. The highest obtained standard deviation within the Verbal scale for boys is 16.7 IQ points at age 12½. Similar discrepancies, but of a really minor nature, are reflected for girls and boys within the Verbal, Performance, and Full scales. Seashore et al. comment that such discrepancies are due to sampling and that the data might be smoothed in establishing the distribution of scale scores and IQ's without biasing results.

Somewhat more noticeable differences were found between boys and girls on each scale, however. Generally, Wechsler found that boys tended to obtain higher IQ's on the average than girls. Greater differences were found at the older age levels than at the younger ones between boys and girls, but even here differences tended to be small. The maximum difference found between boys and girls is at age eight and one half on Full Scale scores, where the boys obtain a mean of 102.1 and the girls a mean of 97.6. This is a 4½ IQ point difference. The corresponding standard deviations are 15.5 for boys and 15.8 for girls. Causes for such differences are speculative, and Seashore et al. present the following possibilities.

> How shall one interpret these sex differences? Three explanations come to mind:
> A. The tests are fair to both boys and girls, and boys actually do excel girls, especially at the later ages.
> B. Boys and girls are the same in mental ability, but the chosen test items turned out to be slightly biased in favor of the boys.
> C. Again, assuming that general ability is not sex differentiated, the sampling of boys was somehow chosen with a slight bias. (Seashore, Wesman, and Doppelt, 1950)

There are no data available to these authors to signify which possibility is most acceptable. They point out that probably both B and C are plausible.

Still, even where such differences are found, they are small enough that by and large the possibility of sex differences seems unrealistic. For this reason, separate norms for boys and girls in clinical or educational utilization of the WISC seems quite unnecessary.

Seashore et al. also consider the intelligence quotients obtained in the sample by children from rural and urban areas. The data agree with those reported in other studies where children in urban areas tend to score higher in such tests than those from rural areas. This difference is 6 IQ points overall on the Verbal scale, 4 IQ points on the Performance scale, and 5.6 IQ points on the Full scale. The urban sample also shows greater range for each of the scales though the actual obtained differences in standard deviations are negligible. The importance of the differences obtained between rural and urban children may be a matter of some significance. Whether or not the conditions obtaining in 1949 are still found today is a factor needing empirical verification. There is at least a possibility that the obtained IQ differences between rural and urban children of some twenty-odd years ago would not be found today. Seashore et al. do not comment on the differences obtained between rural and urban children beyond the fact that this agrees with other studies.

Finally, Seashore et al. consider the intelligence quotients obtained within the sample as compared to fathers' occupations. Again, other research had found differences in mean obtained IQ depending upon the occupational level of the father. Generally speaking, the higher the occupational level the higher the mean IQ. For the sample used in the norming of the WISC, differences found are not as large between occupational groups as in other studies. This includes the data reported by Terman and Merrill for the 1937 Revision of the Stanford-Binet. Differences do tend to be somewhat larger for mean scores on the Verbal scale than for mean scores on the Performance scale.

Essentially similar findings, though of less magnitude, are reported for Performance IQ's. Because the Full scale represents a combination of Verbal and Performance scales, consequent comments must be similar.

The matter of social importance for the findings reported by Seashore et al. are not considered particularly by them. They simply point out that whatever social implications may be drawn, this should not bias one to the fact that there is a considerable overlap in the distributions of IQ's for occupational groups represented in the standardizing sample. It might be wise to emphasize again at this point that only white children are represented in the sample. As was stated for urban-rural relationships, whether or not the differences obtained in 1950 are appropriate now is a matter of conjecture and in need of empirical verification.

FEEBLE-MINDED AND SUPERIOR CHILDREN. As discussed in prior chapters, Wechsler classifies children who obtain IQ's under 70 as psychometrically feeble-minded. In the statistical sense used by him, some 2.2

percent of the general population should meet this criterion. In selecting the sample for standardization of the WISC, Wechsler included some 2½ percent (N = 55) of individuals who were known to be deficient. Within this group ten children obtained Verbal IQ's above 70, twelve children obtained Performance IQ's above 70, but only four obtained IQ's above 70 on the Full scale. This would indicate that in only four of the fifty-five cases, assuming the institutionalization and assignment to special class criteria to be accurate, would there be error in the psychometric diagnosis. Within the remainder of the sample, some nineteen children achieved a Full scale score below 70. These children would, apparently, be misdiagnosed by the psychometric results.

If one considers the psychometric diagnosis as being more accurate, the total numer of cases who would be diagnosed as feeble-minded by the test would be 70, 3.2 percent of the total sample. Seashore et al. consider that this does not deviate far from a generally accepted criterion of about three percent of the general population being deficient.

There is a problem of the matter of floor on the WISC. The lowest possible IQ which may be obtained is 45. For individuals who would obtain scale scores yielding IQ's less than 45 Seashore et al. suggest the notation of IQ 44 or below. This raises some problem in the use of the WISC for discrimination of children of very low ability. Probably some other test will be necessary to make more accurate discrimination than the WISC can provide for children with IQ's below 50.

In the same way there is the problem of a ceiling for children who are quite bright. Though a subsample of feeble-minded was included purposely in the norming procedures, no such group of highly superior children was included. Wechsler operated on the assumption that children who are truly superior in ability will be enrolled in the school system and will enter the sample in the accurate proportion anyway. On a statistical basis, as before, approximately 2.2 percent of the general population should be superior in ability. However, only 1.5 percent of the total sample obtained IQ's above 130. On the Verbal scale the actual obtained percentage was 2.1, while for the Performance scale it was 1.1. The highest obtainable IQ in the tables for the WISC is 156. Children who perform at a level yielding scale scores above this point Seashore et al. suggest being recorded as 156, or above. They point out that differentiation above this point probably is not necessary, and indeed it seems unreasonable to quarrel with their position. However, in those situations where some degree of differentiation above IQ's of 150 seems necessary, some other test should be employed for this purpose. The WISC simply does not contain sufficient floor nor ceiling for certain decisions to be made about children who are most atypical in the general population.

Seashore et al. discuss this matter of floor and ceiling by pointing out that many psychologists may be disturbed by the limitations. As they point out, however, any range of IQ is arbitrary depending upon the limits set by the test author. Wechsler, in deciding on a mean of 100 and a standard deviation of 15 IQ points and with his statistical definitions of classification, determined the limits found. He felt it better to use a standard deviation of 15 because of its approximation to the kind of empirical standard deviation obtained by Terman and Merrill with the Stanford Revisions. Obviously, if he had used a standard deviation of 20 the limits would have been considerably extended. Comparability across tests seemed more important to him, since meaning of scores between the WISC and the Stanford Revision should be established.

Characteristics of the WISC

Wechsler has maintained for many years the position that the mental age offers no information not available from the IQ and at the same time contains many more possible sources of error. He believes that the intelligent quotient in many respects is even more usable than mental age since it does give a clear reflection of an individual's rank within a group of described characteristics. By the use of scale scores and distributions of IQ determined on statistical grounds, the deviation IQ has been advocated by him and adopted even in the current revision of the Stanford-Binet.

Theoretically, Wechsler has consistently taken the position that there is some global nature to intelligence. He maintains that the rationale underlying the WISC reflects this global concept. At the same time, general intelligence may not be equated with intellectual abilities measured by any test including the WISC. Entering any measure of intellectual ability are certain nonintellective factors such as persistence, drive, energy level, and the like. Where test constructors have attempted to control and eliminate such factors, the validity of the test is reduced in Wechsler's estimation. Though he concedes that intellectual capacity may represent a unitary trait, the concept of general intelligence certainly is not unitary. To Wechsler, intelligence is a part of some greater entity which he labels personality. He assumes, then, that intelligence may not be extracted from the rest of the personality of the individual and the WISC reflects some attempt to account for other factors which may contribute to effective utilization of ability by the individual.

The organization of the WISC is one portion of this theoretical position. Weights which he has assigned to each subtest, and which he calls impartial since they are equal weights, also are attempts to account for factors which enter total effective ability. He makes it clear that the subtests do not reflect primary abilities in the sense in which the Thurstones used them, nor is there any particular importance to the order in which the subtests are presented. What is needed is some broader concept of general abilities than has been commonly recognized, and Wechsler believes that the WISC, with the positions cited above taken by him, offers just such a broader view. His experience in developing and using the Bellevue scale in the clinical setting and the experience reported by other clinicians with this scale indicate the importance of nonintellective factors in assessing the performance of the individual, and the need for some psychometric recognition of these factors.

ORGANIZATION OF THE SCALE. Twelve subtests comprise the Wechsler Intelligence Scale for Children. These are divided into two subgroups known known as Verbal and Performance scales. As one would assume, Wechsler maintains that the Verbal and Performance scales tap somewhat different abilities. At the same time other factors, including nonintellective ones, also enter subtest performance on both the Verbal and Performance scales.

The Verbal scale consists of the following subtests: (1) Information, (2) Comprehension, (3) Arithmetic, (4) Similarities, (5) Vocabulary, and (6) Digit Span. The Performance scale includes the following subtests: (1) Picture Completion, (2) Picture Arrangement, (3) Block Design, (4) Object Assembly, (5) Coding, and (6) Mazes. In standardizing the WISC, all twelve of these subtests were administered to every individual in the standardization sample. To use all twelve subtests requires more time than is warranted by the psychometric return, the ranking of the individual in his age group. As a result, the scale normally is used with ten subtests: the first five Verbal and the first four Performance, plus either coding or mazes. Digit span and mazes were excluded from the total examination for purposes of establishing IQ tables because they showed relatively low correlations with other subtests in the total scale plus the extensive time needed for performance on the mazes subtest. This does not mean that both the digit span and mazes test will not be used; indeed, Wechsler believes that in clinical situations there is a good bit of qualitative and diagnostic information which may be obtained by their administration. However, if all subtests are used it is necessary to prorate the various scores in order to determine an accurate IQ for the individual in his age group. Wechsler explains that the psychometrist may use either the coding or the maze test depending upon his preferences and the kind of information desired, if the total scale is not being administered.

SUBTEST INTERCORRELATIONS. Intercorrelations among the subtests subdivided according to Verbal, Performance, and Full scale are reported at three age levels by Wechsler in the Manual for the WISC. The three age levels selected are 7½, 10½, and 13½. He gives no reason for not reporting the intercorrelations at the other age levels. It is worth noting that he would probably have increased the size of these correlations if he had combined across age levels; for example, ages 5½ through 7½ rather than age 7½ alone. There is a question of the size of correlation coefficient desirable under such circumstances. By and large, one would wish some degree of correlation between subtests to reflect the fact that they are measuring the same quality, but the correlation coefficient should be low enough that they are not apparently measuring the same thing. By contrast, the correlation of any subtest with total score should be relatively large. However, to state exact correlation coefficients desirable would be hazardous at best, since no one has been able to empirically determine what the "best" value may be.

SCORE STABILITY. The reliability of scores seems important for two reasons: estimates of errors of measurement and potential validity. In a scale like the WISC, reliability estimates should be reported not only for Full Scale score and for Verbal and Performance scores but for subtest scores as well. This information Wechsler has provided for the norming sample at the three age levels of 7½, 10½, and 13½. His position is that such information is vital to the psychometrist as a means of more capably utilizing test scores. With the statistical definition of classifications of intelligence which he has used and the position that subtest scores may have value for differential prediction, the information is crucial.

With only one form of the WISC, reliability coefficients had to be estimated either by the split-half technique or test-retest. Wechsler chose the former, the split-half technique, with correction for attenuation by the Spearman-Brown formula. One problem with the split-half technique is that it tends to spuriously overestimate reliability as compared with alternate forms estimates. Such overestimates may be even further exaggerated by the limited number of items in each of the subtests. As will be noted from examination of Table 8-1, subtest reliabilities at all ages are considerably less than for scale and full-scale scores. Additionally, reliability estimates are lower at age 7½ than at age 13½. As a result, the standard errors of measurement, reported as scale-score values in the subtest, are quite high when considering the possibility of differential diagnosis. If for example one wished to estimate the scale score value at age 7½ for the comprehension subtest such that the true score would lie within a 99 percent confidence interval, about six scale-score points would have to be added and subtracted from the obtained value to make certain that the child's score was estimated within the true range for repeated performances. If he obtains a scale score of ten on comprehension, then his true score probably lies between 4 and 16 scale score points. Of course, the psychometrist may use a less stringent estimate. The less stringency in the estimate, the greater the possibility of error. Obviously, where great stringency is used, the subtest scores are not

TABLE 8-1
RELIABILITY ESTIMATES AND STANDARD ERRORS OF MEASUREMENT FOR THE WISC

Subtest	Age 7½ (N = 200)		Age 10½ (N = 200)		Age 13½ (N = 200)	
	r	SE_m*	r	SE_m*	r	SE_m*
Information	.66	1.75	.80	1.34	.82	1.27
Comprehension	.59	1.92	.73	1.56	.71	1.62
Arithmetic	.63	1.82	.84	1.20	.77	1.44
Comparison (similarities)	.66	1.75	.81	1.31	.79	1.37
Vocabulary	.77	1.44	.91	0.90	.90	0.95
Digit span	.60	1.90	.59	1.92	.50	2.12
Verbal score (without digit span)	88	5.19	.96	3.00	.96	3.00
Picture completion	.59	1.92	.66	1.75	.68	1.70
Picture arrangement	.72	1.59	.71	1.62	.72	1.59
Block design	.84	1.20	.87	1.08	.88	1.04
Object assembly	.63	1.82	.63	1.82	.71	1.62
Coding	.60	1.90	—	—	—	—
Mazes	.79	1.37	.81	1.31	.75	1.50
Performance score (without coding and mazes)	.86	5.61	.89	4.98	.90	4.74
Full scale score (without digit span, coding and mazes)	.92	4.25	.95	3.36	.94	3.68

From Wechsler, 1949

*Reported in scale-score units for subtests and in IQ points for Verbal, Performance, and Full scale.

reliable enough for individual prediction. This issue is a central one to any attempt at comparative analysis among subtests.

This argument may be extended to difference scores between subtests. As Thorndike and Hagen (1955) have noted, difference scores remove common elements between tests and therefore expand the role of error in the procedure. Figure 8-1 is an example of the results of using difference scores.

The use of diagnostic differences or "signs" between subtest values is a matter not only of reliability, but intercorrelation as well. The higher the degree of intercorrelation between subtests and the lower the reliability of separate subtests, the less likely that differences between them will have any meaning at all. Regardless of one's position on differential diagnosis, the employment of formulas designed to indicate the stability of score and the stability of differences between scores is essential in any such procedure. Unfortunately, very few psychometrists seem to employ any such rigorous analyses. As a result, many of the kinds of diagnoses being made may be in great error and actually do harm to individuals.

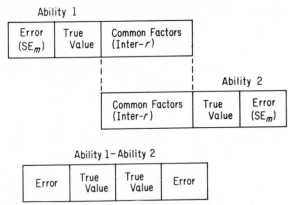

Fig. 8-1. Demonstration of proportions of score values entering difference scores. (Adapted from Thorndike and Hagen, 1955.)

Wechsler is first of all, to be commended for including the information, and for quite frank statements about the limitations in considering scores on separate tests and differences between scores. For instance, Wechsler (1949, p. 14) points out that the reliabilities of the Verbal and Performance scales and Full scale are considerably better than for any given subtest and therefore more confidence may be placed in statements derived from such scores. It should be noted as well that the standard errors of measurement were reported in IQ points for Verbal score, Performance score, and Full Scale score. All of the subtests are reported in scale-score values. For ages other than the specific ones chosen by Wechsler, reliabilities and standard errors for the nearest age group should be used.

The Preschool and Primary Scale of Intelligence

The WISC was designed to offer the kind of information obtainable on adults with the WAIS for children of school age. No test was available that would allow an implementation of Wechsler's statistical definitions of intelligence nor an estimate of the ability of the individual to adapt to his environment. For this reason a number of psychologists advocated a standardization of the WISC for children under the ages of six. Wechsler reports that he considered this need (Wechsler, 1967, p. iii) and decided that a scale devised and separately standardized for children under age 6 would be superior to a downward extension of the WISC. This does not mean that the essential concepts and measurement procedures followed in the WPPSI are in any disagreement with the WISC or the WAIS. In fact, the general form and even much of the content of the WPPSI are closely related to the WISC. Assumptions made about the nature and expression of intelligence are employed in this scale, but with separate standardizations on children between the ages of 4 and 6½.

Rationale for the Scale

Wechsler gives reason for a separate scale for the age range from 4 to 6 in the introduction to the WPPSI (Wechsler, 1967, pp. 1–2). He speaks of this age range, for example, as representing a "nodel period" in the intellectual development of the individual. To him, this age range is a particularly important period in its own right, though obviously it is related to succeeding developmental periods as reflected in the measurement procedures followed by him. There is a kind of intellectual awareness on the part of the child that differentiates him from the infant. The child is now what Wechsler calls a "little man." There are a great many features of the environment with which the child can cope reasonably and well, particularly in situations where practical intelligence must be put to work. Wechsler maintains that the child has now begun to think for himself, and that as he makes mistakes he is able to use them experientially to correct his responses in future situations. Intellectually, the child is now ready to deal with a variety of tasks which are reasonably difficult, a matter reflecting both intellectual development and interest in awareness of the environment. It is during this period as well that the child embarks upon the formal education procedure. This not only offers expansion of opportunities and experiences but also puts him into a social context which he has not experienced until this time.

All in all, according to Wechsler, the child is in a position to express himself and to deal with a variety of situations if his interest and attention are aroused. The ability to express himself intellectually is not restricted to specific behaviors nor to limited measures, but are much broader-ranging. Under this umbrella, the reasoning and procedures underlying the WAIS and the WISC now become applicable to the measurement of the intelligence of the preschool age child, the group for which the WPPSI is specifically designed.

The Preschool and Primary Scale includes, then, both a verbal and performance subscale. Within each of these subscales, tests are found which reflect the content of the WISC. Indeed, only the Sentences subtest in the Verbal scale, intended as a supplementary test, and Animal House and Geometric Design in the Performance scale are new tests. The relation of the WPPSI to the WISC is evident from the number of items common to the two tests. Except for the three new tests included in the WPPSI, nearly all the subtests share approximately half of their items commonly with the WISC. Differences between the tests in this regard thus depend upon the standardization procedures.

The WPPSI is intended to serve the same purposes and play the same role as the WISC. The psychometrist administers a series of subtests, each of which is intended to measure an ability differing somewhat from the other subtests and yet contributing highly to total score. Separate scores for Verbal and Performance scales are obtained, and these may be used for analysis under appropriate circumstances. A combination of Verbal and Performance scale scores into the Full Scale score gives an estimate of the individual's ability to deal effectively with his environment. Wechsler makes the point that the verbal and performance scales are not measuring different kinds of intelligence but different expressions which may have diagnostic significance. The same argument is extended into the subtests themselves. One role of subtest performance is to indicate to the psychometrist how the individual's competencies and various intellectual abilities may contribute to or influence his total functioning. Once again the ability of the test to do this job is dependent upon the demonstrated validity of the subtests selected for the purpose in mind.

Under the rationale already discussed, Wechsler points out that children in the age ranges 4 to 6 may be tested on a scale which yields a value reflecting the degree of presence or of "moreness and lessness" as he puts it. He assumes that such is, indeed, the fact and reports that he spent some three years in research intended to demonstrate the validity of the assumption. Primarily, this centered around administering the WISC to children beginning at age 4 and gathering some evidence that it was usable for the younger age group. To Wechsler, this evidence indicates that intellectual abilities of the type measured by the WISC are found in the child by the time he is four years of age and may be measured under the appropriate circumstances. However, the degree to which such abilities are expressed may not be identical for a child of age 4, say, with the child of age 9. For this reason, separate norming was necessary. There is the basic assumption, however, that mental abilities as defined by Wechsler are continuous beginning at age 4 and may be measured with the same kinds of tasks as at later age levels.

Wechsler's quarrels with the mental-age concept and his acceptance of the IQ as a measure of intellectual ability are repeated in the manual in the same form in which they have been presented on prior occasions.

Scale Standardization

Perhaps the most central feature which would differentiate the WPPSI from the WISC are the procedures followed in standardization and consequent development of IQ tables. As Wechsler notes, there is something more of a problem than usual in the attempts to find a representative sample of children below school age. A stratified sampling procedure was followed as one of the best means to reach the criterion of representation. The same control variables are found with the WPPSI as with the WISC plus one additional variable which is of considerable significance in considering the norming procedures.

AGE AND SEX. As with the WISC, 100 boys and 100 girls were used at each of the age levels selected for standardization. Rather than birthdates, however, Wechsler uses half-year increments from 4 through 6½ for the WPPSI. A total sample of some 1,200 cases is included in the standardization, although considerably more children than this were tested in the development of the scale.

GEOGRAPHIC REGION. The four major regions of the country geographically were used in the standardization of the WPPSI.

URBAN-RURAL RESIDENCE. Communities containing a population of at least 2,500 were put into the urban category along with suburbs of large cities and cities. Other communities were considered rural.

FATHER'S OCCUPATION. Though the same kinds of categories for occupational placement as had been used for the WISC were repeated, the order was changed. This order agrees with the 1960 census and the groupings for occupational purposes made within that census.

Indeed, all data reported with the standardization of the WPPSI are based upon 1960 census data. As was true with the WISC, representation for all the above variables was included simultaneously in the sample used.

COLOR. The most distinct differences in the standardization of the WPPSI from all preceding scales is the fact that both white and nonwhite children were included in the standardizing group. The nonwhites and whites were proportional on the basis of ratios for color reported in the 1960 census for the various age ranges included in the standardization sample. Whether or not a pronounced effect on the norms results from this step will have to wait further research. One way to answer this question is by testing children with the WPPSI and at a later time testing with the WISC and determining the degree of agreement between the two kinds of measures. There is, at least for the first time, a norm which is indeed more representative of various subgroups in the United States.

Using the WPPSI

As was true with the WISC, Wechsler presents tables indicating the percentage of the U.S. population in the various categories of the 1960 census and in the sample at the different age levels used by him. The agreement, upon inspection, is most marked, and insofar as the variables selected do control for sources of variation not desirable in test scores reported, the sample is quite representative.

Given the appropriate raw scores for the standardization level at each age level, the distribution was forced to fit a scale-score distribution with a range from zero to 20, a mean of 10, and a standard deviation of 3. This is the procedure followed by Wechsler in both the WAIS and the WISC, and the minor irregularities noted by him in the plot were corrected by smoothing the curve. In turn, the scale scores for the various ages were fitted to an IQ distribution with a mean of 100 and a standard deviation of 15. As is true with the WISC, children obtaining scale-score values at the extremes are reported as simply having IQ's under 45 or over 155. All children in the standardizing sample fell within 3⅔ standard deviations in IQ points according to Wechsler.

As is also true with the WISC, a child may obtain a raw score of zero on the WPPSI and yet receive some scale-score value greater than zero. For the first time Wechsler comments upon this condition and specifically within the context of the intellectual performance of a child in the age range 4 to 6. He observes that no child may receive a scale score less than 5 on either the Verbal or Performance scale because even a zero raw score is assigned a scale score of at least 1. In certain instances, the scale score assigned to a zero raw score is 4. He takes the position that a raw score of zero does not indicate a complete absence of the ability measured by the subtest. Instead, it should be assumed by the psychometrist that the obtained raw score simply indicates an inability to determine the level at which the child can function on that subtest. He uses the example of a child whose score is zero on vocabulary, pointing out that the child may know the meaning of a few words even if he is not able to define the specific word used in the subtest.

There is, of course, a considerable area for debate with Wechsler's assumptions and position in this regard. However, he does make it clear that unless a child obtains some raw-score values greater than zero on at least two of the verbal subtests, the psychometrist should not attempt to compute a verbal IQ for him. Instead the child should be reported as insufficiently tested or as untested.

The occurrence of such cases will be primarily at the lower age levels. In addition, performances of zero on so many subtests should be quite rare. Whether or not performance on only two of five subtests is sufficient for the psychometrist to draw some conclusions about the child's abilities to function may be left to the conscience of the psychometrist. There are, as has been stressed over and over in this series, various sources of error even under the best of conditions. Personally, the present author would not attempt to use scores on either the WPPSI or the WISC where so little information was gained as discussed in this context. Perhaps the notable exception to this is some conclusion, substantiated by considerable external evidence, of mental defiency on the part of the child.

Diagnosis of Mental Deficiency

Wechsler's consideration of diagnosing deficiency in a preschool age child is thus worthy of consideration at this point. Wechsler believes that such a diagnosis is usually not difficult for the very young child, either medically or psychometrically. There is a danger that other conditions may be responsible for behavior than deficiency as such, and this inability to differentiate between mental deficiency and, say, schizophrenia may pose a considerable problem. The differentiation may depend upon some observation and data collection over a period of several years prior to the time the child enters school. The final decision, of course, would determine the educational program to which the child will be exposed.

Unfortunately, as Wechsler points out, very frequently not even the most gross kind of information is available to school officials at the time of original admission to school. This would be particularly true for the child who may be considered to be borderline in mental ability. Because of assumptions made by teachers and school officials and the tradition associated with certain kinds of decision making, the child may have reached the upper primary grades before there is some agreement that perhaps he cannot benefit from the normal school program. Identification prior to entering school, if it is valid, would be of considerable importance to the child and his welfare.

The question now becomes: to what degree will the preschool and primary scale of intelligence devised by Wechsler help to overcome some of these problems? As Wechsler himself agrees, diagnosing some gross degree of mental deficiency really is not difficult. It is not even necessary always to administer a test in order to note some behavioral deficiencies on the part of the child. For those cases approaching borderline, and those consequently of greatest educational significance, the ability to validly diagnose some degree of mental deficiency will depend upon the appropriateness and suitablity of the tests used. Wechsler, having made-this point, maintains that the efficiency of this test in such diagnoses depends upon how retarded intellectually the child is and the age at which he is tested with the WPPSI. In order to apply the scale, some minimal maturation must have been achieved for each of those functions or abilities measured by the test. This minimum in all cases is not achieved before age 3, according to Wechsler. He then states: ". . . in terms of overall functioning level, this equates to an IQ of 75 at age 4, 60 at age 5, and 50 at age 6. For children with endowments below these levels, the WPPSI may prove too difficult and may have to be supplemented and sometimes replaced, by other measures" (Wechsler, 1967, p. 44). Under such circumstances, the utility of the WPPSI for some quite significant decisions of the child must be held in abeyance. As research is gathered over the next decade or so, a more definitive position may be taken and incorporated in the psychometric appraisal.

Reliability Estimates

Wechsler reports reliability coefficients and standard errors of measurement for each of the subtests, the Verbal and Performance scales, and Full scale IQ at each of the age levels for the standardization group. Reporting the information at each of the half-year levels tested is an improvement even over the procedure followed with the WISC, and a fact for which Wechsler must be commended. The reliabilities obtained, again on the split-half basis with correction except for one subtest, are surprisingly high. The resulting standard errors of measurement are most encouraging. The standard errors of measurement for subtests are reported in Scale score values while for the Verbal, Performance and Full Scale scores, the standard error of measurement is in terms of IQ points.

Once again Wechsler cautions the psychometrist to consider reliability and standard error in interpreting any individual score and particularly when difference scores are considered. For psychometric uses, he presents a table of differences between scale scores required for statistical significance at a 15 percent confidence level. For differences between Verbal and Performance IQ's, evidence is tabled for significance at both the 15 percent and the 5 percent level. Whether or not a 15 percent level is stringent enough for the psychometrist is a matter to be individually determined. The appropriate formulas for more stringent values are available. It should be noted that the table for differences reported by Wechsler is for the average values for all age groups and not for each age group separately. It would seem most appropriate for the psychometrist to use the reported standard errors available at each age level and apply these on a consistent confidence level for the appropriate age of the child.

Wechsler also reports intercorrelations with the various subtests at each of the age levels used in the standardization. Additionally, a table of average intercorrelations for all six age groups is given and indicates low to moderate relationships for the subtests. The relation of subtests to Verbal, Performance, and Full Scale score tends to be at least somewhat higher for most subtests. This condition must hold in order to indicate something about the relation of the individual subtest to total score.

Wechsler also includes some data relevant to a test-retest reliability obtained over a period of approximately three months for children who ranged in age from five years three months to five years nine months. Over the eleven-week time interval, some mean increases in scale-score values and standard deviations were noted for most of the subtests. There was also some increase in mean IQ over the period with the performance IQ increasing almost seven points. The Full Scale IQ increased about three and one half points and the Verbal IQ about three points. Wechsler does not comment on the significance of the data. The test-retest reliability coefficients tend to be lower than the split-half coefficients reported for the 5½-year-old group. Wechsler reports these obtained test-retest coefficients in terms of the estimated stability coefficient for the standardization group at age 5½. There is not discussion of the significance of this feature.

Finally, congruent validity coefficients are reported for the WPPSI with the Stanford-Binet IQ, the Peabody Picture Vocabulary Test IQ, and the French Pictorial Test of Intelligence. These are reported by subtests, and by Verbal, Performance, and Full Scale IQ. The significance and meaning of the correlation of a subtest score with Stanford-Binet total IQ or French Pictorial Test of Intelligence IQ seems somewhat dubious. More significant are the Verbal, Performance, and Full Scale IQ values as correlated with these tests. As is usually the case, the Wechsler Scale, IQ's yield correlation coefficients in the 70's for Verbal and Full Scale IQ, and in the 50's for Performance IQ with the Stanford-Binet. Correlations with the Peabody and French Pictorial Test of Intelligence were considerably lower. This simply signifies that the WPPSI apparently measures a common, but somewhat different, performance from the Stanford-Binet.

Subtest Characteristics

Considering the subtest labels and content in the preschool scale and their similarity to subtest labels and content back to the Bellevue scales, one must assume that characteristics described by Wechsler are as applicable for the child four to six years of age as they are for the adult in the Bellevue Clinic. Indeed, as noted before, Wechsler does assume that there is a considerable agreement in intellectual abilities for the child and the adult, the major difference being in degree. Wechsler calls attention to a congruence with the WISC in the fact that primary modification in the preschool scale involved adding easier items so as to adapt the subtests for younger children and to eliminate those items which would clearly be beyond the abilities of children from age 4 to 6. However, some changes were made in content, according to Wechsler, or in mode of administration, for arithmetic, similarities, mazes, and block design. Changes in these subtests are discussed by him.

ARITHMETIC. The change here is the addition of four items at the beginning of the test to provide a floor. Each of the cards contains pictures of objects which Wechsler believes measures basic quantitative concepts without requiring the child to have explicit ability to deal with numbers. The questions asked of the child require him to show a relative value rather than a numerical one. The items are intended primarily to give some opportunity for 4- 4½-year-old children to succeed.

SIMILARITIES. Wechsler discusses the fact that before age 6 or so children have considerable difficulty in verbally explaining similarities even though their behavior indicates a grasp of the essential function. Difficulty in devising items for such a subtest lies in identifying appropriate content, not in the adequacy of the measure for use with young children. He has found that the use of an analogy is suitable for very young children and satisfies the requirements of a similarities subtest. Of the sixteen items in the subtest, ten of them are of the simple analogy type in which the child completes a statement with an appropriate word but without having to explain how things are alike.

MAZES. Again, the principal difference is through adding easier items. For the young child, a horizontal maze which requires him to move only in one direction is used rather than the more common and complex square.

Wechsler makes some interesting statements, though he offers no sources of substantiation, relative to this procedure. He points out that a child under age 6 may be very much confused when presented with the usual kind of maze where he must begin at the center and work outward through several paths. He comments that the child may experience some frustration by being fenced in or held to a limited development of spatial orientation. Below age 6, according to Wechsler, the child has a tendency to proceed without interruption in a horizontal direction. He adds that the young child moves more naturally in a horizontal direction and that it is interruption of this normal behavior rather than the fact that the child lacks the ability to determine appropriate escape routes, which does not allow him to complete the usual maze problem. Whether or not the explanation is accurate, Wechsler has found a pragmatic basis by which mazes may be included in the testing of the very young child.

BLOCK DESIGN. The young child grasps the idea of a pattern on a plain surface without difficulty, according to Wechsler, but use of such materials as the Kohs blocks introduces a three-dimensional aspect to the pattern that disturbs the child's performance. Even demonstrating to the child at age 6 the correct assembly of a pattern is insufficient. For this reason, a flat block with only two sides is used in the preschool-scale block-design task.

Considering the changes from the WISC, one would have to conclude that the changes are indeed minor. They represent an attempt to add enough floor for young children that even those with the least intellectual abilities may be expected to provide some adequate performance for scoring. In all other ways, the purposes and intellectual abilities sampled by the items of the subtests may be considered congruent with the WISC, the WAIS, and the Bellevue Scales.

There are, however, three tasks in the WPPSI which have not been used by Wechsler before. He discusses the purposes of including such tasks and the abilities which he believes they sample.

ANIMAL HOUSE. The task labeled Animal House is similar to the Coding task used on the WISC. In the case of the preschool subtest, the child associates a sign with a symbol and Wechsler reports that this kind of task is a measure of learning ability. A basic factor in performance on this task is memory (as it is in every task, of course) but Wechsler adds that attention, awareness of the goal to be reached, and concentration ability may also be involved. He offers no evidence that these kinds of traits have been identified in any empirical fashion and related directly to performance on the subtest.

The task was administered twice to each child although only performance on the first testing was used in establishing norms. The nature of the task allows a second administration by the examiner as a means of determining the acquisition ease for the individual child. Under certain conditions, Wechsler reports, the second test may be given to indicate whether or not the child is a relatively slow or relatively fast learner. Indeed, he expects to find the performance on this subtest will correlate with the child's learning rate in school. He does not report the degree to which such a correlation should exist. Under no circumstance should the score obtained on a second testing of Animal House be used in computing the IQ. Since Coding has been reported by some clinicians to be associated with organic deficit under limited circumstances, Wechsler believes that a very poor performance on this task may suggest the need to independently determine whether or not the child has a deficit of an organic nature.

GEOMETRIC DESIGN. Wechsler reports that he included a task of geometric designs in the scale because of correlation with other measures of ability. There is the additional matter that performance on designs of this nature is not so heavily dependent upon the abilities used in verbal tasks. Wechsler reports that such a test will indicate some of the child's more specialized abilities and disabilities. He says that the abilities measured by this subtest are based upon the perceptual and visual motor organization of the child, a factor closely related to chronological age. He maintains that deficiencies of a large nature, particularly in performance on geometric designs, may indicate something about a behavioral deficiency and/or organic deficit on the part of the child. After age 5 or so, certain more pronounced differences in performance tend to disappear.

He comments that an effort was made to include items which would allow for the perception of rather complex patterns and thus more than just visual motor features. However, to avoid possible conflict with other tests designed to measure perception of pattern, Wechsler reports that scoring is based upon objective criteria in the main and all kinds of diagnostic implications were avoided.

SENTENCES. The sentences task was included as a suitable substitute for young children for digit span. In the case of sentences, some credit could be given for partial recall and again a floor could be established. Wechsler adds that this kinds of scoring fits in with his belief that ability should be measured in terms of amount of presence rather than all or none. This, of course, is a feature of the point scale advocated ever since Yerkes first described its potential strengths.

All in all, the addition of the so-called new tasks in the preschool scale occur as substitutes for other tasks in the WISC. It would seem that the preschool scale may be used with the same strengths as are found for the WISC. Obviously, the same limitations also exist.

References

Seashore, H., A. Wesman, and J. Doppelt. "The Standardization of the Wechsler Intelligence Scale for Children," *Journal of Consulting Psychology,* Vol. 14 (1950), pp. 99–110.

Thorndike, R. L., and Elizabeth Hagen. *Measurement and Evaluation in Psychology and Education.* New York: Wiley, 1955.

Wechsler, D. *Intelligence Scale for Children: Manual.* New York: Psychological Corporation, 1949.

Wechsler, D. *Manual for the Wechsler Pre-School and Primary Scale of Intelligence.* New York: Psychological Corporation, 1967.

9

The Current Wechsler Scales: The WAIS

That Wechsler's method of scaling extended to children has been widely accepted and used is a manifest fact. Essentially, as outlined in the preceding chapter, however, the scales for children represent an application of the Wechsler approach based upon his conceptions of adult expressions of intelligence. For this reason, any final decisions about the contribution of Wechsler and the adequacy of this contribution to the field of measurement must be placed upon the adult intelligence scale. The base of the WAIS rests in the Bellevue scales; there is relatively little that is really new in the adult scale currently being used. There has been a considerable addition of clinical knowledge and use, and some refinement in the rationale Wechsler uses to explain certain assumptions inherent in the building of the test. For example, he notes that his ideas about the nature of intelligence have changed very little since the introduction of the Bellevue scales (Wechsler, 1958, p. vii). There has been a change, as expressed by him, in terms of the belief that intelligence is some aspect of total personality rather than a separate entity. For this reason, then, Wechsler conceives of intelligence as being an effect rather than a cause, and that intelligence, whatever the effect, is a product of certain abilities interacting with each other and influenced by those nonintellective factors that he has spoken of in much of his writing. The principal problem facing the psychologist dealing with the concept of intelligence today, then, is the determination of how the various abilities interact to produce the effect which we label intelligence. At the present time Wechsler sees no valid way to answer such a question. He continues to pay his debt and tribute to the theory of Spearman.

The Nature of Intelligence

Though his basic conception of the construct of intelligence has changed little over the years, Wechsler does provide some extension and extrapolation of his basic contentions. To some degree this portion of discussion will be repetitious of the Chapter on Wechsler in Part I and the chapter on the Bellevue scales in this Part II. Basically, such repetition is necessary in order to reflect the current position of Wechsler on the nature and expression of intelligence.

Wechsler pays tribute to Binet's historical contribution to the measurement of ability in terms of his attempts to measure with less regard for a precise definition which might guide the efforts. As he further points out, this has been the approach taken by most test constructors since the original work of Binet. We are now in the position to measure the construct with many kinds of items and subtests not conceived of nor employed by Binet in his original efforts. Furthermore, according to Wechsler, we now have reached the point where we have a great deal more knowledge about what it is that we actually measure with our test: the factors that are represented in whatever measures are devised. This psychometric progress has had two important outcomes. First of all, the discovered factors or elements of intelligence which have now been identified do not coincide with the traits originally ascribed to the construct of intelligence. Where Binet spoke of complex mental faculties of reasoning, comprehension, and the like, we now use much more precise terminology for the item content making up a factor. The second of the discoveries of some importance as a result of the years of work with the construct is that it is possible now to express the various factors and elements in a fairly simple and straightforward form. Indeed, as Wechsler also observes, for many psychologists we have simply succeeded in stirring up confusion. We seem to be no better off in terms of defining the true meaning of intelligence than we were in 1895. He dismisses this position by adducing that there are many scientific constructs which are not proven yet which are quite adequately used. Indeed, the role of a definition to Wechsler may be confined to the fact that a definition does not describe the trait itself but merely what the trait involves, and consequently some of the behaviors which would represent it. In this regard definitions of intelligence, including Wechsler's own definition, would be acceptable.

Within this context, Wechsler retains the definition he has used for some years: "Intelligence, operationally defined, is the aggregate or global capacity of the individual to act purposefully, to think rationally and to deal effectively with his environment . . ." (Wechsler, 1958, p. 7). In view of the discussion preceding this definition, it is important that the adequacy of the definition be judged on the outcomes of purposeful action, rational thinking, and effective dealing with the environment. Insofar as one is able to define behaviorally these outcomes and to measure them with some degree of accuracy, the definition is acceptable for its operational purposes. Perhaps it should be repeated that such outcomes will not *prove* the accuracy of the definition, but only lend support to its operational acceptance. Other definitions with other kinds of outcomes behaviorally may indeed be just as acceptable by the same criteria. There is a place for both definitions and both kinds of tests under such conditions.

The first outcome of importance, that of purposeful action, Wechsler denotes as being necessary but certainly not all-inclusive. Many kinds of purposeful actions really do not reflect much about intelligent behavior. Purpose, or direction toward a goal, must be further supported by rational thinking, which must involve some degree of insightful behavior in the Wechsler viewpoint. Finally, the purpose in action and the insight that distinguishes its qualities must be applied to environmental conditions so that the organism behaves effectively. Under these conditions, intelligence has been best expressed. It is worthy of note that these are not separate continua but interrelated expressions of intelligence.

There is the further matter that intelligence is some capacity of an aggregate or global nature because it is made up of a number of separate abilities. Each of these abilities may be defined and measured, but Wechsler points out again that merely measuring and summing the performance on tests of the abilities will not give us an adequate reflection of the aggregate or global capacity itself. He continues to reject the bundle hypothesis for the same reasons that he has done so for many years.

DISTINCTION BETWEEN ABILITIES AND GENERAL INTELLIGENCE. Wechsler sees a difference between some general intellectual factor such as Spearman's *g* and the abilities which are used to estimate this quality. The tests designed to measure intellectual abilities, regardless of their structure, reflect other factors than some general quality, and these factors must be explained and accounted for in order adequately to predict human behavior. Wechsler says that there are a number of sources of information about the kinds of factors influencing intellectual performance. The first source is one of clinical experience. He again uses the example of two individuals attaining the same score but being classified in different ways. Accurate and adequate clinical diagnosis is dependent upon much more than the intellectual abilities which enter into behavior. In recent years, Wechsler says, new correlational techniques and factor analysis have allowed the first demonstrations of what the other factors may be—their nature and measurement. As such studies are carried on, the weight to be assigned such factors and given scores may be determined.

In addition to the clinical evidence, there is the empirical evidence as well. In this context, he repeats the evidence and arguments provided for variance unaccounted for in correlational studies. As before, he assumes that the variance which is not accounted for by the correlation between ability measures must reflect certain nonintellectual factors at work in the measure itself. Wechsler then remarks that it is obvious that whatever we are measuring with our tests is not some simple quantity which is directly expressed in this score. It must be whatever abilities are expressed in the score plus a great deal more. Indeed, whatever the quality is it must be put to work in various settings and situations with all their content, purpose, form, meaning. Wechsler says if this position is accepted, it implies that intelligence is some biological function in the very widest sense of the term. He maintains that this practical implication has been an hypothesis used by him in the design and construction of his scales. Although the test cannot measure all the attributes making up general intelligence, Wechsler believes that it does give sufficient information of portions of the practical definition to allow a reasonable estimate of an individual's global capacity.

RELATING ABILITY TO INTELLIGENCE. The practical situation exists that any measure of what we call intelligence is dependent upon performance on specific kinds of items and subtests. A battery of such tests may be administered and the scores used as the basis for estimating the level of intelligence. As Wechsler indicates, we begin with what we believe to be a series of measures of aptitude and somehow wind up with the IQ (Wechsler, 1958, p. 15). The reason for this, he says, is that we use our ability measures as a tool to discover something more fundamental, as a basis for projection about the individual well beyond the performance itself. A vocabulary test then is used not alone or even primarily to discover how many words the individual knows but as a reflection of some more basic capacity which is a part of the general ability to function adequately. The same is true of any other kinds of items or series of subtests which are included within the scale.

Wechsler adds: "The tentative answer we are suggesting is that intelligence can be measured by way of abilities because what we are concerned with essentially is not the abilities themselves but what enters into or emerges from them . . ." (Wechsler, 1958, p. 15). The extent of the problem is stated later in this fashion:

> . . . the thing we seek to measure when we measure intelligence is the net result of the complex interaction between the various factors entering into intelligent behavior. In practice we measure this resultant fact by means of tests of ability. An intelligence scale is an assembled battery of such tests; the intelligence rating obtained from them is a numerical

expression of their combined contribution. Although the amounts contributed by each test may be, and usually are, expressed as a single sum, the factors which determine the scores ought not, strictly speaking, to be so combined, since the result is not a linear function of these factors. . . . (Wechsler, 1958, p. 16).

Despite these problems, intelligence tests remain usable because the behaviors demonstrated in performance are some reflection of the trait we wish to measure and predict. Some kinds of tasks will be superior to other kinds of tasks in this job of estimation. The tasks which have proven most successful and which have been perpetuated in the variety of tests available, according to Wechsler, are those that allow the individual to give some reflection of his capacity to act purposefully, think rationally, and deal effectively with his environment.

The Role of the IQ

Wechsler again discusses his reason for rejecting the mental-age concept and the adoption of the deviation IQ as the score expression in his scales. Since this position has been explained before (see Part I of this series), his summary of the purpose of the IQ would seem sufficient to reflect the current position of Wechsler.

Wechsler states that the IQ serves the purpose of furnishing some measure of relative brightness, relative in the sense of the position of the individual within a group of known characteristics. But since the particular IQ only describes the rank of the individual in a specific group, it cannot be used to define a level of particular brightness as such. Whatever meaning is attached to the number expressed as IQ is conventional in nature, though certainly utilizing criteria which may be arbitrarily devised. The point is, as aptly stated by Wechsler, that the number denoting IQ is not what is important but what the number actually defines: the behavioral meaning which may be ascribed to the IQ and the validity of that behavioral meaning.

Within this context, the IQ serves as a means for classifying intelligence within the assumptions and arbitrary decisions made for the derivation and designation of relative brightness. The classification scheme of IQ's used by Wechsler, primarily statistical in nature, is the same for the adult scale as it is for the children's scales. The discussion of classification of intelligence in Chapter 8 of the present text is adequate for the purpose of understanding IQ classification with the WAIS.

Characteristics of the Adult Scale

The content of the WAIS is highly similar to the Bellevue scale discussed in a previous chapter. To avoid repetition, only a brief survey of the scales, subtests within the scales, and the presumed abilities measured by these scales will be detailed here.

Wechsler comments that several problems enter the selection of subtests used to measure certain abilities implied by the theoretical position of the test constructor. Briefly, these include attention to both theoretical and statistical matters, characteristics of items suitable for a point scale, ceiling and floor effects, and the suitability of the test as a measure of intelligence. A much more complete discussion of these matters will be found in Chapter 7.

Procedures followed in standardizing the Bellevue scales were repeated with the WAIS. An item was included in the WAIS if it met the following three criteria: (1) aviable research demonstrating the satisfactory correlation of a given test with total measures of ability, (2) variety and diversity in measurement so that the test might be used with all kinds of abilities and not limited to only a select group, and (3) the kind of errors made by the individual can be demonstrated to be related to certain diagnostic predictions. This last point is important from the standpoint that identity in performance as expressed in score may reflect marked differences in performance item by item and subtest by subtest. Wechsler assumes an importance to this difference in the means or pattern by which the individual achieves whatever total score he achieves. Even the correct response to an item by two individuals may have different connotations of some diagnostic importance. The subtests of the WAIS take on added significance for inclusion if they demonstrate some possibilities for such diagnosis, in Wechsler's view.

The Subtests of the Scale

There are eleven subtests in the Wechsler Adult Intelligence Scale, all administered under normal conditions. Under conditions where a given subtest is invalid or may not be used with an individual, prorating of scores among the remaining subtests of the subscale may be done. There are six verbal and five performance scale subtests, and Wechsler states in the Manual (Wechsler, 1955, p. 31) that there must be at least five verbal and four performance subtest scores for the computation of a full scale score.

INFORMATION TEST. The information subtest is intended to sample the individual's range of information and Wechsler notes that such tests have been widely used in mental testing for many years. Though educational level and background will determine the score obtained by the individual to some extent, Wechsler maintains that this dependence is not a source of serious objection to the inclusion of the Information subtest in a scale of this nature. The issue is more one of the kinds of items used and their reliance upon general sources of information rather than highly specific ones as in the educational setting. He holds that the items used in the WAIS are of the type that may be answered through the kinds of common opportunities presented in a culture such as ours.

Where the Wechsler-Bellevue I subtest of information had twenty-five items, the WAIS information subtest has twenty-nine. He began with a pool of items believed to represent appropriate information questions, administered these to individuals who had been measured with acceptable ability tests, and retained those items which showed an appropriate discrimination in terms of successes and failures. Essentially, the item was retained if the higher-ability groups showed significantly more individuals getting the item correct than the lower-ability group. At the same time, there are some items at the lower end which discriminate really only between borderline and defectives and items at the upper end which will discriminate only between average and superior. The procedure and results resemble very closely the percentage-passing concept used in the placement of items in the original Binet scales and the Stanford Revision.

Wechsler reports that the information test is one of the most satisfactory in the battery. It holds well with increases in age, as would be expected if the items in fact represent general experiences available to the population, and shows a most satisfactory correlation with total score.

COMPREHENSION. As with information, Wechsler reports that the comprehension subtest has been a very popular one in the development of scales. In the WAIS, ten of the original twelve items in the Wechsler Bellevue I comprehension subtest were retained with four new ones being added, giving a total of fourteen items for this subtest. Of the additions, the interpretation of proverbs constituted the majority of the items. The difficulty of explaining a proverb adds to the possible ceiling since two such items were included at the upper end of the scale.

In speculating about the mental trait measured by such a subtest, Wechsler points out that the assumption was made in the Army Alpha that a comprehension test measures common sense on the part of the individual. This might be more adequately explained as having knowledge from past experience of a very practical nature and being able to evaluate one's past experience in environmental problem situations. Whatever the measure, Wechsler says that the questions are the kind that most adults will have had an experience with at some time in the past. So commonly do these experiences occur that translation into foreign languages have not required very major changes in the item content for this comprehension subtest. Though low education level is not a deterrent to performance, poor ability to express oneself with language does usually yield a low score on the subtest. As with information, the comprehension subtest does not show a significant drop with increasing age, again probably due to its general experiental nature, and the drop that occurs late in life is relatively small.

ARITHMETICAL REASONING. The solution of arithmetic problems is viewed by many persons, according to Wechsler, as a sign of mental alertness. He maintains the importance of such a subtest in a scale because performance on such tasks will correlate quite well with a global measure of ability. Such a subtest also has the advantage of ease in construction and standardization. The biggest drawback to such a subtest, of course, is the fact that educational level and background are correlated quite well with such performance. Certain occupational groups have an advantage in performance on such a subtest because of the importance of dealing with numbers quite frequently in their day to day activities. A final drawback reported by Wechsler is the fact that individual scores may be influenced by the attention level of the individual and even by certain temperament-emotional states. How much the latter condition is the outgrowth of the former ones is not clear. Wechsler does report, however, that adults find such a task contains considerable face validity and are frequently interested in attempting to perform well on such a task.

The items included by him in this subtest are made as practical as possible and require no reading on the part of the individual. Since educational level does affect performance, nearly all of the items contain arithmetical skills commonly taught in the elementary school. Indeed, Wechsler maintains that the average adult could acquire such skills on his own if he wished to do so. There are fourteen items in this subtest, as compared with ten in the Wechsler-Bellevue I Scale. Most of the additions are at the beginning of the subtest, for purposes of floor, and in the intermediate positions.

MEMORY SPAN. Wechsler points out that the digit-span test has been one of the most popular in tests, particularly of an individual sort, since Binet devised the original scale. He attests its popularity to ease of administration, scoring, and apparently specific nature of the ability tested. Yet it is among the poorest of all single measures for estimating general ability. Indeed, it correlates poorly with other measures of ability, apparently because it contains very little of a factor such as g.

Despite these limitations, Wechsler decided to maintain the subtest in the WAIS for two reasons. The first of these involves its utility with low levels of intellectual functioning. He reports that adults who are unable to retain as many as five digits forward and three backward will usually be found to be feeble-minded or mentally disturbed except for those special cases of organic disease or defects. The second reason, somewhat related to the first, extends the argument to special difficulties with repetition of digits either forward or backward and the possible diagnostic significance of such inept performance. Wechsler specifically mentions the kinds of memory defects which he observes in clinical symptoms of an organic nature, and the marked reduction in performance in memory span as an early indication of mental impairment and deterioration (Wechsler, 1958, p. 71). However, low scores are not always indicative of such conditions since they may also be due to anxiety or inattention. Success is dependent upon a relatively high degree of concentration, according to Wechsler, and such a lack would be pertinent to anxiety states. Particularly will these nonorganic conditions be noted with the repetition of digits backward.

In the Wechsler scales, digits forward and backward are presented as part of the same task and a summed score used as the estimate for the subject. This procedure puts somewhat less emphasis on this task in the total score, deservedly so when one considers the low correlations of the memory span test with general ability and total score.

SIMILARITIES. This subtest has not been as widely used in scales of ability as the other subtests have been. Wechsler argues that this is difficult to understand, since the various studies done report correlations of a relatively high level between similarities and measures of general intellectual ability. While it is true that language ability influences performance on the subtest, this fact should be no more than a minor consideration in its inclusion in the scale. Much more important is some kind of complex mental ability to recognize commonality in elements and combine these in some generalized form. Quite familiar common words may be used in such a task and yet show great difficulty if appropriately paired.

The WAIS similarities subtest contains thirteen comparisons whereas the Wechsler-Bellevue I had twelve. Ten items are shared commonly between the two scales. Again, Wechsler defends the inclusion on the basis of administrative ease and face validity to the average adult. He reports that investigations have indicated a substantial amount of *g* entering the performance of the individual. In addition, certain qualitative features are found in the scale which make it even more important as a means of estimating ability. The examiner may distinguish sometimes broad differences in the quality of the common element reported by the individual. In this regard, Wechsler uses as an example the comparison of banana and orange on the one hand as fruit and on the other as both having a skin. Though either is correct, they would not receive the same amount of credit on the point scale basis employed by Wechsler.

PICTURE ARRANGEMENT. Picture arrangement, as the title indicates, requires the individual to arrange pictures in an order that tells a chronologically correct story. The items used are of the type found in comic strips and in the daily newspapers. There are eight items in the WAIS (compared to seven in the Wechsler-Bellevue), ranging in length from three pictures to six pictures. Time limits are included for correct solution, with bonus points awarded for more rapid correct performance. The issue of scoring in the Wechsler scales will be considered as a later part of the present chapter.

Wechsler reports that more than twice the number of items finally included in the WAIS were used as the basis of tryouts. The selection was intended to reflect interesting content, face validity, ease of scoring, and ability to discriminate between high and low levels of ability. Problems resulted which cause Wechsler to state that the final selection does leave a considerable amount to be desired. This is less a matter of the item included in the subtests than it is a matter of the problem existing in all such picture-arrangement tests: the dependence upon the content of the separate parts of the series. Whatever items are included must reflect some marked elements of the cultural background. What will appear to be humorous and common in American culture may be much less so in other cultures. The influence of cultures and subcultures may be fairly significant in the total score achieved by the individual. However, Wechsler reports that surprisingly few changes were necessary in various adaptations and translations into foreign languages. He reports that perhaps cartoons have an international language of their own.

The principal strengths of the picture arrangement test are reflected in the ability to comprehend a total situation and effectively react to it. If the individual cannot get the idea of the story *in toto*, then he cannot perform very well on the task. This feature of realizing the total situation even though trial-and-error behavior may be employed makes the picture-arrangement test different from other measures of comprehension. In this regard, the picture-arrangement test shows only moderate intercorrelation with comprehension subtest scores and indeed a lower correlation coefficient than that found with other subtests for comprehension.

Wechsler also makes the point that the content of the pictures requires the individual to react to some quite human or practical situation. This will involve what many writers have called social intelligence, though Wechsler does not believe there is any such disparate quality. Instead, he would maintain that social intelligence is nothing more than whatever general intelligence the individual has applied to the social situation. His clinical experience indicates to him that the individuals who perform well on a picture-arrangement task such as that in the WAIS very rarely turn out to be mental defective even though as individuals they may perform quite poorly on other kinds of tests.

Picture Completion. Tests requiring a subject to supply some missing element in the picture had been common in intelligence tests. Wechsler believes that the popularity for such a test is justified, although suitable items are sometimes difficult to devise. The problem revolves around the degree of familiarity of the object to the individual. If the object is too familiar, the missing portion is easily spotted and there will be no discrimination among subjects. By contrast, if quite unfamiliar objects are used few persons will pass the item because they do not know enough about the item to recognize any incompleteness.

In standardizing the picture-completion test for the Wechsler-Bellevue I, Wechsler used some fifteen items selected from about thirty-five that had been tried with a number of individuals with known ability level. Discrimination value became the primary basis by which the item was retained or rejected in the final listing. The range of performance found on the items was fairly restricted, a matter which was corrected in the standardization of the WAIS. The picture-completion test used in the WAIS consists of twenty-one items, ten of which are new, and which allow a more complete range of performance.

Picture completion is easy to administer and suffers very little from practice effects. Perhaps its most noteworthy use is with those of lesser degrees of ability, since discrimination is most easily established at low levels. Wechsler ventures that perhaps the test measures something of the perceptual and conceptual abilities of the individual as reflected in visual performance.

BLOCK DESIGN. A block-design test has been included in most so-called nonverbal tests of intelligence. The task as used by Wechsler represents an adaptation of the Kohs procedures. However, to provide economy in administration, Wechsler uses only ten designs in the WAIS, an increase of three over the number found in the Wechsler-Bellevue I. In addition to the limited number of items, Wechsler restricts the colors used in the pattern to two rather than four. All figures are reproduced from a plane surface even though the cubes would allow three-dimensional performance.

Wechsler states that the block-design task is an excellent measure of general ability. Not only does it possess such qualities but it also allows a considerable amount of qualitative analysis, according to him. He states that one can learn a great deal about the individual by watching how he approaches the task and the procedures of solution. He mentions particularly such things as hastiness and impulsivity as compared to deliberateness and care, ease of giving up as compared with persistence, and so on (Wechsler, 1958, p. 80).

Beyond this, he cites considerable diagnostic value for the test. Particularly difficulty will be demonstrated by those who have mental deterioration and senility, and in most cases a brain disease. He believes that in many instances poor performance on the block-design test may be due to some problem in visual motor organization.

DIGIT SYMBOL. Some form of substitution task has been widely used in a variety of psychological tests. Wechsler believes this popularity is justified, particularly when speed and accuracy become the primary measures of competence. There is the possible contaminating feature that speed plus motor coordination and visual acuity are too deterministic with increasing age for an adult intelligence scale to reflect very accurately the individual's true performance. However, Wechsler rejects the possibility that coordination and visual acuity are important, based upon his experiences. The matter of speed of performance remains a significant feature, he maintains. He points out that aged individuals do operate more slowly than younger ones and may be motivated to perform at a slower rate. This matter is not merely one of whether the older individual performs more slowly but, in Wechsler's terms, ". . . whether or not they are also 'slowed up' " (Wechsler, 1958, p. 81).

Using the digit-symbol test over a variety of ages, Wechsler has found a significant and significantly earlier drop in performance than with most other scales of the WAIS. However, digit symbol correlates approximately as well with Verbal, Performance, and Full Scale scores as other subtests do.

The results suggest to Wechsler that an older individual may be penalized when a speed factor is included in a test. But he believes that the penalty should operate and may be defended because the reduction is proportional to the ability of the individual at the age level tested. He accepts the position, then, that not only is an older individual slower but also slowed up mentally. Though one may question (and certainly many authorities have) whether speed should be included in a test of intelligence or whether only power should be emphasized, Wechsler maintains that speed should be included in estimates of ability. This is one of the reasons for including a digit symbol task in the WAIS.

Wechsler reports that individuals who are emotionally unstable and neurotic tend to do rather poorly on the digit-symbol task. There are ninety items in the test, with the individual required to substitute a figure for a given number within 1½ minutes. One reason for such a stringent time limit with so many items is to prevent a ceiling effect.

OBJECT ASSEMBLY. Four objects are included in the object assembly task with the WAIS, an increase of one over the Wechsler Bellevue. These are presented in a specific manner with the pieces of the object cut asymetrically. Again time limits are imposed, and it is possible for the individual to achieve bonus points by completing the task correctly in a limited amount of time. Ths subject is not informed that he may earn bonus points through speeded performance.

Wechsler admits that he hesitated before including this task in the WAIS. A comparison may be drawn with formboards, common to children's intelligence tests, but rejected by Wechsler as appropriate for adults. His reasons for rejection of the formboard with adults is the fact that very often they do not discriminate performance very well between ability levels. However, the combination used in the WAIS shows greater discrimination, though any one alone has low reliability and consequently poor predictive value. Practice effect is a significant feature with the object-assembly task just as it is with form boards with children.

Still, Wechsler reports that the object-assembly task has some compensating features and for these reasons was retained in the WAIS. For one thing, correlations with total score are acceptable, with correlation coefficients primarily in the 50's and 60's. Over all, correlations with other subtests tend to be somewhat lower than is the case throughout the rest of the scale. These low correlation coefficients Wechsler reports as being due primarily to the performance of a restricted group of persons. Perhaps, then, he is correct in asserting that the object-assembly task is poor only for certain types of persons. Performance on the subtests does remain stable to age 40 and begins to drop somewhat after that time.

But the feature cited as most significant by Wechsler for its inclusion in the WAIS are the qualitative features of the task. He cites examiners who have stated that the test is an excellent means of judging thinking and working habits of an individual. Three performance aspects of a personal type are cited by him: (1) being able to perceive the entire figure and understand the relation of parts to the whole, (2) rapid recognition of the total features of the object but an inability to grasp the relationships among the parts, and (3) inability to comprehend the total structure but, after several trial-and-error attempts, a rather sudden realization of the totality and completion of the task. In these circumstances Wechsler believes that the object-assembly task has particularly good clinical value, since it gives some information about the perceptual modes of the individual, the reliance on trial-and-error behavior, and the reaction of the individual to his mistakes.

VOCABULARY. A vocabulary test is generally recognized as the best single estimate of an individual's ability. Though some persons criticize it as being much too dependent upon opportunity and educational level, Wechsler believes this criticism to be unjustified, since even in persons with poor formal education there may be found high vocabulary level. Indeed, in the WAIS the vocabulary test correlates well to moderate with other subtests and rather highly with Verbal and Full Scale scores. Only information rivals it as far as correlation with Verbal and Full Scale scores is concerned.

The vocabulary list in the WAIS consists of 40 items, a new list as compared with the Wechsler-Bellevue I, which had 40 items. Wechsler believes that the task of defining words has qualitative meaning which may be used for diagnostic purposes. He includes in this category certain qualitative levels of definition, an issue first stated by Binet in his early work. Additionally, Wechsler maintains that the quality of a definition gives some indication about the background of the person. But most important may be the reflection of an individual's thinking processes from the character of the definition which he offers. Wechsler believes this has some clinical significance in such cases as schizophrenia, where the formal aspect of the language disturbance is believed to be of diagnostic significance.

In scoring, of course, any acceptable response is scored plus. It is true in the WAIS vocabulary scale that differential values may be assigned depending upon the quality of the response. However, there is no consistent approach to the difference between a two-point and a one-point response. In some instances, multiple citations lead to two points credit; in others, some more inclusive characteristic or generalized feature will yield a two-point credit. Examiners have some difficulty at times in determining the differences between a two and a one-point response for any particular vocabulary item eith the WAIS.

Vocabulary performance tends to hold with increased age, although probably reflecting something of the importance of the function in day-to-day life activities.

Standardization Data

The procedures followed in standardizing the WAIS are essentially those used in standardizing the Wechsler-Bellevue I (see Chapter 7). However, certain refinements occurred in the WAIS standardization that make it superior to the Bellevue procedures.

Some 1,700 individuals of both sexes, fifty subjects less than with the Wechsler-Bellevue I, were used in standardizing the WAIS. The range consisted of groups from age 16 through age 64, although the numbers actually employed are not evenly distributed for each age, as is evident from the inspection of Table 9-1. It will be noted that there are 100 males and 100 females for age 16 and 17 together; the same is true for ages 18 and 19 together, while age group 20 through 24 utilizes the same number, and each bracket after that time includes a ten-year interval. One outcome of this procedure will be the spurious increase in estimated reliability. For the 300 males and females comprising the sample between ages 25 and 34, for example, we do not know how many twenty-five year-olds, how many twenty-six-year-olds, how many twenty-seven-year-olds, and so on, comprise the sample. All we know is that some 300 subjects between ages 25 and 34 were used. It is possible that all 300 were age 30, or some combination in between.

Some 475 individuals above age 60 were also included in the standardization procedure for the WAIS.

TABLE 9-1
DISTRIBUTION OF SUBJECTS USED IN WAIS STANDARDIZATION SAMPLE

Age Group	Male	Female	Total
16–17	100	100	200
18–19	100	100	200
20–24	100	100	200
25–34	150	150	300
35–44	150	150	300
45–54	150	150	300
55–64	100	100	200
Total	850	850	1,700

From Wechsler, 1958, p. 87.

Whatever the distribution of subjects within the age brackets, certain control variables were then utilized as a means of assuring representative norms. These are the same factors as were used with the Bellevue scale, with somewhat better controls. The first of these variables is age. As Wechsler indicates, prior adult scales had tended to treat all individuals beyond a certain age, usually age 16, as the same age group. The WAIS corrects at least partially for this limitation by having different age groups in the norming. Interpretation of results for the fifty-year-old made with the WAIS is apt to be much more reliable than it had been with prior scales simply because there are performance data for individuals between 45 and 54. The same is true of course of other individual ages beyond age 16.

The second control factor is that of educational level. The position that education is the primary factor in intelligence test performance is not completely accepted by Wechsler, although he admits the correlation between performance and educational level. He believes, however, that the issue is not one of whether education influences test scores so much as it is a matter of the differential effects that such a factor as education has on intelligence-test performance at successive age levels. Very few studies have been done where educational level has been held constant. Wechsler does report one study (Wechsler, 1958, pp. 136–137) indicating that any decline of ability with age is very little related to the educational level of the individuals in the sample. The issue of course is not settled by such limited data, although the rationale Wechsler presents is logical and feasible until such data are forthcoming.

Of greater importance to Wechsler is the need to consider educational level as some kind of variable in standardizing the test. There are other correlated variables which must also be considered. These include occupation, sex, and age along with geographical distribution, and Wechsler attempts to consider them all simultaneously. Tables are presented by Wechsler in the Manual (1955, pp. 6–11) indicating the distribution of the sample percentagewise for the control variables mentioned above.

The third control factor mentioned by Wechsler is one of possible sex differences. Certain items have been demonstrated to yield rather marked differences in performance between males and females, particularly in children. Less definitive data is available on adults. Wechsler concludes that even where such differences exist when total score is considered there tends to be cancellation and overall total equality. The reasons for this are not clear. In the Wechsler-Bellevue I, women tended to score higher than men at about every age. Research reported following the publication of the Wechsler-Bellevue I found less indication of such differences than Wechsler had found with the standardization group. With the publication of the WAIS, standardization data indicated somewhat superior male performance at each age level. Full Scale scores, averaged across the Bellevue I and the WAIS, indicate no differences between the sexes. Wechsler notes that individual subtests, however, do show some sex differences, with women succeeding better on certain subtests and men on others. He considers this matter in great detail in a separate chapter of his text (Wechsler, 1958, pp. 144–151).

The results with the WAIS indicate to Wechsler that women may use a somewhat different kind of intellectual resource or perhaps some different degree of a sexlike ability to perform in their use of intelligence. This difference is akin to hhe assertion that men and women tend to behave and think differently. Wechsler agrees that the evidence is not clear on this latter point, would need greater testing, and would be more precise if a greater variety of subtests were available to study such differences. In any event, he does set up a group of subtests showing a "maleness" factor and a "femaleness" factor for comparative purposes. One may examine masculinity-femininity components of the individual in his test performance if one wishes. It might be added that considerable caution should be employed when one attempts such an analysis.

A final group of factors, interacting to some degree and therefore difficult to discriminate, included race, social background, and economic status. Weschsler maintains that separate norms probably should be provided for significant components of each of these factors. However, knowledge of such labels as "race" is not sufficient to provide the possibility of clear distinctions and separate normings. (It is true, however, that the preschool and primary scale of intelligence does include a proportional number of nonwhites in the standardizing sample. This represents a significant and important trend in standardization of more current tests.)

One of the changes which represents progress is the fact that Wechsler utilized a sample not largely restricted to New York City in the standardization of the WAIS. Indeed, subjects now come from all over the country, roughly in proportion to geographical distribution and ur-ban-rural representation. Ths appropriate data concerning the percent-age of the standardizing group in these categories will be found in the WAIS Manual (Wechsler, 1965, pp. 6–11). The norms recorded with the WAIS are probably much more usable for adults in other parts of the country than the Wechsler-Bellevue I was. All of the subjects used by Wechsler in the standardization were volunteers. He excluded any known mentally disturbed or hospitalized patient, but did include about 2 per-cent of the sample as known defectives in order to establish sufficient floor for the use of the test for possible diagnosis of mental retardation.

Statistical Data

The Wechsler scales are point scales (see Chapter 5). Certain as-sumptions underlie the selection of particular subtests which will be utilized in the point scale, and the weight which must be assigned to each of these subtests. Wechsler reports (1958, p. 93) that he decided to accord equal weights to subtests once the various tests were conceived to be suitable for measuring ability.

He explains this decision on the basis of a theory which he calls *assortative,* as opposed to a *heirarchial* theory. In this assortative theory upon which he nows relies he states that there is no implication that the subtests are equally effective or "good" measures of ability. The only necessary implication is that each of the subtests yield a comprehensive measure of general ability. The essential purpose of each subtest then is to make a significant contribution to the total score; only to a lesser degree does the subtest have significant qualities about ability in its own right. It is for this reason that he includes subtests such as object assembly and digit span for which there seems less defensible reason for inclusion.

In the case of object assembly and digit span, Wechsler maintains that they contribute to the comprehensive measurement of the intellectual competence of the individual to behave effectively in his environment. On this basis one must question to some degree the utility of individual subtests for stating various qualitative features about the individual.

Regardless of the theory and consequent assumptions underlying the selecton and weighting of subtests, Wechsler holds that where there are sufficient numbers of subtests the weight assigned to any particular one is not a significant contributor to the total score. At the same time, the individual of lower ability on the trait measured by a particular subtest will not be penalized because of the opportunity to score well on the variety of other subtests. The procedure used, once items had been finally selected and included in the subtests, was to force all distributions of raw scores for the subtests into a standardized distribution of scale scores with a mean of ten and a standard deviation of three. Thus in the WAIS each subtest makes an equal contribution to total score. Correlation coefficients reporting degree of relationship with total score are therefore ignored by this procedure. Whether or not one agrees with the procedure followed by Wechsler is less important at this stage than to understand the way in which he has operated. With an understanding of such a limitation, a decision may be made about the extent and specific purposes for which such a task may be used.

Given these assumptions and procedures, certain statistical results may be considered for their reflection of intellectual functioning as measured by the WAIS. The first of these has to do with the performance variable as it relates directly to age. Wechsler reported with the Wechsler-Bellevue I that maximum functioning on the test occurred around age 25 and then showed a gradual but steady drop to age 75. The same result, as must be expected, is found with the WAIS. He has plotted a curve (Wechsler, 1958, p. 96) which indicates mean scores in scale values from age 16 through 75 and the standard deviations of these scale scores. These values are for Full scale only. As before, maximum performance on the average is reached around age 25 and shows a steady decrement to age 75.

Along with the decline in mean scores with advancing age, there is a change in variability for scale performance as well. Full scale standard deviations tend to systematically increase from ages 16 to 59 for the Wechsler-Bellevue I Scale. However, with the WAIS the fluctuations are smaller and much more irregular by age group. It is true as well that standard deviations for Full Scale scores are higher with the WAIS than with the Wechsler-Bellevue I, though eleven subtests are reported for WAIS data whereas only ten are included in the Wechsler-Bellevue I data.

Wechsler reports an increase in variability beyond age 40, a fact which agrees with a number of other functions of old age. He makes the careful point that the variability associated with age is not discussed in terms of IQ, the score yielded by the test, but in absolute test performance. IQ's as computed by Wechsler are independent of age and a given IQ represents the same rank regardless of the age of the individual concerned.

This is simply another way of saying that in the WAIS the mean IQ is 100, the standard deviation of the IQ is 15 points, for each age level for which data are available. This condition is one that is forced by the assumptions made by Wechsler. One may speak more meaningfully of the constancy of the IQ under this procedure, and attempt to disclose reasons for changes in IQ over time if there is a significant change. This is a feature of the deviation IQ previously discussed in terms both of Binet and Wechsler scales.

RELIABILITY ESTIMATES. Split-half reliability coefficients were computed for the WAIS by Full, Verbal, and Performance scales, and each subtest. Additionally, Wechsler reports standard errors of measurement for all scores. Reliability estimates and standard errors are reported for three age groups: ages 18 and 19, ages 25 through 34, and ages 45 through 54 (Wechsler, 1955, p. 13).

The reliabilty estimate for the Full scale IQ is .97, a most satisfactory estimate. Verbal IQ's yield reliability estimates of .96 for each of the age groups, while Performance IQ's have reliability coefficients of .93 for the two younger age groups and .94 for the oldest one. The size of these coefficients indicates quite stable performance by groups, and the plausibility of some reasonably accurate predictions about the individual.

The subdivision of scores into subparts tends to consistently yield lower reliabilities and higher standard error. The same is true with the WAIS as it is of other tests. Thus when reliabilities of subtests on the WAIS are considered, much greater caution must be exercised with any kind of predictions, either group or individual. By and large, verbal subtests show greater reliability estimates than performance subtests for all three age groups. For the age group 18 and 19, Information, Vocabulary, and Digit Symbol show estimates in the 90's. However, the reliability coefficient for the Digit Symbol test is an estimate based upon a correction applied to obtained coefficients for two separate groups. As such, the reliability estimate may be exaggerated even beyond the usual split-half inflation. Correlation coefficients in the 80's were found for Similarities, Picture Completion, and Block Design. Correlations in the 70's were obtained for Comprehension, Arithmetic, and Digit Span. Correlation coefficients only in the 60's were found for Picture Arrangement and Object Assembly.

For the age group 25 through 34, correlation coefficients for subtests in the 90's were found for Information and Vocabulary. Coefficients in the 80's were found for Arithmetic, Similarities, Picture Completion, and Block Design, in the 70's for Comprehension, Picture Arrangment and Object Assembly, and a correlation of .66 for Digit Span. Again no reliability estimate is reported for Digit Symbol.

The lower the estimated reliability the higher the standard error of measurement. For subtests obtaining reliabilities only in the 60's and

70's, a caution must be stated for any prediction about the individual. There is a chance that significant error may be made where difference scores are computed in any fashion. Wechsler reflects this idea of caution with the following statement (Wechsler, 1958, pp. 101 and 102).

> While the reliability of the WAIS and the Wechsler-Bellevue I scales as a whole (Full, Verbal, and Performance) is quite satisfactory, that of the individual subtests, with some exceptions, leaves much to be desired. The low reliability of some of the W-B I and WAIS tests is primarily due to the fact that most of these subtests contain too few items, particularly as regards the number of items available for any given level of performance—an inevitable consequence of the time limit set for the scales as a whole. The low reliabilities of the subtests nevertheless bring up the question of legitimacy of using individual test scores for establishing clinical diagnoses. The compelling answer to this question is that tests of low reliability cannot be so used with any degree of confidence. But it must also be borne in mind that diagnostic patterning does not depend entirely upon the reliability of the subtest employed. Equally important are the validity of the individual subtests and the number of other tests brought into the configurational relationships which one is seeking to establish.

Wechsler further treats of this issue in a separate chapter on clinical diagnoses which will be considered later in the present chapter.

As noted earlier, the lower the reliability estimate the higher the standard error of measurement. In some instances the standard errors of measurement are so large as to be untrustworthy on the scales provided by Wechsler. All standard errors for subtests, for example, are provided in terms of scale scores. The scale-score distribution arbitrarily decided upon by Wechsler has a mean of 10, a standard deviation of 3, and a range of zero through 20.

To consider a single example, we will use the subtest with the lowest reliability estimate and the highest standard error, the digit span score for age group 25 through 34. The reliability estimate is .66 for this task at this age level, with a standard error of measure of 1.75 scale-score points. Assume that an individual obtains a scale score of 10 on the digit span. If we use a stringent limit to control as much as possible for error, we would take a band of within $+3$ standard errors. Doing so with this task would indicate that the individual's true score on digit span in scale-score units probably lies between 4 and 16. Obviously, very little faith can be put in any such score. Though the greatest standard error has been considered in this example, it is unfortunately true that most of the subtests have standard errors in excess of one scale-score unit, indicating great limitations in any attempt to interpret the meaning of performance on a single subtest.

Differences between subtests for some kind of differential prediction also are suspect with such standard errors. Indeed, as illustrated in Part I of this series, difference scores tend to enlarge the role of error since commonality will be removed. Wechsler comments on difference scores in this fashion:

> The reliability coefficients presented in this table should be carefully considered by the clinician when interpreting the scores earned on separate tests or differences between scores. The smaller the reliability of a given score, the less confidence one can have in the judgments made concerning a subject's true ability based upon that particular test. Judgments with respect to *differences between scores* on two tests of moderate reliability must be made with considerable caution—the lower the reliabilities of the scores, the more likelihood there is that the difference between them is due to chance rather than to any real difference in the abilities possessed by the subject. As may be seen by reference to the reliability table, this caution is more necessary for some tests than for others. It is least necessary when working with the composite Verbal, Performance, and Full Scale scores, which are highly reliable. (Wechsler, 1955, p. 13)

Wechsler continues his discussion in the Manual with reference to the standard errors of measurement and their interpretation. He warns that because certain standard errors are quite large relatively, it is necessary to be particularly cautious in attempting to compare differences between or within profiles of individual examinees.

VALIDITY ESTIMATES. In discussion of validity of the Wechsler Bellevue and WAIS as adult tests of intelligence, Wechsler describes the usual procedure of correlating the new test and its scores with an already accepted test with scores for the same individual. He informs us that whether or not the correlation coefficient obtained is of any significance will depend upon the criterion originally specified. The new test may not be so in need of validation as the matter of testing in general. Still, he reports correlation coefficients from a number of selected studies of the WAIS and the Wechsler-Bellevue with selected and widely recognized tests. These include the Stanford-Binet, 1937 Revision, certain group tests, and Raven's Progressive Matrices. These correlations are moderate to good, although the samples used for validating purposes are not always congruent.

Wechsler also discusses certain independent criteria which have been suggested for determining the validity of a given test. He mentions some three independent criteria of this nature, all of which he believes are met by both the Wechsler-Bellevue I and the WAIS. The first such external criterion is the congruence between test performance and rating of individuals by independent judges. With children's tests such as the Binet, for example, teacher ratings have been used as one evidence of validity when the comparison has been favorable to the Stanford-Binet. Wechsler asserts that this seems a perfectly logical procedure except that it is somewhat paradoxical. The reasons for the original development of the Binet scales was to correct for poor judgments, including those of teachers, in determining the abilities of children. The corrective has now become the proof, as Wechsler aptly observes. This type of circularity is not reserved just for teachers but to any selected group of authorities who determine both purpose and judgment.

A second criterion of an external nature considered by Wechsler is the approximation of test performance to the usually conceived growth curves for mental ability. For children, such comparisons may be justified, Wechsler believes, but their application to adults is less defensible. What represents normal growth curves for the adult simply had not been available. It is interesting to note that the Wechsler-Bellevue I and WAIS have been the source for such plots that have been widely accepted with adult groups.

Finally, Wechsler cites a third type of validity criterion in terms of the comparison of test scores with socioeconomic factors. Individuals belonging to high socioeconomic groups, those who have achieved best in life, tend to score higher on intelligence tests. Those who belong to lesser socioeconomic groupings tend to score lower. This argument has been rejected in quite recent times as merely another circular reflection of bias in the test reflected from society. As an added bit of data for this third criterion, Wechsler cites the agreement between test scores and those individuals labeled mentally defective.

Each of these criteria has been rejected at one time or another on the basis of the same kind of circularity that Wechsler applies to agreement with teacher judgments. Nevertheless, Wechsler concludes that the adult scales devised by him meet the criteria which he has cited and therefore illustrate something of the validity of the test. He does exercise caution by advising that such "validity judgments" are only a minimum. He indicates that in the final analysis the validity of the test will be most dependent upon its use in practical situations for predictive purposes and the consequent evaluation which is made of the test by psychologists who need information and who use it in making judgments.

Clinical Uses of the WAIS

Wechsler has proposed that a Full Scale score based upon both Verbal and Performance tasks will yield a better estimate of the functioning of the individual than will either alone. The primary reason for inclusion of a performance scale, then, is to increase the efficiency of the Full Scale score. However, the Wechsler Adult Scale is also a point scale, and as such includes subtests for both Verbal and Performance scales. The subtests were chosen for some at least presumed utility and diagnostic work for clinicians. Indeed, one might say that the current use of the Wechsler scales emphasizes much more the diagnostic and clinical possibilities than the increased precision of total score. With the concept of the IQ in some disrepute, it is not unusual to find the more stable estimate represented by Full scale, Verbal, and Performance IQ's relegated to a position of unimportance while analysis of subtest scores for differential prediction becomes paramount. Whether or not such a system is warranted depends upon some features of the scale discussed in prior chapters, and demonstration of clinical validity. In this volume the validity of clinical claims will not be considered as much as some presentation of Wechsler's arguments for clinical applications.

Wechsler maintains that beyond the primary purpose of a stable estimate of an individual's global intellectual capacity, an intelligence test should also give information of greater utility than the IQ or MA. The position that observational material may be used for interpretation beyond the scoring of items as right or wrong and the summing for a total score is not new; Binet advocated it with the very first scales which he proposed. It is an idea which has been accepted and promulgated with all scales since. Wechsler mentions as specific kinds of information derived from observation by the experienced examiner such features as the reaction and type of response of the examinee, perhaps some specialized abilities or disabilities as reflected in specific items or subtest content, and perhaps even some basis for describing personality traits. He does admit that at this point in time (that is, in 1958, although the statement still is pertinent) such observations are dependent for their validity upon the examiner's experience as a clinician and his wisdom in using observational techniques. Given such a state of affairs, one might wonder whether the conclusions have anything to do with the tests as such; might not the examiner come to the same conclusion through a conversational period quite aside from the administration of a standardized test? Regardless of one's position on this issue, the presumption of utility of observational data is widely held.

Wechsler also says that this dependence upon examiner competence is apt to remain true to some degree for many years to come. However, the test can play a role in the validity of such observations if there is inherent within the test at least some minimum possibilities. All tests do not yield the same possibilities, as Wechsler tries to indicate. Indeed, within a test such as the WAIS, certain subtests will be more amenable to elicitation of qualitative materials than will others. Perhaps what does the job at one time may not do the job at another time, or with a different person. As a result, Wechsler proposes that some composite scale which requires a variety of performances by the individual will be more usable for the qualitative interpretation of behavior than will another kind of test. The Wechsler-Bellevue I and the WAIS he believes reflect such possibilities.

Qualitative data must remain inferential to a large degree. The qualities observed by the examiner will depend in part upon the assumed content of the test used. Examinee's responses to such items must further be interpreted by the examiner as to their significance. Wechsler makes the point that the examiner must be very careful to avoid employing a personal interpretation which lacks validity and indeed may not even be validated in any fashion. Even if the examiner attempts controls he must still bear in mind the fact that any behavior and therefore any response may have a multiplicity of causes rather than a single one. There is no rigid formula which may be applied for each individual, for each subtest, for each item.

ROLE OF THE IQ. Within this context, Wechsler discusses the reliability of the IQ and its value in a scale such as the WAIS. He points out first that an IQ signifies the rank of an individual within his own age group, and therefore the IQ becomes a reflection of relative degree of brightness. If the IQ were to signify only this, it would not be very defensible as a measure. Wechsler believes that in addition to the role of ranking individuals it also becomes a kind of comprehensive statement of his overall functioning ability. To some degree, then, the IQ is a shorthand expression of certain behavioral outcomes which are reasonably stable and which may be independently verified from other sources. Insofar as any score expression, including the IQ, stands the trial of independent validation of behavioral significance, then it becomes a meaningful and usable score.

Since the IQ does serve as a kind of best estimate of the person's intellectual functioning in general, Wechsler says that one would suppose it to be one of the most important kinds of information derived from the test itself. In recent years, however, the IQ has been less and less accepted, more and more slandered. As a result, according to Wechsler, it has lost caste such that clinical workers tend to pay little heed to the numerical value expressed as IQ for varying reasons, none of which are totally acceptable to him. He points out some of the quarrels and myths that he believes to be misleading; such matters as the unalterable value one is born with at birth and which persists to death. As he points out, no competent psychologist in the testing movement has ever made such a claim nor would any competent individual. Instead, this argument represents something of a twist on certain demonstrable contentions related to stability of the IQ for groups.

He also considers the legitimacy of using the IQ for determination of ability with those persons who might be considered disturbed. Many persons have raised a question about this procedure since, if a person is disturbed, the score must in certain ways be inaccurate. An answer to such a question, Wechsler says, depends upon the particular aspects desired. First of all one may question the intellectual level of the individual prior to the disturbance. Second, one may be concerned about the evaluation of the present level of the individual regardless of the cause, and the prediction to be made about behavior in some future context. Wechsler believes that either position may be decided in terms of test scores, although other sources are also available to answer the questions.

Wechsler believes, then, that the IQ indeed has considerable value, and perhaps primarily because of its use in diagnosis. Some interpretation must occur, as is true with any quantitative measure, but he makes it clear that such interpretations should be based upon objective findings not upon bias or misconception. The aim of the IQ is to define some aspect of functioning overall for the individual. To him, the IQ helps to define the general assets and liabilities possessed by the individual. Only secondarily does it represent any specialized abilities or disabilities, only secondarily may it be used in conjunction with interests or the kind of training the individual should undergo because of his specialized abilities. He concludes with the statement: ". . . the fact that a subject has an IQ of 110 rather than 90 is ordinarily more important than whether he does well or poorly on a particular test, and this holds for the mentally ill as well as for the normal individual." (Wechsler, 1958, p. 159).

Comparison of Verbal and Performance Scales

Having presented the preceding arguments for care in any attempts to utilize part scores, Wechsler then proceeds to those conditions under which such analysis may be appropriate. He feels that one of the more useful features of the WAIS and the Wechsler-Bellevue is the fact that information is available for both verbal and performance subtests. He makes very clear that the inclusion of both verbal and performance scales was not based upon some theoretical assumption of differences in kinds of intelligence reflected in the two scales but rather on the assumption that certain individuals, through their experiences, are better able to deal with objects than they are to deal with verbal symbols. He cites certain studies that indicate by factor analysis that there may be a more fundamental dichotomy than verbal and performance in the scale despite overlap between tests. In any event, inferences may be drawn about the abilities reflected in the subtests and they may be grouped in certain ways to yield functional clusters usable for a variety of purposes.

From clinical experience, Wechsler reports that persons who have mental disorders generally show greater impairment on the Performance subtests than on the Verbal subtests. There are some exceptions to this finding clinically, though he believes that it is particularly true for the psychoses of all types and for organic brain disease. To some degree neurosis reflects such a breakdown in Performance tests as well. How much of a difference makes a difference then becomes the issue. Wechsler concludes—on a rule of thumb apparently more than on any other kind of evidence—that a difference of fifteen IQ points in either direction may be diagnostically important. On a statistical basis, such a discrepancy would occur by chance some thirteen times in one hundred. More stringent probability levels could be established very easily by the psychometrist, but whether much would be gained is doubtful. It cannot be overemphasized that Wechsler would draw no conclusions simply because of a difference of 15 or more IQ points. The differences would indicate the need for some independent determination of whether in fact one of the conditions described is accurate for the individual or whether the case represents one of those thirteen in one hundred conditions. As he states it, "All this means, of course, that the significance between a subject's verbal and performance score cannot be interpreted carte blanche, but only after due weight is given to the various factors which may have contributed to it." (Wechsler, 1958, p. 160).

Variability and Pattern Analysis

In introducing the concept of pattern analysis, Wechsler discusses test variability and the concept of scatter. Though intratest variability is important in many respects, most of the clinical use of tests such as the WAIS has depended upon intertest variability, the more common term for which is "scatter." The procedure followed will determine certain outcomes of scatter on consequent decisions made. Wechsler says that the most generally accepted approach to evaluating intertest variability has been to sum the average deviation for each subtest from the overall mean for total test performance. Thus on the verbal scale of the WAIS one might determine the mean standard score for the Verbal scale and compare the obtained scale score for each subtest to that mean. Greater departure from that mean might have significance for some diagnostic conclusions.

This procedure, which is somewhat more rigorous than other procedures tried, does not always yield large differences in test variability that might be expected between normal individuals and those with some aberration. Wechsler proposes that several reasons may account for this lack of significant differences. Perhaps the first of these would be considered the lack of adequate controls used by the clinician. In many cases there will be too few subjects to allow control, in other cases there may be too great heterogeneity for either normal or abnormal groups. Finally, there is always the possibility that there exists some bias in the sample unrecognized by the clinician. He may generalize from his very small group, with limited behavioral signs, and thus not find the same signs in other individuals of the same type but outside his group.

An issue lies in the determination of necessary difference from the mean. This is the same issue that we have faced in other contexts of the use of the Wechsler scales. As has happened so frequently before, the conclusion drawn by Wechsler seems to be based on convenience and observation rather than any empirical data. In any event, Wechsler says that for most purposes a deviation of two or more scale-score units from the mean of the scale scores will operate as a reasonable difference. The psychometrist may choose a greater difference if he wishes to increase the precision of his diagnosis. Considering the availability of statistical means of determining significance of such differences, a more precise method can and should be used by the psychometrist. Wechsler reports a table of differences of significance at the 15 percent level between pairs of scores, and other tables have been computed affording even greater rigor. Any psychometrist may compute the significance of the difference between pairs of scores using formulas available.

Whatever limits are chosen, the departure of a subtest score from the mean of the subtest is the basis upon which patterning is most often accomplished. Wechsler says that pattern analysis is a means for identifying diagnostically *different* groups. The importance of such a step lies in being able to identify an individual belonging, or who should belong, to such a group. If the procedure is accurate, performance on different subtests comprising the battery should be usable for differential diagnosis. The number of individuals identified accurately by the subtest pattern will determine the accuracy of the procedure. The problem, of course, is to avoid including individuals who do not belong to the group and to avoid excluding individuals who do belong to the group. In all clinical settings and in the use of clinical instruments, this problem looms large indeed.

As Wechsler says, any attempt to analyze by pattern for diagnostic purposes assumes that the test scores used may be combined to yield unique combinations. Those combinations which are of behavioral importance must be extracted from all of the possible combinations, many of which would not be of particular importance. Part of the problem, Wechsler claims, lies in the fact that so many combinations are possible. For example, with ten tests and three dichotomies more than 175,000 test combinations are possible (Wechsler, 1958, p. 165). Where intercorrelations exist among the subtests the possibility of combinations is less than for independent tests, but even so there would still remain too many possibilities to be of any great utility. In actual fact, all the possible combinations for the WAIS have not been computed. Wechsler has used a much more pragmatic procedure.

The procedures Wechsler employed are not true instances of patterning, according to his own statement. He states that what is desired is the identification of certain unique combinations of subtest performance which are diagnostic of clinical entities. Discovering such combinations through some random procedure would yield small returns. If one reduced the number of tests, the combinations possible would be lessened and the chances of random identification better. But as he advises, reduction in number of tests is not feasible until direct relationships between tests and clinical syndromes are discovered, and this has not yet occurred. An alternative, then, is to reduce the number of dichotomies. This could be more easily done, he believes, but only if there has been some prior identification of at least reasonably reliable cutoff points within the test scores.

In actual fact, then, Wechsler has followed what he calls a "piecemeal procedure." He has attempted to find tests which may be associated with diagnostic syndromes. Initially, using his own observations and those of other clinicians, he attempted to list those tests in which clinical categories tended to do relatively well or relatively poorly as compared with individuals who are not labeled by the clinical category. He submits that this is not patterning, although many persons have referred to it as such in the literature. Instead it is a preliminary step which may allow eventual patterning, doing little more than offering some clues to the kinds of tests which might be combined for configurational properties representing the diagnostic category.

One danger in such a procedure is the fact that overlap between possible combinations often will occur. The degree of overlap will determine the number of individuals who belong to but are not assigned to the category. These are individuals who possess the relevant behaviors but are not identified by the test scores. Wechsler admits this to be something of a problem but says that we should also remember that in differential diagnosis the greater concern should be how well rather than how many. His point is well taken, since it will be a quite rigorous measure and there will be less chance of error in identification. The problem, of course, is that a number of individuals who should be included in the category will be left out by the rigor of the procedure. As Wechsler observes, the search for unique patterns which will be valid will almost certainly identify only a small percentage of the total possible population to whom it may be applied. The procedure will be valid and is therefore more justifiable than a less reliable and valid procedure would be.

The problems concerned with missing certain individuals in the population who should belong to the diagnostic category may be corrected in certain ways by using Wechsler's "method of successive sieves." Rather than only one portion of the data being employed for diagnosis, in this approach several successive screenings dealing with different portions of the data will be undertaken. The continued procedure will tend to identify more individuals in the population who should be included in the category. How many more will depend upon the competencies of the test.

As already alluded to, there is always the danger of including persons in the diagnostic category who do not belong. This is the concept of false positives so frequently cited in clinical literature. Wechsler maintains that a certain amount of such misidentification is unavoidable because of the uncertainty of criteria and the unreliability of measures. Again, however, the use of the method of successive sieves will tend to identify those individuals who actually should not be retained in the diagnostic category, since they will meet only a few of the total number of sieves.

Wechsler maintains that differential diagnosis is much less difficult for a clinician who is well trained and experienced than it might appear to the layman. For one thing, the experienced clinician has dealt with a large number of cases already, has observed a number of behavioral signs of various clinical conditions, and consequently can apply this experience to any given case. In addition, he will have a number of sources of information available to him from case records and past histories in most instances that will help to exclude certain potential diagnoses and lend some degree of possibility to others. Having delimited the number of possible diagnoses which may be applied, he may then differentiate among these more quickly and accurately with test data and with external criteria. Wechsler gives a number of examples of test characteristics which may be found in different clinical groups. He stresses that these are not patterns and should not be used in that fashion. Essentially, the descriptions represent the application of his method of successive sieves to try to include maximum identification with the minimum number of test performances. In some instances, he believes, the descriptions are well verified clinically and quite usable. Others are much less well supported.

One final comment about the role of test interpretation seems pertinent at this point. Wechsler conceives of test items as representing a certain amount of projective material, at least to a degree and with selected items. To the clinician, he says, this is a positive factor while to the test constructor it is a source of error. He holds that both the clinician and the test constructor are correct to some degree at least.

An intelligence test gains in value in proportion to the amount of information it gives, other than overall rating of intellectual level; at the same time it suffers if it is at the mercy of factors other than the basic abilities which it is trying to measure. The question, of course, is to what extent these factors influence the final results or contribute to the better understanding of the individual. In the writer's opinion, both the over-sensitized clinician and the matter-of-fact statistician are likely to overestimate the impact of personality variables on test performance. (Wechsler, 1958, p. 79)

Wechsler maintains that such variables are of importance. As he has said in other instances, motivational factors, affect, and other such behaviors have their influence on test scores. To Wechsler they are not sources of error at all, but aspects of the global intellectual capacity of the individual that would be operating. Admittedly, we do not identify their weight or role at this time in intelligence tests. This does not deny either their importance or their necessity to test performance.

References

Wechsler, D. *Manual for the Wechsler Adult Intelligence Scale.* New York: Psychological Corporation, 1955.

Wechsler, D. *The Measurement and Appraisal of Adult Intelligence.* Baltimore: Williams & Wilkins, 1958.

Subject Index

Ability levels
  average
    1916 Revision, 25, 27–29
    1937 Revision, 69
    Wechsler-Bellevue, 130
  borderline
    1916 Revision, 25, 27–29
    1937 Revision, 69
    Wechsler-Bellevue, 130
  bright normal, Wechsler-Bellevue, 130
  dull normal
    1916 Revision, 25, 29
    Wechsler-Bellevue, 130
  feeble-minded
    1916 Revision, 25, 27–29
    WISC, 154–156
  high average, 1937 Revision, 69
  low average, 1937 Revision, 69
  mentally deficient
    1937 Revision, 69
    Wechsler-Bellevue, 130
  superior
    1916 Revision, 25, 29–30
    1937 Revision, 69
    Wechsler-Bellevue, 130
    WISC, 154–156
  very superior
    1916 Revision, 25
    1937 Revision, 69
    Wechsler-Bellevue, 130
Army Alpha, 96–98, 100

Binet method, 10, 12–14, 36
  limitations, 14–16

Deviation IQ, 62, 73–76, 123–124
  classification, 68–69, 128–135
  limitations, 133
  role, 175, 194–195
  use, 77–78, 133–135
  variability, 66–67
Differential diagnosis, 66, 97–98, 139,
    146–149, 193–194, 196–200

Differential diagnosis *(continued)*
  related to WAIS scales, 195–196
  signs, 148–149, 159–160

Full scale
  WAIS, 188, 190, 192–195
  Wechsler-Bellevue, 106, 122–123, 126,
    130, 133–135, 137, 146, 148
  WISC, 152, 154–156, 158
  WPPSI, 162

Intelligence
  abilities versus *g*, 173–174
  adult, 99–103
  composition, 171
  distribution of, 1916 Revision, 19–20
  nonintellective factors, 133–135, 137,
    171, 174
  problems of classification, 128–130
  statistical concept, 131–133
  using subtests, 65

Mental age, 12–14, 18–19, 42–43, 45–47,
    63, 137
  and achievement, 24, 100
  limitations, 90–91, 101–103
  use, 76–77, 78–81
Mental deficiency, 136–139, 165–166
  defining, 136
  psychometric classification, 137
  statistical definition, 137–139
  types, 138–139
Mental deterioration, 139–145
  definition, 139, 144
  determination, 141–142
  differential test score method, 143–144
  and subtest performance, 140–141
Mental growth, 75–76

Norming, control variables
  1937 Revision, 40–42
  WAIS, 185–187

201

Author Index